Studies in applied regional science

This series in applied regional, urban and
environmental analysis aims to provide
regional scientists with a set of adequate tools
for empirical regional analysis and for practical
regional planning problems. The major
emphasis in this series will be upon the
applicability of theories and methods in the
field of regional science; these will be
presented in a form which can be readily used
by practitioners. Both new applications of
existing knowledge and newly developed ideas
will be published in the series.

D1674365

Studies in applied regional science Vol. 1

On the use of input-output models for regional planning

W.A. Schaffer
Professor of economics,
Georgia Institute of Technology

With the assistance of

E.A. Laurent, C.F. Floyd,
E.M. Sutter Jr., C.K. Hamby
and R.C. Herbert

Martinus Nijhoff Social Sciences Division
Leiden 1976

ISBN 90 207 0626 8

Photoset in Malta by Interprint (Malta) Ltd.

Printed in the Netherlands

To Samuel

Preface

This book attempts to show, in a style acceptable to both academics and hurried planning executives, how simple analytic tools may be used to bridge the substantial gap between producing an input-output table and using one. In pursuing this goal, we eschew all discussions of complex programming models, for example, and concentrate on, above all, interpretation of the transactions table itself, on such common tools as multipliers, impact analysis, projections models, and self-sufficiency analysis, and on a few innovations such as income-per-employee indices, development simulators, and market analysis routines. Our primary purpose has been to show how planners, both private and public, can use regional input-output analysis quickly and to their advantage.

The Georgia Interindustry Study was sponsored by the Office of Planning and Budget and the Department of Industry and Trade of the State of Georgia; their support is gratefully acknowledged. The final study report, of which this book represents a substantial revision, benefited enormously from the support and incisive criticisms of Dr. William W. Nash, then with the Office of Planning and Budget; his efforts are warmly appreciated.

Many other officials in Georgia government contributed to this study, including: Louis Schneider and Kenneth P. Johnson in the Office of Planning and Budget; James O. Bohanan, James Butler, George Rogers, and H.W. Wiley in the Department of Industry and Trade; Joe Woodall and Corine Cross in the Department of Labor; William M. Nixon in the Department of Audits; and J.B. Murray and R.E. Davis of the Department of Mines, Mining, and Geology. Also helpful were: James D. Cooper of the U.S. Bureau of Mines; Frank H. Welton of the Georgia Agribusiness Council; Dr. Bill R. Miller of the College of Agriculture and Elizabeth E. Barnes and the late Dr. William B. Keeling of the Division of Research, University of Georgia.

Direct assistance in collecting data has been given by Dr. Susan Johnson, Stanlee L. Schaffer, Lawrence H. Hoe, and William M. Arrants. We have benefited substantially from earlier work with Dr. Kong Chu, Richard J. Dolce, and William E. Sumner, Jr., work supported in part by a grant from the Economic Development Administration to the Regional Development Program of the College of Industrial Management of the Georgia Institute of Technology. Many of the techniques used in the Study were developed in conjunction with the Hawaii Interindustry Study, which was directed by the senior author; we appreciate the assistance of Dr. Young Joun and others on the staff of the

Department of Planning and Economic Development of the State of Hawaii.

Mrs. Sarah Born typed this manuscript. We acknowledge her patience through many drafts and we appreciate the care with which she has made innumerable changes.

I gratefully share the credit for the contents of this work. Dr. Laurent contributed his experiences with the Charleston input-output model in formulating our tools, in contributing parts of earlier drafts long since assimilated, and in collecting and amassing much of the data; Andy was my internal watchdog and critic. Dr. Floyd gave direct assistance in formulating our projection model and was responsible for our shift and share analysis. Malcolm Sutter and I worked closely for three years in developing all of the procedures, in constructing the Hawaii model (which was a formative exercise for this work), and in collecting and processing data for this study; he was the master of all computing procedures. Clay Hamby kept the routines alive, altering them for use in constructing subarea models, especially in connection with our highway study. And Ross Herbert made a substantial contribution in reactivating and revising parts of the system to construct the tables used in this volume. I directed the project and wrote the final draft of this book. As principal author, I assume responsibility.

W.A.S.

Contents

Appendices

List of tables

Table

List of illustrations

About the authors

William A. Schaffer, director of the Georgia Interindustry Study, is Professor of Economics at the Georgia Institute of Technology. He holds a Ph.D. in Economics from Duke University and has taught at Oglethorpe and Agnes Scott Colleges. In 1970, Schaffer directed an Interindustry Study of the Hawaiian Economy for the Department of Planning and Economic Development of the State of Hawaii. With special interests in regional economics, he has published studies on the economic impact of baseball on Atlanta and Montreal, on techniques for constructing regional interindustry models, and on the teaching of regional economics. He was the 1972-73 president of the Southern Regional Science Association, and is a member of the Board of Editors of the *Southern Economic Journal* and of the Board of Directors of the *Review of Regional Studies*.

Eugene A. Laurent is Director, Division of Natural Area Acquisition and Resource Planning of the South Carolina Wildlife Resources Department. He holds a Ph.D. in Agricultural Economics from Clemson University and was Assistant Professor at the Environmental Resources Center at Georgia Tech from 1970-72. Laurent constructed an economic-ecologic model of Charleston, South Carolina, in 1969, and has published studies in environmental planning, resource management, and regional input-output analysis.

Charles F. Floyd is Professor of Real Estate at the University of Georgia. He holds a Ph.D. in Economics from the University of North Carolina. Floyd is currently Director of the Georgia Transportation Planning Land-Use Modeling Project, and has published extensively in shift and share analysis and regional development.

Ernest M. Sutter, Jr., is now systems analyst at Computer Management, Inc. A 1970 graduate of the College of Industrial Management at Georgia Tech, he managed computing operations for both the Hawaii Interindustry Study and the Georgia Interindustry Study.

Claybourne K. Hamby is now systems analyst at Mansanto Company, having graduated from Georgia Tech in 1974. He continued refinement of the programs associated with this study and extended their application to substate areas.

Ross C. Herbert is an applications programmer at Georgia Tech while pursuing a degree in Industrial Management. He has been responsible for many of the tables in this book, for aggregating study results to their present level, and for adapting the analytic programs for use with these tables.

1. Introduction

1.1 PURPOSE

This book is intended to show how input-output analysis can provide a sound informational basis for regional planning. We have placed some fairly specific constraints on the presentation. One is that it be self-contained, providing the reader new to regional input-output analysis with a reasonably simple introduction to ·the topic; it is not intended to be an advanced technical treatise. This means that it introduces few new techniques, although it does make some new applications. The other major constraint is that the planners for whom it is intended work in a private-enterprise system, which makes their coercive powers relatively few. This means that they are concerned primarily with information and its use. As a consequence, we emphasize interpretation of a regional input-output model, neglecting a number of procedures, *e.g.* advanced programming and planning models, which would enjoy limited use in the planning system of a state such as Georgia, a politically conservative Southeastern state.

As a case study, this book is complementary to a number of recent publications which should be read by the serious analyst interested in constructing an input-output model. Isard and Langford (1971) provide a number of insights into the construction of input-output models in their recollection of the Philadelphia Study. Richardson (1972) brilliantly summarizes the current status of input-output analysis and regional economics. Smith and Morrison (1975) investigate techniques for constructing tables using secondary data in more detail than reported here. And Miernyk, *et al.* (1970) project economic activity and simulate regional development in far more sophisticated ways than those we consider. We have simply applied many of the techniques discussed elsewhere in great detail to a study of the Georgia economy.

1.2 SIGNIFICANCE OF THE GEORGIA ECONOMIC MODEL

The Georgia Economic Model is the final product of the Georgia Interindustry Study. The study identifies sales and purchase patterns in the State in 1970. Systematically assembled and supplemented, this data forms the Georgia Economic Model, showing the dependence of industries in the State upon one another and upon industries outside the State for markets and inputs.

The Georgia Economic Model is useful in a number of ways to businessmen, to area planners, and to state planning and development agencies. *First*, it compiles in a consistent framework a series of facts about the Georgia economy. This basic economic information system is organized around a transactions, or input-output, table which identifies consumption patterns, the industry structure, income sources, and nonmarket transfers in the Georgia economy. Through it, several important questions can be answered. What is Georgia's gross state product? Who received this income and what are its major sources? The system also outlines the economic structure of the State, showing who buys Georgia products, who provides the inputs needed in making these outputs, and how production takes place.

Second, the Georgia input-output table is the basis for the Georgia Market Information System, through which market analyses can be provided for over 100 industry groups. Available to businessmen and development agencies, these analyses identify the sizes of Georgia markets, show the portions being served locally, project Georgia markets and production to 1980, and outline the markets and outputs of these industries in the Southeast in 1970.

Third, the Georgia Economic Model shows the importance of the various industries in the State and indicates the impact of changes in the demands for Georgia products on industry outputs, employment, personal incomes, and state and local government revenues.

Fourth, the Georgia Economic Model has been made into a computer-based 'development simulator' which can be used to show the effects of changes in the economic structure of the State on other industries, on employment, and on personal and government incomes. The development simulator permits a testing of development programs for planning economic growth in Georgia.

Fifth, the Georgia Economic Model has been used to produce a series of baseline projections of the Georgia economy in 1980. These projections show the growth which might be derived from national growth patterns, and they stress both the need for planning and the importance of continued and stronger efforts by the Georgia Department of Industry and Trade and the other planning and development agencies in the State.

And *sixth*, the Georgia Economic Model represents a substantial step forward by the State government. The series of programs designed for using this economic information system makes this the most sophisticated and powerful planning tool in the Southeast. The Georgia Economic Model is a critical element in the overall planning system required for promoting orderly growth in a complex state economy; to facilitate its integration into other data systems in the State, the Model has been developed with care to provide for ease in use, in modification, and in revision. The system can be extended to answer critical environmental questions and to project occupation needs for use in manpower planning and development. Refined and linked with existing data sources, the projection model can become a major instrument of state policy.

1.3 ORGANIZATION OF THIS BOOK

Using a five-industry transactions table, the next chapter establishes the logic of regional input-output models. Chapter 3 examines the procedures used in constructing the Georgia transactions table, showing the evolution of a nonsurvey estimating technique into a survey-based one. In Chapter 4, we interpret the empirical relations identified for Georgia in a 28-industry transactions table; our emphasis is the usefulness of the table as an accounting framework. Chapter 5 outlines and discusses the numerous possible multipliers which might be computed. The projection model presented in Chapter 6 is an elementary 'baseline' model intended to show how projections are made and how shift and share analysis may be integrated into the system.

Identifying a strategy for development is the topic of Chapter 7, which shows how skyline charts and multipliers may be used by the planner. Chapter 8 introduces a simple computer-based development simulator which provides a starting point for an impact analysis; in addition, we discuss analysis of the impact of public projects. Using the transactions table as a basis for market analysis is the topic of Chapter 9, which outlines in detail the steps required in this transformation. A final chapter comments briefly on extensions not made in this study but which could further assist the planner.

As appendices, we have included notes on constructing regional income and product accounts for use in input-output tables, an essay on shift and share analysis by Charles F. Floyd, and a set of input-output tables.

2. The logic of input-output models

Relying on a 5-industry aggregation of the 28-industry table for Georgia, this chapter presents the logic of a regional input-output model. First, we look at the table as an accounting system for an economy. Then we rationalize the use of a model and examine the construction of a regional input-output model. The chapter closes with a brief look at economic change in input-output models as a prelude to later chapters.

2.2 THE STATE TRANSACTIONS TABLE

A state input-output model shows the interactions of industries in a state with each other, with industries outside the state, and with final-demand sectors. The central element in this model is a state transactions table such as that shown in Table 2.2a. To avoid overwhelming the reader with details, we have aggregated the Georgia transactions table beyond the 28-industry level used later in this book. Twenty-eight industries are combined into five broad industries, six final-payments sectors are presented as three, and six final-demand sectors are shown as three.

Each row in this table accounts for the sales by the industry named at its left to the industries identified across the top of the table and to the final consumers listed in the right-hand section of the table. Intermediate goods are sold to local industries for use in producing other products, while finished goods are sold to final consumers. Goods exported from the state to other parts of the nation and the world are listed under exports in the final-demand section, regardless of their stage of production. The sum of a row is the total output or total sales of an industry.

Thus, the sales by the extractive industry (a combination of agricultural, forestry, fishing, and mining industries) of Georgia are shown in row one of Table 2.2a. Of the total output worth $1,674 million, over 35 percent is sold to light manufacturing (which processes it for further sale), and over 35 percent is sold outside the state. The remaining sales are largely to other industries within the broad extractive industry itself.

Each column in Table 2.2a records the purchases, or inputs, of the industry

Table 2.2a Aggregated interindustry transactions, Georgia, 1970.

In millions of dollars	Purchasing industry						Final demand				Total outputs
	Extractive industry (1)	Construction (2)	Manufacturing (3)	Trade (4)	Services (5)	Total local sales	Household expenditures	Other local final demand	Exports	Total final demand	
Selling industry											
Extractive industry (1)	182.9	30.9	599.0	6.1	73.1	892.0	98.5	87.9	595.8	782.2	1,674.2
Construction (2)	13.9	.9	42.7	13.8	292.9	364.2	0.0	1,802.6	352.7	2,155.4	2,519.6
Manufacturing (3)	141.9	413.8	1,390.4	109.9	356.1	2,412.0	1,275.2	1,130.4	9,344.0	11,749.5	14,161.5
Trade (4)	52.3	224.2	520.4	71.9	256.9	1,125.7	2,563.4	160.8	970.4	3,694.6	4,820.3
Services (5)	102.0	220.9	862.1	558.3	1,990.1	3,733.4	4,262.3	522.8	2,828.3	7,613.4	11,346.8
Total local purchases	492.9	890.8	3,414.6	760.0	2,969.1	8,527.3	8,199.3	3,704.5	14,091.3	25,995.1	34,522.3
Final payments											
Households	595.0	665.0	3,695.5	2,385.0	4,603.1	11,943.6	99.7	2,523.7	0.0	2,623.3	14,567.0
Other payments	261.1	240.6	1,623.5	1,364.8	2,402.2	5,892.2	(3,789.2)	(943.2)	(1,097.5)	(5,829.8)	5,892.2
Imports	325.2	773.2	5,427.9	310.5	1,372.4	8,159.2	3,777.8	1,056.8	-12,993.8	-8,159.2	0.0
Total final payments	1,181.2	1,628.8	10,747.0	4,060.3	8,377.7	25,995.1	3,877.5	3,580.5	-12,993.8	-5,535.8	20,459.2
Total inputs	1,674.2	2,519.6	14,161.6	4,820.3	11,346.8	34,522.3	12,076.8	7,285.0	1,097.5	20,459.2	54,981.5

Notes:
1. Based on *Georgia Interindustry Study*.
2. Other payments by final-demand sectors (in parentheses) are not included in totals.
3. Totals may not add due to rounding.

identified at the top of the column from the industries named at the left. Payments by the industry to employees, holders of capital, and governments are contained in the first two rows of the final-payments section of the table. These payments constitute the 'value added' by the industry in question. Purchases from industries outside the state are identified in the last row of the final-payments section and are called 'imports.' These imports may be either of goods not produced at all in the state or of goods produced in quantities insufficient to meet local needs. The sum of the entries in each column represents the total purchases by the industry in question. Since profits, losses, depreciation, taxes, etc., are recorded in the table as final payments, the total purchases and payments must equal total sales. Inputs equal outputs; hence the term 'input-output.'

For example, the purchases and payments of the extractive industry in Georgia are shown in column 1 of Table 2.2a. Since this industry is almost 90 percent agriculture, the column reflects large intraindustry transactions (purchases of feeder stocks, baby chicks, grains, etc.), substantial purchases from light manufacturing (feeds), and a large payment to households for labor and proprietors' income. Georgia farmers also import from outside the state large amounts of feeds and other supplies. Notice that the total inputs is the same as the total outputs identified in row 1.

Now, with this brief introduction to a state transactions table, let us look at the table as an accounting system for an economy.[1] Figure 2.2a shows an input-output table in skeleton form and divided into four quadrants. Quadrant I describes *consumer behavior*, identifying consumption patterns of households and such other local final users of goods as private investors and governments. Another important part of Quadrant I is the export column, which shows sales to other industries and consumers outside the state economy. Since these goods would not normally reappear in the state in the same form, these sales are regarded as final. According to economic-base theory, in which final demand is the motivating force in an economy, we would look in this quadrant for activity-generating forces and we would especially examine the government and export sectors.

.Quadrant II depicts *production relationships* in the economy, showing the ways that raw materials and intermediate goods are combined to produce outputs for sale to other industries and to ultimate consumers. This is the most important quadrant in an input-output table. For regions and states, it typically ranges in size between 30 and 39 industries.[2] Quadrant II is the basis for the input-output model itself.

Quadrant III shows *incomes* of primary units in the economy, including the incomes of households, the depreciation and retained earnings of industries, and the taxes paid to various levels of government. These payments are also called value added; since they are so hard to identify individually, these

PROCESSING   FINAL DEMAND

	PROCESSING	FINAL DEMAND	TOTAL OUTPUTS
PROCESSING	II INTERINDUSTRY STRUCTURE	I CONSUMP- TION PATTERNS	
PAYMENTS	III INCOMES	IV TRANSFERS	
	TOTAL INPUTS		

Figure 2.2a   The transactions table as a picture of the economy.

incomes are frequently recorded as one value-added row. The quadrant also includes payments to industries outside the economy for materials and intermediate goods which are imported into the state. Since all of these payments to resource owners and to outsiders leave the industrial system of the state, they are called 'final payments.'

Quadrant IV identifies primarily *nonmarket transfers* between sectors of the economy and might properly be labeled the 'social transfers' quadrant. Here we see gifts, savings, and taxes of households; we see the surpluses and deficits of governments, their payments to households, and intergovernmental transfers. The quadrant also typically includes purchases by final-demand sectors from industries outside the state.

A glance across Table 2.2a yields several interesting points about Georgia, and about input-output tables. First, out of a total output of over $34 billion, Georgia's manufacturing output in 1970 was valued at over $14 billion and its service output at over $11 billion, indicating that Georgia's economy is dominated by the manufacturing and service industries. Even so, Georgia is not a major manufacturing or service economy by national standards. Table 2.2b compares the origins of gross income or value added in Georgia and the United

States. Georgia has larger contributions to value added from trade and government than does the nation, and smaller contributions from the extractive industries, construction, manufacturing, utilities, and services. This deviation from the national pattern is an expression of the state's still modest stage of development and its central position in the Southeast.

Table 2.2b Industrial origins of value added in Georgia, 1970, and the United States, 1966.

Sector	Georgia, in percent of GSP	U.S., in percent of GNP
Agriculture, mining	4.2	5.2
Construction	4.4	5.6
Manufacturing	26.0	28.9
Transportation, utilities	7.7	8.1
Trade	18.3	14.6
Services	25.6	26.9
Government	13.7	10.7

Sources: Computed from the Georgia input-output table and from *Input-Output Transactions: 1966*, Staff Paper in Economics and Statistics, No. 19, February 1972, Bureau of Economic Analysis, U.S. Department of Commerce.

It is useful to note that the 'importance' of an industry is completely dependent on the definitions and aggregation patterns employed in constructing a table. By enlarging the table and altering sector definitions, we could change the apparent importance of industries. For example, by combining the agricultural industries with the food-processing industry (normally in manufacturing), we could make the 'agriculture-based' industry larger than any of the components of the 'trade' or 'service' industries. In fact, in the 28-industry version of the Georgia table, the five largest industries in terms of output are: 1. trade, 2. finance, insurance, and real estate, 3. services, 4. textile mill products, and 5. transportation equipment.

A second interesting item in Table 2.2a is the gross state product (GSP) of Georgia. Analogous in concept to the gross national product, GSP can be defined as total production without duplication, or as the economic product of all factors of production residing in the state. It can also be seen as the total final payments (adjusted for imports) in the state, $20.459 billion. Alternatively, it is also the total final demand by ultimate consumers of the state's products (net of imports). The GSP accounts are discussed further in section 4.5.

In summary, an input-output table traces the paths by which incomes flow through the economy. Quadrant I is where the spending cycle begins and is where finished goods go to satisfy the needs of final consumers. Quadrant III is where the production cycle starts, with households and other resource owners, including governments, receiving payments for their contributions to the production process. Quadrant II traces production relationships, describing the technology of production in the economy. It outlines the market sector of the economy. Quadrant IV identifies nonmarket flows of money, showing purchases of labor inputs by governments, taxes paid by households, surpluses and deficits of governments, and transfers between governments and other governments and people.

2.3 THE RATIONALE FOR A MODEL: ANALYSIS VS. DESCRIPTION

While the Georgia transactions table describes the economy and yields interesting bits of information for a particular point in time, in itself it has no analytic content. That is, it does not permit us to answer questions concerning the reaction of the economy to change. Let the transactions table represent the economy in equilibrium and subject it to a shock, say a cutback in defense expenditures or an increase in tourism. When the repercussions of the shock have moved through the economy, what will be its new 'equilibrium position?' In other words, which industries will be larger or smaller and whose income or employment will have changed? Such analysis requires an economic model, which we can now proceed to construct.

2.4 PREPARING THE TRANSACTIONS TABLE: CLOSING WITH
RESPECT TO HOUSEHOLDS

As we shall see, it is important to include in the interindustry structure (Quadrant II) all economic activities which make buying decisions primarily on the basis of their incomes. These activities are called *endogenous* since their behavior is determined *within* the system. Other activities, such as federal government expenditures or exports, are based on decisions made *outside* the system and so are called *exogenous* activities. Activities which are labeled 'industries' are normally considered to be endogenous and those which are labeled 'final-demand sectors' are normally considered to be exogenous. But sometimes it is not so easy to classify activities.

The household sector is a case in point. While traditionally classified as a final-demand sector, it is frequently treated in regional economic models as an 'industry.' Households sell labor, managerial skills, and privately owned resources; they receive in payment wages and salaries, dividends, rents, proprietors' income, etc. And to produce these resources, they buy food, clothing, automobiles, housing, services, and other consumer goods. Exceeded in total expenditures only by the manufacturing sector, the household sector is obviously a critical part of the Georgia economy. So we move the household row and column into the interindustry part of the transactions table and treat households as another industry in the Georgia Economic Model. In the aggregated transactions table (2.2a), the household sector would thus become the sixth 'industry' in the aggregated model, and the model would then be 'closed with respect to households.'

The state and local government sectors (included in 'other final demand' and 'other final payments' in our aggregated table) also are difficult to classify. While we leave them in the exogenous part of the table now, primarily for simplicity, they are included in the endogenous part of the table in the detailed forecasting model.

2.5 THE ECONOMIC MODEL

An economic model is based on three sets of relations: 1. definitions or identities, 2. technical or behavioral conditions, and 3. equilibrium conditions. A model thus is an extension of a description of an economy through a set of assumptions such that it can be used to trace the effects of disequilibrating forces. Each set of relations can be easily identified in the Georgia Economic Model.[3]

2.5.1 Identities: the transactions table

The state transactions table as extended above (in 2.4) provides our set of identities: it defines the economy of Georgia in 1970. Now let's express these relations in simple algebra. Let x_{ij} be the sales of industry i to industry j, y_i the sales of industry i to final demand (ultimate consumers), and x_i the total sales of industry i. Then we can define the sales of Georgia industries in terms of the following equations:

$$x_{11} + x_{12} + x_{13} + x_{14} + x_{15} + x_{16} + y_1 = x_1$$

$$x_{21} + x_{22} + x_{23} + x_{24} + x_{25} + x_{26} + y_2 = x_2$$

$$x_{31} + x_{32} + x_{33} + x_{34} + x_{35} + x_{36} + y_3 = x_3$$

$$x_{41} + x_{42} + x_{43} + x_{44} + x_{45} + x_{46} + y_4 = x_4$$

$$x_{51} + x_{52} + x_{53} + x_{54} + x_{55} + x_{56} + y_5 = x_5$$

$$x_{61} + x_{62} + x_{63} + x_{64} + x_{65} + x_{66} + y_6 = x_6$$

This set of identities can be seen symbolically in the top six rows of Figure 2.5a and numerically in the five industry rows and in the household row (now 'industry' six) of the Georgia transactions table (Table 2.2a). Since we are now primarily concerned with Quadrant II, we have reduced Quadrant I to one column in these tables and we have dropped the various intermediate totals.

As can be seen, Figure 2.5a and the above set of equations differ in only two ways: 1. the arithmetic operators are implicit in the table, and 2. the table includes values for other final payments (v_j) and imports (m_j), completing the accounting framework.

2.5.2 Technical conditions: the direct-requirements table

Now, say that we have estimated what final demand will be at some later date $(y_1', y_2', y_3', y_4', y_5', y_6')$ and that we wish to identify the effect of this demand on the economy. We would like to know the gross outputs of industries (that is, the values of x_1' through x_6') in Georgia at that time. It is obvious that little additional information can be gleaned from the transactions table. We have six equations and 48 variables, of which only six (the y's) now have assigned values. The minimum requirement for a solution to this system is that the number of equations equals the number of unknowns; therefore, we must reduce the number of unknown variables by 42.

To do this, we introduce a set of technical conditions. Assume that the pattern of purchases identified in 1970 is stable. We can now define a set of values called 'direct requirements,' or 'production coefficients:'

$$a_{ij} = \frac{x_{ij}}{x_j} \; .$$

Selling industry		Purchasing industry → Agriculture, mining (1)	Construction (2)	Manufacturing (3)	Trade (4)	Services (5)	Households (6)	Final demand	Total outputs
Agriculture, mining	(1)	x_{11}	x_{12}	x_{13}	x_{14}	x_{15}	x_{16}	y_1	x_1
Construction	(2)	x_{21}	x_{22}	x_{23}	x_{24}	x_{25}	x_{26}	y_2	x_2
Manufacturing	(3)	x_{31}	x_{32}	x_{33}	x_{34}	x_{35}	x_{36}	y_3	x_3
Trade	(4)	x_{41}	x_{42}	x_{43}	x_{44}	x_{45}	x_{46}	y_4	x_4
Services	(5)	x_{51}	x_{52}	x_{53}	x_{54}	x_{55}	x_{56}	y_5	x_5
Households	(6)	x_{61}	x_{62}	x_{63}	x_{64}	x_{65}	x_{66}	y_6	x_6
Other final payments		v_1	v_2	v_3	v_4	v_5	v_6	(v_d)	v
Imports		m_1	m_2	m_3	m_4	m_5	m_6	$-m$	0
Total inputs		x_1	x_2	x_3	x_4	x_5	x_6	y	

Figure 2.5a Algebraic transactions table.

Table 2.5a records these a_{ij} coefficients for the aggregated Georgia model. We have simply divided each value in a column by the total inputs (total output) of the industry represented in the column. These numbers show the proportions in which the establishments in each industry combine the goods and services which they purchase to produce their own products.

Notice that we can define x_{ij}, the sales by industry i to industry j, in another way. It can be written as $x_{ij} = a_{ij} \cdot x_j$. That is, if the manufacturing sector purchases 6.1 percent of its inputs from the service sector (a_{53}), and if manufacturing purchases a total of \$14,162 million worth of inputs (x_3), then its purchases from the service sector would have to amount to \$862 million, or 6.1 percent of \$14,162 million. If the proportions in which industries buy their inputs remain reasonably stable over time, then we can define purchases by industry i from industry j in the future as $x'_{ij} = a_{ij} \cdot x'_j$. As we shall see, this simple assumption solves our problem.

Table 2.5a Direct requirements of Georgia industries, 1970 (in percent).

		Purchasing industry					
		Agriculture, mining	Construction	Manufacturing	Trade	Services	Households
		(1)	(2)	(3)	(4)	(5)	(6)
Agriculture, mining	(1)	10.9	1.2	4.2	.1	.6	.6
Construction	(2)	.8	*	.3	.3	2.6	.0
Manufacturing	(3)	8.5	16.4	9.8	2.3	3.1	8.0
Trade	(4)	3.1	8.9	3.7	·1.5	2.3	16.2
Services	(5)	6.1	8.8	6.1	11.6	17.5	26.9
Households	(6)	35.5	26.4	26.1	49.5	40.6	.6
Total local purchases		64.9	61.7	50.2	65.3	66.8	52.3
Other payments		15.6	9.6	11.5	28.3	21.2	23.9
Imports		19.4	28.7	38.3	6.4	12.1	23.8
Total inputs		100.0	100.0	100.0	100.0	100.0	100.0

Selling industry (left vertical label)

* Less than .05.

2.5.3 Equilibrium condition: supply equals demand

Note that along the way we have implicitly stated the equilibrium condition. This condition is that anticipated demand equals supply, or that the gross output of an industry equals its sales (in algebra, $x_j = x_i$, where $i = j$). Over any long period of time in a market economy, it is irrational to produce more than is used and impractical to consume more than is produced. Under normal conditions, an economy faced with a change in demand will react by changing supply. When anticipations are fulfilled, the economy is in a state of equilibrium.

2.5.4 Solution to the system: the total-requirements table

Since we assume the production coefficients to be stable over time, we can rewrite the equation system to apply to a later period by substituting y'_i for y_i, x'_i for x_i, and $x'_{ij} = a_{ij} \cdot x'_j$ for x_{ij} in each of our equations:

$$a_{11} \cdot x'_1 + a_{12} \cdot x'_2 + a_{13} \cdot x'_3 + a_{14} \cdot x'_4 + a_{15} \cdot x'_5 + a_{16} \cdot x'_6 + y'_1 = x'_1$$

$$a_{21} \cdot x'_1 + a_{22} \cdot x'_2 + a_{23} \cdot x'_3 + a_{24} \cdot x'_4 + a_{25} \cdot x'_5 + a_{26} \cdot x'_6 + y'_2 = x'_2$$

$$a_{31} \cdot x'_1 + a_{32} \cdot x'_2 + a_{33} \cdot x'_3 + a_{34} \cdot x'_4 + a_{35} \cdot x'_5 + a_{36} \cdot x'_6 + y'_3 = x'_3$$

$$a_{41} \cdot x'_1 + a_{42} \cdot x'_2 + a_{43} \cdot x'_3 + a_{44} \cdot x'_4 + a_{45} \cdot x'_5 + a_{46} \cdot x'_6 + y'_4 = x'_4$$

$$a_{51} \cdot x'_1 + a_{52} \cdot x'_2 + a_{53} \cdot x'_3 + a_{54} \cdot x'_4 + a_{55} \cdot x'_5 + a_{56} \cdot x'_6 + y'_5 = x'_5$$

$$a_{61} \cdot x'_1 + a_{62} \cdot x'_2 + a_{63} \cdot x'_3 + a_{64} \cdot x'_4 + a_{65} \cdot x'_5 + a_{66} \cdot x'_6 + y'_6 = x'_6$$

The prime applied to each variable indicates 'future' value. The power of our assumption that the technology of production is constant is now clear. With it, we have reduced the number of unknowns from 48 to six, the x'_i's, and can proceed to solve the system and thus to determine the outputs of Georgia industries in the future.

A full, mathematical explanation of the solution to this system is discussed in Chapter 5. For now, we note that the formal solution, which is computed in terms of matrix algebra, is analogous to one in simple algebra. Say we wish to solve the following equation for x:

$$x = a \cdot x + y .$$

We subtract $a \cdot x$ from both sides of the equation,

$$x - a \cdot x = y ,$$

factor x from the terms on the left,

$$x(1 - a) = y ,$$

and divide both sides by $(1 - a)$ to get

$$x = y/(1 - a) ,$$

the solution for x in terms of y. Now if we visualize x as the column vector of total sales in Figure 2.5a, y as the column vector of final demand, and a as the table of a_{ij}'s computed above, then we can write an analogous solution to our system of equations:

$$x = (I - a)^{-1} \cdot y .$$

Here, I is the identity matrix, which is the matrix equivalent to the number 1, and the exponent (-1) shows that the parenthetic expression is inverted, or divided into another identity matrix. The term $(I - a)$ is sometimes called the 'Leontief matrix' in recognition of Wassily Leontief, the originator of input-output economics; $(I - a)^{-1}$, of course, is called the 'Leontief inverse.' A more descriptive title is 'total-requirements table.'

Table 2.5b Total requirements per dollar of delivery to final demand, Georgia, 1970.

		Delivering industry					
		Agriculture, mining	Construction	Manufacturing	Trade	Services	Households
		(1)	(2)	(3)	(4)	(5)	(6)
Supporting industry	Agriculture, mining (1)	1.14	.03	.06	.02	.02	.02
	Construction (2)	.02	1.01	.01	.02	.04	.01
	Manufacturing (3)	.19	.26	1.18	.12	.13	.15
	Trade (4)	.17	.21	.14	1.16	.17	.25
	Services (5)	.35	.35	.28	.43	1.49	.50
	Households (6)	.69	.60	.52	.80	.75	1.38
	Total output	2.54	2.46	2.19	2.55	2.60	2.32

Table 2.5b shows the total-requirements matrix for the aggregated model of Georgia. Each entry shows the purchases from the industry named on the left by the industry numbered across the top for each dollar of delivery to final demand. To illustrate the use of Table 2.5b, let us assume that the demand for the output of the manufacturing sector increases by $100. If the economy is to satisfy this demand, the gross output of the agriculture and mining sector must increase by $6, of the construction sector by $1, of the

manufacturing sector itself by an additional $18, of the trade sector by $14, of the service sector by $28, and of households by $52. These estimates are obtained by multiplying column 3 in Table 2.5b by $100. The total change in output in the economy is $219.

Now that we have developed the logic of a state input-output model and can see that it is a means for tracing the effects on local industries of changes in the economy, let us go back and examine the effect of closing the model with respect to households. Recall that we have included the household sector as the sixth industry in the model. Under these conditions, the total-requirements table traces the flows of goods and services required to accommodate changes in final demand through all industries and through households as well. What if the household sector had been left in final demand? What if we had continued to treat it as exogenous to the system rather than endogenous?

Table 2.5c Total requirements per dollar of delivery to final demand, Georgia, 1970 (based on interindustry transactions excluding households).

			Delivering industry				
			Agriculture, mining (1)	Construction (2)	Manufacturing (3)	Trade (4)	Services (5)
Supporting industry	Agriculture, mining	(1)	1.13	.02	.05	*	.01
	Construction	(2)	.01	1.01	.01	.01	.03
	Manufacturing	(3)	.11	.19	1.12	.03	.05
	Trade	(4)	.04	.10	.05	1.02	.03
	Services	(5)	.10	.14	.09	.15	1.23
	Total output		1.40	1.46	1.32	1.21	1.35

* Less than .005.

Table 2.5c reports a total-requirements table which is based on a five-industry version of Table 2.5a, the direct-requirements matrix. Examination of the column sums in the rows entitled 'total output' in each table reveals the importance of the household sector in generating new activity in the economy. Table 2.5d compares these tables. Just including the household sector in the inverted table leads to increases in output by the processing industries (1 through 5) of 27 to 45 percent. When we include households as an industry and count the flows through it as output, the percent increase in output rises to from 66 to 111 percent of the flows based on the table excluding households. As we shall see later in a more detailed discussion of multipliers, income flows induced by households are important to a regional input-output analysis.

2.5.5 Summary and transition

This section has been intended to show the logic of economic models and to demonstrate how the tables representing an input-output model are developed. The state transactions table, seen here as Table 2.2a, is presented as Table I in the more detailed formulations of the model. The direct-requirements table, here Table 2.5a, becomes Table II. In the detailed model, Table III is the total-requirements table excluding households, here Table 2.5c; it shows the direct and indirect requirements from other industries for each dollar of delivery to final demand. The final detailed table, Table IV, is the total-requirements table with the household sector included as an industry, here Table 2.5b; it shows the direct, indirect, and induced requirements per dollar of delivery to final demand. 'Induced' means caused by household consumption; it is a term used to distinguish Table IV, the extended inverse, from Table III, which more conservatively includes only clearly identified processing industries.

Table 2.5d Comparison of total-requirements matrices excluding and including the household sector.

Delivering industry	Sum of industry total requirements		Percent increase due to households (3)	Total requirements including households (4)	Total percent increase due to households (5)
	Including households (1)	Excluding households (2)			
Agriculture, mining	1.40	1.85	32	2.54	81
Construction	1.46	1.86	27	2.46	68
Manufacturing	1.32	1.67	27	2.19	66
Trade	1.21	1.75	45	2.55	111
Services	1.35	1.85	37	2.60	93
Households	-	1.22	-	2.32	-

Sources:
Column (1): Column sums, Table 2.5c.
Column (2): Column sums, Table 2.5b less household row entries.
Column (3): Column (2) divided by Column (1), less one, and expressed as a percent.
Column (4): Column sums, Table 2.5b.
Column (5): Column (4) divided by Column (1), less one, and expressed as a percent.

2.6 ECONOMIC CHANGE IN INPUT-OUTPUT MODELS

2.6.1 Causes vs. consequences of change

An input-output model is designed to trace the effects of changes in an economy which has been represented in an input-output table. Such models show the consequences of change in terms of flows of monies through an economy and in terms of incomes generated for primary resource owners. The models themselves do not show the causes of change; these causes are exogenous to the system.

Economic change as traced through an input-output model can take two forms: 1. structural change or 2. change in final demand. Change in the economic structure of an area (state) can be initiated in several ways. It can be through public investment in schools, highways, public facilities, etc., or it can be through private investment in new production facilities, or it can be through changes in the marketing structure of the economy. Changes in final demand are basically changes in government expenditure patterns and changes in the demands by other areas for the goods produced in the state.

2.6.2 Structural change

Structural change in an input-output context can be interpreted to mean 'changes in regional production coefficients.' In turn, this can be interpreted as either changes in technology or changes in marketing patterns or both. Let us see what this means in terms of the direct-requirements matrix, or the a matrix of our earlier discussion (2.5.2). Recall that a_{ij} is the proportion of total inputs purchased from industry i by industry j in Georgia. We can treat this regional production coefficient as the product of two other coefficients and write it symbolically as $a_{ij} = p_{ij} \cdot r_{ij}$. The 'technical production coefficient,' p_{ij}, shows the proportion of inputs purchased from industry i by industry j without regard to the location of industry i, while the 'regional trade coefficient,' r_{ij}, shows the proportion of that purchase made in Georgia.

A change in technology, or a change in p_{ij}, could be illustrated by a shift from glass bottles to metal cans by the soft-drink industry. But a change in location of purchase, or a change in r_{ij}, would be illustrated by a shift from metal cans made in Baltimore to metal cans produced in Atlanta.

The above changes are couched in terms of existing industries. Another way in which change can take place is through the introduction of new plants or even new industries. The introduction of a new plant into an existing industry has the effect of changing the production and trade patterns of the aggregated industry to reflect more of the transactions specific to the detailed industry of which the new plant is a member. For example, consider the manufacturing sector of our highly aggregated five-industry model. As presented, it reflects the combination of all manufacturing activities in Georgia in 1970. The introduction of new plants in the transportation-equipment industry would change the combination of purchases presently made in the manufacturing sector. The same statement might be made concerning the purchase pattern displayed by the transportation-equipment industry if a new aircraft-producing plant were established (or an old one were to cease operation).

The addition of a completely new industry to the system means adding another row and column to the interindustry table to represent the new industry. This is done in a manner similar to that involved in closing the table with respect to households.

To account for structural changes which are caused by changes in technology or in marketing requires a revision of the interindustry flows table and is best accomplished when a biennial revision is made.

To account for structural changes which are caused by addition of new plants in either old or new industries, we have programmed a 'development simulator' which is presented in Chapter 8.

2.6.3 Changes in final demand

Accounting for structural changes in an input-output model requires substantial skill and familiarity with the mechanics of the model on the part of the analyst. This is not the case when accounting for the effects of changes in final demand. It can easily be accomplished with the inverse matrix, or the total-requirements table, Table 2.5b in this chapter or Table IV in the detailed model.

Two kinds of changes can be traced. One form is a set of long-run changes in the demands for the outputs of all industries. This set takes the form of the y' vector discussed in section 2.5 above and represents our best judgment of the export demands for the products of our industries in some later year, say 1980. Using the formula

$$x' = (I - a)^{-1} \cdot y' \, ,$$

we can easily derive projections of the expected gross outputs (x_i') of industries in the later year. This process is discussed in more detail in Chapter 6, which outlines our *forecasting model*.

The other form which change in final demand might take is an assumed change in the final demand for the output of one industry. Say we wish to know the effect on the economy of a $100,000 increase in the demand for floor coverings. We would simply go to the detailed 28-industry tables and look for the column sum for the floor-covering industry in Table IV, 'the total-requirements matrix. The entry is 2.2234; multiplied by $ 100,000, it shows that these additional sales of carpets outside of Georgia would increase the outputs of Georgia industries by a total of $222,340. A look at the household row in that same column would have yielded a household-income coefficient of .4136, meaning that the additional carpet sales would have increased local household incomes by $41,360.

The example can be pursued on a more gross level by looking at Table 2.5b and assuming a $100,000 increase in the output of the manufacturing sector. As pointed out in section 2.5.4, the output multiplier in manufacturing is 2.19, meaning that the $100,000 change in export demand yields $219,000 in additional business to Georgia firms. The household-income coefficient of .52 means that household incomes increase by $52,000. The differences between these figures and those in the above paragraph show the consequences of aggregation, which conceals a substantial amount of variation in the detailed tables.

We discuss the *multiplier model* in more detail in Chapters 5 and 8.

NOTES

1. The notion of an input-output table as a double-entry accounting system appears throughout the literature. We were first introduced to the 'quadrant' sectoring of a transactions table by Marvin Hoffenberg, one of the architects of the 1947 U.S. input-output study, at a meeting of the Western Regional Science Association several years ago. Good discussions appear in Miernyk, *et al.* (1967), Fuerst (1955), and Liebling (1955).
2. Based on unpublished compilation by Philip Bourque.
3. Much of this explanation of input-output models is based on a similar review for the interindustry model of Hawaii (Schaffer, *et al.,* 1972b). That, in turn, had several origins. Our presentation of an economic model as a set of relations evolved from lectures at Duke University by the late Charles Ferguson. The clearest outline of an input-output model as the solution of a set of simultaneous equations is in Isard (1960). And although the distinction between regional production coefficients and technical coefficients is common to most discussions, we have enjoyed the comments of Bourque and Cox (1970). An abbreviated version of this chapter appeared in the *Atlanta Economic Review* (Schaffer, Laurent, and Sutter, 1973).

3. Constructing the transactions table

3.1 GENERAL APPROACH

As with any large statistical undertaking, the Georgia Interindustry Study depends on a number of data sources, both primary and secondary. Here we document our approach to melding these data into a consistent representation of the Georgia economy. This approach is based on research conducted in the Regional Development Program of the College of Industrial Management at Georgia Tech and on experience gained in constructing a similar system at the Department of Planning and Economic Development of the State of Hawaii. We also draw extensively on the experience of one of the team members (Eugene A. Laurent) in constructing an input-output model of Charleston, South Carolina.

The system permits us first to develop an input-output table wholly from secondary (published) data and then to evolve from this first estimate a table embodying as much primary data as can be obtained with available resources. Ultimately, the system could be completely survey-based. We feel that our approach is both useful and interesting.

This chapter summarizes our computing techniques, and provides a few comments on our data sources and a general overview of the system. A system flowchart is used to identify more precisely the elements in the system while at the same time conveying a feeling for the system as a whole.

3.2 LOCAL- AND PRIMARY-DATA SOURCES

The Georgia Interindustry Study depends for primary data on a survey of manufacturing firms in the state and on unpublished sources at the Georgia Department of Labor and the Georgia Department of Revenue.

In the survey, contacts were made with over 240 firms. Mail questionnaires were returned by 93 firms out of 700 in a stratified sample selected from the *Georgia Manufacturing Directory* (Cheatham, 1971). Personal interviews were conducted by three senior team members with executives in 150 large manufacturing firms, with most of these contacts being made during a series of tours around the state during the summer quarter, 1971. An important feature of these tours was visits with the eight field offices of the Industrial

Development Division (IDD) of the Georgia Institute of Technology and with the staffs of the 19 Area Development and Planning Commissions (APDC's) in Georgia. The IDD field offices maintain files on major firms in their areas containing lists of products, employment, markets, major customers and suppliers, contacts, and special characteristics. We were given access to these files under standard rules regarding disclosure. Interviews with the development specialists in many APDC's were invaluable preliminaries to firm interviews and frequently were adequate in themselves to form trade patterns.

Primary data on over 400 other firms were provided by the Georgia Department of Revenue. While the identity of each firm remained unknown to us, the sample was spread across all nonagricultural industries in the state. We were provided in each case with a set of final-payment ratios and a range of dollar sales by the firm. These data, supplemented by interview-gathered data, formed the basis for our detailed final-payment sectors.

In addition, the Georgia Department of Labor gave us access to its unpublished data on employment and wages and salaries classified by detailed industry, subject to the rules governing disclosure of confidential data. Combined with the final-payments ratios noted above, these data became the primary source for gross-output estimates.

We did not survey the nonmanufacturing industries. But in certain cases, *e.g.* agriculture and mining, we relied on local industry and government experts in preparing data for these industries, and in almost all cases expert opinion was sought in developing export estimates.

Because of the many and diverse sources used in this study, we have not devised a table of response rates, as has become fashionable for regional studies. For us, the table would be misleading since reporting actual full-interview responses would conceal the wealth of information available to us otherwise, and listing all contacts and sources would obviously stretch the point of the table.

3.3 SECONDARY-DATA SOURCES

Our principal secondary-data source is the Bureau of Economic Analysis [formerly the Office of Business Economics (OBE)], U.S. Department of Commerce, which provided three basic sets of data: the 367-industry national input-output tables for 1963, price indices for most industries between 1963 and 1970, and the worksheets underlying personal-income estimates in Georgia. In addition, we have used the *Census of Manufactures, County Business Patterns*, the *Minerals Yearbook, Farm Income Situation, State Government Finance, Government Finance,* the *Georgia Auditor's Report,* and many other published documents. The following comments outline the nature of the national input-output table and identify some of the problems associated with its use.

3.3.1 *The national input-output table as an initial data base*

Since we generally adopted the format, definitions, and conventions of the U.S. Input-Output Study, we should identify some of the peculiarities of the national table before discussing its use for regional studies. The following comments are based on a description by the National Economics Division (1969).

Trade. The trade industry is a 'margin industry.' That is, it is an industry producing an output measured in terms of total margins, or operating expenses plus profit. If actual flows of goods were traced to and from the trade industry, the detailed connections would be between trade and the producing industries, while the consuming industries and final users would make most of their purchases from the trade industry. Since it is desirable to show the links between industries, and between industries and final markets, commodities are shown as if moving directly from producer to user, by-passing trade. The value added by the trade industry is then recorded as a separate transaction, so the purchaser appears to have purchased two things, the commodity itself and the service of the tradesman who bridges the gap between producer and consumer.

This definition is no particular problem for the analyst constructing a regional table. In fact, it is common to all regional interindustry studies. As far as we know, only Harmston and Lund (1967, pp. 51-2) have suggested the alternative treatment, and this for the special case of a very small area or community in which trade dominates.

The only problems with trade as a margin industry are 1. that it is difficult to explain to a layman and 2. that a 'bridge' may be needed to properly interpret the impact of an exogenous sale.[1] This bridge would show the trade margin associated with a commodity sale and would permit the analyst to trace the impact of the sale through both the producing and trade industries. For example, a bridge would be needed to trace the effect of a purchase by a tourist of a locally made souvenir since a large part of the purchase price would no doubt be the trade markup. But this is a problem of interpretation, not construction, and is discussed further in section 8.4.

Valuation of transactions. Transactions are recorded in producers' prices, which include excise taxes collected and paid by the producer but exclude the distribution costs which make up the difference between producers' and purchasers' prices. Under this system the individual inputs into a consuming industry are valued at producers' prices and the trade margins and transportation costs associated with these inputs all appear as purchases by the consuming industry from the trade industry and the transportation industry.

This convention also applies to regional input-output tables. With fully survey-based tables, the analyst might in fact estimate trade margins by comparing cells in a purchasers' prices table (based on a survey of purchasers) with the corresponding cells in a producers' prices table (based on a survey of producers). But no matter how the valuation is made, all modern regional input-output tables are based on producers' prices.

One particularly good feature of the national input-output tables is the availability on computer tape of the margins associated with each individual cell in the table. We have made use of these entries in constructing our margin industries.

Secondary products or activities. In the national study, an establishment is classified according to the Standard Industrial Classification (SIC) in an industry based on its principal activity, and its entire output is counted as part of the output of that industry. The output which determines its classification is called its primary product, while its other outputs are called secondary products. It is in the treatment of secondary products that most regional tables differ from the national table. In the national table, secondary products are normally 'transferred' from their producing industries to the industries in which they are primary. In some cases, when secondary production is large and considerably different from the primary output, both the secondary products and their associated inputs are subtracted from the producing industry and added to the industries in which they are primary.

Obviously, this procedure is complex and highly dependent on a strong, experienced, and well-financed statistical organization. These are characteristics not typical of groups constructing regional input-output tables. Even the directors of the Philadelphia Input-Output Study, the largest and most expensive regional study to date, were not prepared to handle secondary products.

As a general rule, then, regional input-output studies focus on the production and sale of the outputs of establishments classified into industries on the basis of their primary products. These outputs include both primary and secondary products. At the level of aggregation used in most regional studies this is not necessarily a severe problem, since at the two-digit classification level many primary and secondary products may not be distinguishable.

Imports. Imports are classified in two ways in the U.S. table. Imports competitive with products produced by U.S. industries are treated as secondary products. That is, they are shown as if purchased by the industries producing substitutable products domestically. On the other hand, imports which are not competitive with domestic products are shown as purchased directly by the consuming industry in the final market.

Gross output and input. The gross output of an industry includes not only the total primary and secondary output of the industry but also the secondary products and imports transferred into the industry and distributed as part of the output of the industry.

The gross input of an industry is the sum of purchases by the industry, value added by the industry, and the producers' value of the secondary products and substitutable imports transferred into the industry.

These definitions differ from those used in the normal regional study only through the inclusion of secondary products.

Format and availability. Finally, having considered the major definitions and conventions associated with the U.S. table, we should note its availability. The latest U.S. table available as this study commenced in 1970 was the 1963 table. It was available at three levels of aggregation: 85 industries, 367 industries, and 478 industries. The 85-industry version matched the 1958 study in size and definition and is the officially published table. The 367-industry table, published in a supplement to the *Survey of Current Business*, contained industries defined in sufficient detail to be associated with SIC industries on the three- and four-digit level. It has ten final-demand sectors and one value-added row. Along with matrices of interindustry transfers and detailed margins, it is available on a computer tape from the National Economics Division. Although a 478-industry table, with expanded construction and manufacturing industries, was also available, we chose to work with the 367-industry data for fear of exceeding our computing budget.

3.3.2 Problems in using the national table

Several problems are inherent in estimating regional interindustry transactions from the national input-output table. Let us examine a few of these problems and explore alternatives for solving them. The problems arise from two basic sources, changes over time and differences over space.

Technology. Technological change is defined simply as changes in the physical requirements for production. For example, consider a shift from glass bottles to metal cans in the soft-drink industry, or from glass bottles to plastic containers for certain chemical products such as common household bleach. The problem arises primarily because of the time lag involved in constructing the national table (five years for the 1958 study and six years for the 1963 study).

Outside a full-scale survey, we can account for technological change by conducting a series of corrective interviews with representatives of major industries in the regional economy. We will show that this partial solution to the technology problem is also a solution to the other problems cited below.

Differences in the technology of production between plants in different regions may also exist, but their importance is generally considered to be small. Technological change flows fairly rapidly between regions in an open economy. Plants in rapidly developing areas adopt new technologies and may thus differ slightly from those in older, more established areas. Steel production is more efficient in Germany and Japan than in the United States.

One indicator of spatial differences in technology for an industry may be a comparison of the distribution of plants by size in the region relative to the nation. We have not made this comparison in Georgia. Our assumption is that the scales of operation for plants in the state are reasonably similar to those for plants in the nation.

Critics of the use of national tables in constructing regional models have not been harsh in applying this criticism regarding technological change. Since a lag of at least two years normally occurs in producing a survey-based table, this criticism also applies to survey-based studies, at least with respect to technological change over time. In fact, the method used in this study may yield results superior to those of the typical survey. By roughly estimating transactions from national patterns and correcting these estimates on the basis of interviews with selected industry experts, we could complete a regional input-output study, or update an old transactions table, within months of the interview period.

Product mix. A more telling criticism of regional tables constructed from a national table has been based on the product-mix question. For most studies, regardless of the means of construction, the question is a serious one.

The problem is concerned with the level of aggregation of the national industry and, to some extent, of the regional industry. For example, food and kindred products is one industry in the 1958 national study. Since the industries subsumed under this title show substantial geographical variation, the use of this one industry as a basis for identifying the transactions within a region is quite inaccurate. The producing of cheese involves a series of transactions quite different from those necessary to the canning of fruit.

The product-mix problem is of much less consequence with the 1963 national table than with the 1958 study. For 1958, the data are available only in 85-industry detail; for 1963, the data are available at two additional levels of aggregation. The 367-industry table reduces the product-mix problem by substantially expanding the industry detail. Here the one food and kindred products industry of 1958 is divided into 32 industries; the alcoholic-beverages industry can be contrasted with the soft-drink industry. The unpublished 478-industry table helps even more. Continuing our example, 41 food industries are available in this table. The malt-liquor industry, a subset of the alcoholic-beverages industry, can be contrasted with the wine industry, another subset employing another production technology.

The 367-industry table forms the basis for our state study and resolves the product-mix question fairly effectively. With more resources than were available to us, the data required for this study could have been gathered in sufficient detail to permit use of the 478-industry table with its expanded construction and manufacturing industries.

One clear advantage of our procedures is our ability to work with industries defined in fine detail. As long as the industry can be defined by four-digit SIC code and its gross output can be approximated, the industry can be considered

for inclusion in our model. The transactions data which might be considered confidential has already been collected on a national level. The analyst basing his study exclusively on a survey is not so fortunate and must carefully define his industries in such a way that his respondents are protected. In his case, the data derived from the survey are transactions data. If the number of firms in the industry is insufficient to avoid disclosing data collected on a confidential basis, then this industry must be combined with others; some of its individual character is lost and the ability of the input-output table to demonstrate interdependence among economic units is impaired.

Survey-based regional input-output models are thus seldom constructed to show more than 50 industries. Using our techniques, any number of industries can be included initially. As interviews are conducted, the table can then be aggregated as necessary to avoid disclosing confidential data.

Prices. Since transactions are expressed in value terms, changes (and differences) in prices can have an important effect on transactions over time. If not accounted for, price changes can have a serious effect on interindustry relationships.

While the technology problem can only be alleviated by applying local judgment, price changes can be partially accounted for by updating the national table with price indices. This updating is accomplished by multiplying each row in the national transactions matrix by the appropriate price index. The process is described in more detail in the next section.

Definitions. Definitions cause several problems, primarily those dealing with transfers of secondary products, with industry classification, with margins, and with the final-payments sector.

The transfers problem is perhaps the most troublesome. In the national table, the secondary products of an industry (establishment) are transferred to the industry for which the transferred products are primary. Thus the cotton industry 'produces' housing for resident owners of cotton farms. The imputed value of this clearly secondary product is 'sold' (transferred) by the cotton industry to the owner-occupied dwelling industry, to which the product is primary. The problem in constructing regional tables arises: 1. if an industry which does not exist in the state transfers a secondary product to a local industry (*e.g.*, if the copper-mining industry, which does not exist in Georgia, transfers the imputed value of housing produced at copper mines to the owner-occupied dwelling industry in Georgia) or 2. if the industry into which a secondary product of a local industry is transferred does not exist in the region. In both cases, regional imports would be distorted. Several alternative solutions exist.

One solution is to follow the common procedure used in most regional studies, which is not to transfer secondary products. This particular solution involves establishing the sales pattern associated with the secondary product (the row of the industry into which the product is transferred) and distributing the secondary product according to this pattern as part of the sales of the primary industry. But while this procedure may yield a table characteristic of most regional studies, it also yields a table defined in a way substantially different from its national basis.

Another 'solution' is to demonstrate that the problem is insignificant. This can be accomplished by showing that transfers of secondary products between local industries and nonlocal industries do not exist or exist at such a magnitude that they can be either ignored or corrected in the interview process.

Our solution calls for slightly modifying the method used by the Bureau of Economic Analysis in handling transfers. In the local-transactions matrix and in the corresponding competitive-imports matrix, we have retained the national definitions. That is, we continue to transfer secondary products into the industries in which they are primary. Our assumption is that transfers are imported and exported in the same proportions as are the corresponding primary products. But, with the exceptions of the foreign-imports row and the dummy-industry columns, we have eliminated transfers altogether from the noncompetitive-imports matrix. The transfers in this matrix are from a nonlocal producing industry into a local consuming industry. In the context of a relatively closed national economy, these transfers had meaning; in the context of an open regional economy, they erroneously imply an irrational physical transfer of goods or services.

The problem regarding industry definitions is basically one of convenience. For example, federal-government enterprises, which is an industry consisting of the post office and other such product-producing and revenue-collecting activities, is separated from federal-government purchases. The former is treated as endogenous while the latter are exogenous; the federal enterprises fit into the market economy while the federal purchases are based on political decisions. This division is proper; nevertheless it presents some problems in that it requires additional data collection. Another example is the 'dummy industries' which were defined in the national study to account for business entertainment and travel, office supplies, scrap and second-hand goods, etc., all of which are items whose industry of origin is not easily identified. Regional analysts relying on surveys typically slough off such fine problems by aggregating. The regional analyst using the national table as his base is not so fortunate; he must face the problem forthrightly and explain his actions.

Difficulties of definition are also found in the margin industries, which include wholesale trade, retail trade, and transportation. These have been defined on fairly gross terms and were not treated with finer detail in the 1963 study. For regional purposes, it would be convenient to have more detail.

The transportation industry reports the transportation margin for production in the entire nation. To the extent that transportation costs differ for

Georgia industries, this margin should be adjusted. Further, this industry should be divided into two components, one local and the other nonlocal, to account for the use of nonlocal transportation to and from the state.

A final definitional shortcoming, as mentioned earlier, is in the definition of the final-payments, or value-added, sector of the national table. The more interesting applications of regional input-output analysis require that value added be divided into its component parts: wages and salaries, profits, depreciation, state and local taxes, federal taxes, etc. We have had to rely on local, primary data for this division.

3.3.3 Adjusting for price changes

One serious question facing the regional analyst using an older table is what to do about price changes. The answer depends on his assumption regarding elasticity of demand, among other things. For example, if the analyst chooses not to adjust transactions for price changes, he may implicitly have assumed a unit elasticity of demand for all products, substitutability among certain inputs, and price changes which are consistent with these substitutions. The possibilities are boundless, and the analyst could easily become trapped in a theoretical maze. Therefore, we retreat to the only practical solution available to us. Variation in prices can influence our assumed equality between the technology expressed in the 1963 national study and the technology of production for Georgia in 1970 in two ways: 1. prices can change over time and 2. prices can vary over space. Since we do not have reliable comparisons of prices in Georgia with those in the rest of the nation, we are unable to account for spatial variation in industry prices. But we do have indices comparing prices over time for the nation and can consequently account for temporal variation in prices.

These price indices are based on the unpublished data used in deriving implicit price deflators for estimates of gross national product. We should note their detail. For all manufacturing industries except ordnance and accessories, the price indices have been computed on the 367-industry level. (The basic data is available for most four-digit industries; we have aggregated as required.) We use the price index for aircraft and parts as a proxy for the index for the ordnance industry. For the remaining nonextractive industries, we obtained data from the Bureau of Economic Analysis sufficient to construct indices on the 85-industry level. Indices for the extractive industries were constructed from published information in the *Survey of Current Business* and the *U.S. Minerals Yearbook*.

Our method is simple and resembles the 'double-deflation' method used by the Office of Business Economics in computing industry gross product in constant dollars:

The gross product of an industry measured from the income side is not directly convertible to constant dollars because its components − employee compensation, interest, profits, depreciation, etc. – are not factorable into quantity and unit price suitable for this purpose. Gross product can be adjusted indirectly for price changes, however, by deflating output and purchases separately. Both the output and the purchases consist of specifiable goods and services that can be analyzed into quantity and price. The difference between the two deflated figures is gross product in constant dollars. This method is known as the 'double deflation' method.

Let x_{ij} represent the value of cell ij in the national transactions matrix for 1963, c_{if} the value of cell if in the final-demand matrix, v_j the value added by industry j, and p_i the 1970 price index (1963 base) for industry i. A prime denotes value expressed in 1970 prices, while a 'dot' subscript indicates summation over the replaced subscript. Current (1970) dollar transactions are computed as

$$x'_{ij} = x_{ij} \cdot p_i$$

and

$$c'_{if} = c_{if} \cdot p_i .$$

By definition, gross industry output in 1970 prices (y') is

$$y'_i = x'_{i.} + c'_{i.} .$$

And the column residual is value added in 1970 prices:

$$v_j = y'_j - x'_{.j} .$$

These calculations yield a price-adjusted national transactions table. From this table, production coefficients can be calculated which hold physical production requirements constant. Algebraically, the 1970 production coefficients with technology held constant (a'_{ij}) can be expressed as

$$a'_{ij} = \frac{x_{ij} \cdot p_i}{x_j \cdot p_j}$$

or as

$$a'_{ij} = a_{ij} \cdot \frac{p_i}{p_j} .$$

·3.4 THE ESTIMATING PROCEDURE.[2]

The method used in constructing the Georgia Economic Model has evolved from a nonsurvey procedure to a survey-based one. The procedure resembles the 'rows-only' survey technique introduced by Hansen and Tiebout (1963) while incorporating the best features of a technique based on a detailed national base. This section outlines the conceptual basis for the computing system described in the next section. But first we should look at the problem in graphic terms.

3.4.1 A schematic review of available data

Our transactions table is based on a technology matrix derived from the national table, on estimates of gross outputs constructed from existing data, on gross state product accounts derived in part from published sources, on tax data from unpublished sources, and on survey data on technical relations and regional trade patterns collected from Georgia manufacturers. These data must be carefully integrated to provide a consistent picture of the state economy.

Figure 3.4a shows how these items are related in an input-output framework. View the entire figure as a regional transactions table of the type described in Table 2.2a and Figure 2.2a. Secondary data is recorded in the cross-hatched areas. Total purchases and total sales, developed from employment data and published sources, establish the magnitude of the producing industries; total local final expenditures and total local final payments, developed from published sources, delimit the behavior of final consumers in the state. The remaining local elements of the gross state product accounts appear in the nonmarket transfers quadrant of the table.

Primary data from unpublished sources is identified by a diagonal hatching. This consists mostly of data on final payments, or wages and salaries, profits, and taxes, derived as noted earlier from income-tax sources and the survey. At this point, sufficient basic data exists to produce a state technology matrix, using national interindustry relationships to fill in the remainder of the table.

To develop regional trade patterns and thus to separate imports and exports from local transactions, a nonsurvey technique could now be used. We have done this to produce a first estimate of regional transactions.

But we have drawn on survey-based data to improve these estimates. The stippled area in Figure 3.4a shows the insertion of our manufacturing survey into the system. This substantially reduces the burden forced upon the nonsurvey technique, that of estimating regional trade for the remainder of the state's industries.

3.4.2 The state technology matrix

The input structure of industries in the state is called the 'state technology matrix.' It is commonly designated as the '*A*' matrix. Each A_{ij} indicates the proportion of the total inputs of industry *j* purchased from industry *i*:

$$A_{ij} = \frac{X_{ij}}{X_j}.$$

Note that this A_{ij} is to be distinguished from the a_{ij} of Chapter 2. The table says nothing about the regional origins of inputs; it only identifies the production technologies of industries in the state. The '*a*' matrix is based on purchases within the region.

The process of creating the state technology matrix from the U.S. input-output table involves several steps, some of which we have already discussed: 1. dividing national transactions into two parts, direct allocations and transfers; 2. adjusting for price changes since 1963; 3. rearranging the transactions into local and nonlocal categories; and 4. adjusting the national

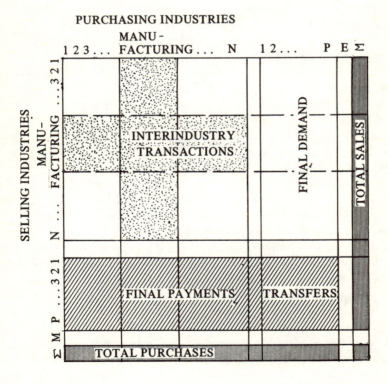

Figure 3.4a Arrangement of secondary and primary data for constructing a regional transactions table.

transactions to account for loss of transfers when the regional model is aggregated. Several comments on these steps are pertinent.

First, since the eventual aggregation of our regional model will necessitate an elimination of transfers between industries which are aggregated, we separate the national transactions into two parts, allocations and transfers. The direct allocations are simply the direct purchases of inputs to the production process. Transfers, as noted earlier, are fictitious sales of goods from producing industries in which the goods are secondary products to industries for which the goods are primary.

To avoid complicated problems in redefining national industries with substantial transfers (such as owner-occupied dwellings, business entertainment, office supplies, etc.), we have worked within a modified version of the framework established by the Bureau of Economic Analysis. Essentially, we eliminate transfers from noncompetitive (nonlocal) industries to local industries, ignore transfers from local industries to nonlocal industries, and assume proportional transfers for industries with competitive imports.

Second, we adjust both the national allocations and national transfers to account for price changes. This adjustment is fully discussed in section 3.3.3.

Third, we divide both matrices into local and nonlocal segments. If an industry exists in the state, we retain it in the local section. If it does not exist in the state, we place its row in the noncompetitive-imports section and delete its column. In the case of Georgia, this rearrangement means that the 367-industry transactions matrix is reduced to one which is 300 industries wide and 367 industries high. The upper 300 rows represent local industries, while the lower 67 industries do not presently produce in Georgia. This arrangement reduces the computer manipulation problem substantially and orders the matrix for best use in the procedure which estimates trade patterns.

Our fourth step is to account for the disappearance of transfers with aggregation. Since we present the study in a 28-industry format while computing the basic regional-transactions table at the 367-industry level, a number of combinations are necessary. If industry one transfers its secondary product to industry two for distribution, and if those industries are aggregated, then the fictitious sale becomes unreasonable in that the 'industry' is now transferring products to itself. (Most industries show some intra-industry sales between establishments. This is acceptable and simply reflects the statistician's inability to count and present everything on an establishment basis. But a transfer from an industry to itself has no logic.) We make zero the transfers which would appear on the diagonal of the aggregated matrix and add the remaining elements in the transfers matrix to the direct-allocations matrix. The result is a modified total-transactions table which will not show intra-industry transfers when aggregated.

Finally, it is but a simple matter to divide each entry in a column by the corresponding gross industry output to obtain a first estimate of the state technical coefficients. As seen later, these coefficients are subject to revision as corrections are discovered; but for now, this technology matrix will do as a basis for the next section.

3.4.3 Estimating regional trade patterns

The regional transactions table, which is the basic table in a regional input-output model, is constructed from the state technology matrix. The state technology matrix identifies the industries which exist in Georgia and divides their purchases into two categories: purchases from industries which exist locally, and purchases from industries which do not exist locally (noncompetitive imports). To complete the regional transactions table, we must now determine the trade pattern with respect to industries which exist in Georgia; that is, we must estimate the exports of these industries and we must estimate imports from nonlocal industries which are competitive to those in Georgia.

We derive the regional transactions table from the state technology matrix in three steps, each moving us closer to the observed trade patterns of industries in the state. First, we use the 'supply-demand pool' technique to construct a first estimate of exports and imports. Then we examine the export column thus computed and compare it with a column of expected values based on observations. Second, we use a variation of the supply-demand pool method, which we call the 'exports-only' technique, to modify our computed exports. This procedure assigns exports and then applies the supply-demand pool technique to estimate the remaining regional transactions and imports. Third, we extend the method to a variation called the 'selected-values' technique. This final modification assigns values to cells in both the regional transactions matrix and the regional final-demand matrix before applying the supply-demand pool technique to the remaining cells in each row. Our final product is a regional transactions table which conforms with available data and which, when no data is available, embodies our best estimates of regional trade.

Basic format. For convenience in presenting our techniques, we symbolically outline the regional system here and define the variables which we will use in describing it.

Our system is static, open, and descriptive. Comparing the region with the rest of the world, the system is based on a regional transactions table of the form sketched in Figure 3.4b. Given a correspondingly defined technology matrix and given estimates of regional outputs (x_i) and regional final demands (y_f), the task is to estimate regional gross flows (x_{ij}), exports (e_i), imports (m_{ij}), and value added (v_j). Or given an input-output system

$$\sum_{j=1}^{s} A_{ij} \cdot X_j + \sum_{f=1}^{t} Y_{if} + E_i = X_i, \quad (i = 1, 2, 3, \ldots s),$$

Outputs / Inputs	Selling industries				Local final demand		Exports	Total sales
	1	2	3 ...	s	1 ...	t		
1	x_{11}	x_{12}	x_{13} ...	x_{1s}	y_{11} ...	y_{1t}	e_1	x_1
2	x_{21}	x_{22}	x_{23} ...	x_{2s}	y_{21} ...	y_{2t}	e_2	x_2
3	x_{31}	x_{32}	x_{33} ...	x_{3s}	y_{31} ...	y_{3t}	e_3	x_3
. . .	.	.	.	.	. . .	.	. . .	. . .
s	x_{s1}	. . .		x_{ss}	y_{s1} ...	y_{st}	e_s	x_s
Value added	v_1	v_2	v_3 ...	v_s	u_1 ...	u_t		
Imports	m_1	m_2	m_3 ...	m_s	p_1 ...	p_t		
Total inputs	x_1	x_2	x_3 ...	x_s	y_1 ...	y_t		

(Purchasing industries)

Figure 3.4b Simplified regional transactions table.

and given a set of regional outputs and demands, we derive the regional input-output system

$$\sum_{j=1}^{s} a_{ij} \cdot x_j + \sum_{f=1}^{t} y_{if} + e_i = x_i, \quad (i = 1, 2, 3, \ldots s).$$

We use lower-case letters to represent variables in the regional system and upper-case letters to refer to variables in the technology matrix. Thus, A_{ij} and a_{ij} are the $s \times s$ production coefficients ($A_{ij} = X_{ij}/X_j$, $a_{ij} = x_{ij}/x_j$) in the technical system and the regional system respectively, X_i and x_i are the outputs of industry i, Y_{if} and y_{if} are the final demands from industry i of consuming sector f, and E_i and e_i are exports. Note that E_i is added only for completeness; in our calculations it has no function.

The above equation systems are in terms of sales, or demands. We can also outline the systems in terms of supply, which is determined by what is purchased, *i.e.* by the production technology. Technically,

$$\sum_{i=1}^{s} X_{ij} + V_j + \sum_{k=1}^{s} N_{kj} = X_j, \quad (j = 1, 2, 3, \ldots s).$$

Here X_{ij} represents the purchases by industry j from industry i within the system of s industries, V_j represents the value added by producers in industry j in the base system, and N_{kj} represents the purchases by industry j from industry k, which is one of r industries existing outside the system (N_{kj} is noncompetitive imports). X_j is the total input (output) of industry j in the base system. In regional terms, the production system can be expressed as

$$\sum_{i=1}^{s} x_{ij} + v_j + \sum_{i=1}^{s} m_{ij} + \sum_{k=1}^{r} n_{kj} = x_j, \quad (j = 1, 2, 3, \ldots s).$$

Our lower-case convention defines all regional variables except m_{ij}, which is competitive imports by industry j from an industry i which exists outside the regional system. Not shown in Figure 3.4b, the variable n_{kj} is defined as $N_{kj} \cdot x_j/X_j$. In the technical system, m_{ij} has no counterpart.

The whole purpose of our trade-pattern calculations is to estimate regional exports, e_i, and then divide $A_{ij} \cdot x_j$, the total purchases from industry i by industry j, into two parts: x_{ij}, which represents local purchases, and m_{ij}, which represents nonlocal purchases.

Supply-demand pool technique. The supply-demand pool technique derives from the concept of regional commodity balances (Isard, 1953). It also is the basis for one of the more well-known nonsurvey models, the Utah model of Moore and Petersen (1955).

Using a base or technical system derived from national transactions, let r_i be the row sum for each industry i of total input requirements (r_{ij} and c_{if})

computed from base production and consumption coefficients for each cell:

$$r_{ij} = x_j \cdot A_{ij}$$

$$c_{if} = y_f \cdot \frac{Y_{if}}{Y_f} .$$

Then the commodity balance (b_i) for each industry can be computed as

$$b_i = x_i - r_i .$$

When b_i is positive, $a_{ij} = A_{ij}$, $x_{ij} = r_{ij}$, $y_{if} = c_{if}$, and $e_i = b_i$, where e_i is exports for industry i. A positive commodity balance represents an exportable surplus.

When the commodity balance is negative, regional production coefficients are computed as proportions of the technical coefficients:

$$a_{ij} = A_{ij} \cdot br_i ,$$

where br_i is defined as x_i/r_i, which we will call the 'balance ratio.' The remainder of total production requirements in each cell is imported as

$$m_{ij} = r_{ij} - a_{ij} \cdot x_j .$$

This pool procedure allocates local production, where adequate, to meet local needs; where the local output is inadequate, it allocates to each purchasing industry j a share of regional output i based on the needs of the purchasing industry itself relative to total needs for output i $(x_{ij} = x_i \cdot r_{ij}/r_i)$.

Exports-only method. Now assume that we have predetermined values for regional exports, e_i, and let us modify the supply-demand pool procedure to account for this knowledge. With e_i now assigned and making a clear claim on supply (x_i), the regional commodity balance should equal zero or less. But in actual practice this condition is not necessarily met. Problems in defining industries and in national statistics as well as errors in estimating exports and industry outputs may upset the balance, forcing a review of our data.

For the exports-only technique, the balance ratio is now computed as

$$br_i^e = \frac{x_i - e_i}{r_i} .$$

Since exports have predetermined values, we estimate local trade as a residual in proportion to needs:

$$x_{ij} = r_{ij} \cdot br_i^e , \text{ and}$$

$$y_{if} = c_{if} \cdot br_i^e .$$

If br_i^e is greater than one, x_{ij} and y_{if} will be larger than expected; that is, they will be larger than the r_{ij} and c_{if} values which are expected to be their upper limits. In this case, some thought should be given to the correctness of estimated exports and the industry gross output. Otherwise, since it is computed as a residual, value added will be reduced to account for this clear overestimate of interindustry purchases.

If br_i^e is less than or equal to one, then a_{ij} and m_{ij} will be computed as in the supply-demand pool procedure.

Selected-values method. Now say that we have prior knowledge not only of exports, but also of certain local transactions which we designate as x'_{ij} or y'_{if}. Since we now are able to asign several values in each row, the balance ratios must be changed to reflect available supply and unsatisfied demand:

$$br_i^s = \frac{x_i - e_i - x'_{ig} \ldots y'_{ih} \ldots}{r_i - r_{ig} \ldots - c_{ih} \ldots} \quad .$$

Note that the predetermined value of exports is subtracted from the numerator but not from the denominator in this formula. This is because total requirements (r_i), or the sum of inputs required by local industries (r_{ij}) and by local final consumers (c_{if}), did not include exports to begin with – there are no predetermined export requirements.

With known values inserted into the regional transactions table and with selected-values balance ratios in hand, we can complete the estimating of regional transactions. For all cells for which values have not been assigned (for those not designated $g \ldots h \ldots$ in the ratio formula),

$$x_{ij} = r_{ij} \cdot br_i^s \text{ and}$$

$$y_{if} = c_{if} \cdot br_i^s \ .$$

And for all cells, we can compute imports as a residual,

$$m_{ij} = r_{ij} - x_{ij} \text{ and}$$

$$p_{if} = c_{if} - y_{if} ,$$

where p_{if} is imports by consuming section f from nonlocal industry i.

In summary, the selected-values method permits us to take advantage of prior knowledge of the exports vector and of a limited number of regional transactions. The procedure assigns these known values and then proportionally allocates the remainder of local production to satisfy local input requirements. Unsatisfied demands are met through imports.

NOTES

1. Bridges are normally not constructed for regional input-output studies, since trade margins are frequently constructed by comparing a sales-survey table with a purchases-survey table. Bridges for the U.S. Input-Output Study can be derived from data in the detailed computer tapes. An example of a personal-consumption-expenditures bridge appears in an article by the National Economics Division (1971).

2. Our procedures have developed over several years, starting with work on nonsurvey techniques by Schaffer and Chu (1969, 1971). The evolution of these techniques to a survey-based procedure is documented in the Hawaii study (Schaffer *et al.*, 1972) and Schaffer (1972a, 1972b). The experience of Laurent in constructing the Charleston model (Hite and Laurent, 1972; Laurent and Hite, 1971) has meant a great deal to this study.

   We spent many hours analyzing other studies, especially those of Washington (Beyers, *et al.*, 1970; Bourque, *et al.*, 1967), West Virginia (Miernyk, *et al.*, 1970), Kansas (Emerson, 1969), New Mexico (Lindberg, 1966a,b), and Utah (Bradley, 1967); our debt to their authors is substantial. We also made good use of the Philadelphia working papers (Isard, Langford, and Romanoff, 1966-68) and wish that the excellent documentation of the Philadelphia experience by Isard and Langford (1971), the excellent synthesis by Richardson (1972), and the recent study by Smith and Morrison (1974) had been available earlier.

4. Input-output relations in the Georgia economy

4.1 INTRODUCTION

This chapter describes the economic structure of Georgia through a more thorough examination of the input-output tables and attempts to interpret some of the relationships uncovered in this examination. In Chapter 2 we pointed out the organization of an input-output table into four quadrants, each describing a part of the economy: Quadrant I identifies consumer behavior, Quadrant II details the interindustry structure of the economy; Quadrant III outlines payments to owners of resources, and Quadrant IV sketches non-market transfers in the economy. This chapter looks at these quadrants to derive an empirical profile of the Georgia economy.

Since many of our comments will point toward export-related activities as critical to a modern economy's success, we comment here on the economic-base theory of regional income determination, or, as it is sometimes called, the 'export-base' theory.[1] The activities of an economy may be divided into two sectors, the basic (or export) sector and the support (or local) sector. Economic-base theory argues that an economy, especially a relatively small and open economy such as a state, must export goods and services if it is to prosper economically. Exporters of locally produced goods and services obtain income from customers outside the economy. This export income then enters the economy to be dispersed in payment for the production of the exported goods in the form of wages and salaries, expenditures for materials and overhead, and profits. But unless the region is entirely self-sufficient, a portion of this circulating income leaks out of the local economy with each transaction in payment for imported goods, supplies, and services. With each round of expenditures made in support of exporting activities, local incomes increase in a continuing but diminishing chain. The impact of an original export sale tends to decrease with each successive round of expenditures as leakages continue; but if we account for all of the incomes accrued locally in this chain, it should be apparent that the export sale has led to increased activities in all industries in the economy.

The state input-output model is a disaggregated economic-base model which permits us to trace in detail the chains of events set off by sales outside the state economy.[2] This tracing is made in terms of multipliers, a point elaborated in Chapter 5. The input-output model also lets us observe the importance of exports and imports to an economy. Large export sales mean that an industry is 'basic' to the state and is an activity-generating industry. Large local sales mean that an industry is a supporting industry which depends on basic industries for its income. Large import purchases mean that an industry is weakly linked to the local economy and contributes little besides wages and salaries to local incomes. Large local purchases mean that an industry is important to many others in the economy.

4.2 FINAL DEMAND

Although not the largest quadrant in terms of number of entries in the transactions table, the final-demand quadrant is the largest in value (by definition, the · final-payments quadrant also has the same value). Total final demand of $25.995 billion accounts for 72.3 percent of the total sales of Georgia industries. Of this sales total, 43.1 percent is exported (with exports including both federal purchases and private sales out of state) and 29.2 percent is consumed locally by households, investors, and state and local government.

4.2.1 Exporting industries

· Exports are the more prominent part of final demand, especially when sales to the federal government are included as exports (as is the case in this discussion). Chart 4.2a records export sales as a percent of total output for each industry. An impressive 16 out of 28 industries sell over 50 percent of their products out of state. The list is topped by the transportation-equipment industry, which sells 89 percent of its output out of state, mostly to the federal government. The apparel industry exports 83 percent of its output, followed closely by the electrical machinery and textiles industries.[3]

But this chart should not be interpreted to mean that Georgia shows an export surplus (exports in excess of imports) in each of her industries. One reason is cross-hauling and competition between producers of similar products. A second reason is that many products are produced in each industry. In Georgia, for example, the petroleum refining industry produces asphalt and asphalt products, paving mixtures, and lubricating oils and greases, selling about $20 million in output out of state; at the same time, Georgia imports over $490 million in gasoline, oil, and other petroleum products.

Table 4.2a shows the net exports by each industry. The largest surplus is in the textile industry, with trade, paper, and apparel following. The state shows major deficits in chemicals, petroleum, metals, and machinery. Various supporting industries and other services also show surpluses, indicating the

Table 4.2a Net exports by industries in Georgia, 1970 (millions of dollars).

INDUSTRY	TOTAL EXPORTS	TOTAL IMPORTS	NET EXPORTS
1 AGRICULTURE (SIC 01, 07-9)	575.54	684.32	-108.78
2 MINING (SIC 10-4)	106.46	29.77	76.70
3 CONTRACT CONSTRUCTION (SIC 15-7)	457.67	195.74	261.93
4 FOOD AND KINDRED PRODUCTS (SIC 20-1)	1126.68	1361.96	-235.29
5 TEXTILE MILL PRODUCTS (SIC 22)	2865.95	755.32	2110.64
6 APPAREL AND RELATED PRODUCTS (SIC 23)	826.87	405.67	421.20
7 LUMBER AND WOOD PRODUCTS (SIC 24)	221.66	233.84	-12.19
8 FURNITURE AND FIXTURES (SIC 25)	134.61	99.94	34.67
9 PAPER AND ALLIED PRODUCTS (SIC 26)	842.93	411.07	431.87
10 PRINTING AND PUBLISHING (SIC 27)	84.24	134.40	-50.15
11 CHEMICALS AND ALLIED PRODUCTS (SIC 28)	395.61	948.15	-552.55
12 PETROLEUM REFINING (SIC 29)	29.23	490.50	-461.27
13 RUBBER AND MISC. PLASTICS (SIC 30)	130.41	184.57	-54.16
14 LEATHER AND LEATHER PRODUCTS (SIC 31)	57.36	97.34	-39.98
15 STONE, CLAY AND GLASS PROD. (SIC 32)	171.54	160.65	10.88
16 PRIMARY METAL INDUSTRIES (SIC 33)	171.17	507.32	-336.15
17 FABRICATED METAL PRODUCTS (SIC 34, 19)	284.48	446.38	-161.91
18 MACHINERY, EXCEPT ELECTRICAL (SIC 35)	265.00	521.42	-256.42
19 ELECTRICAL MACHINERY & EQUIP (SIC 36)	287.09	508.09	-221.00
20 TRANSPORTATION EQUIPMENT (SIC 37)	2222.25	1177.99	1044.27
21 MISCELLANEOUS MANUFACTURING (SIC 38-9)	158.02	298.15	-140.13
22 TRANSPORTATION SERVICES (SIC 40-7)	863.50	530.34	333.16
23 COMMUNICATIONS & UTILITIES (SIC 48-9)	143.20	148.11	-4.91
24 WHOLESALE AND RETAIL TRADE (SIC 50-9)	982.10	91.61	890.49
25 FINANCE, INS., REAL ESTATE (SIC 60-7)	950.75	870.11	80.65
26 SERVICES (SIC 70-9, 80-6, 89)	1048.89	682.26	366.63
27 GOVERNMENT ENTERPRISES	94.62	7.49	87.13
28 UNALLOCATED INDUSTRIES	4.37	134.11	-129.74
29 TOTAL LOCAL PURCHASES	15502.21	12116.62	3385.59

importance of Atlanta, Georgia's capital, as a trade center in the Southeast United States.

The discussion of self-sufficiency in Chapter 7 extends these comments to include both direct and indirect exports and imports.

4.2.2 The economic base of Georgia

Identifying the economic base of a state is not a simple matter. The problem is complicated by the number of approaches which might be taken. As in the preceding section, one approach is to identify the industries which export most of their outputs. A second approach is to look at each industry's exports as a percent of total exports. Table 4.2b presents these percentages.

Private exports are substantially larger than exports to the federal government, so they might be examined first. The largest set of exports in this column appears for textile mill products, which contribute over 20 percent of private exports. The transportation equipment industry contributes almost 10 percent of private exports and is closely followed by food and kindred products with 8 percent of exports. The apparel and related products industry comprises 6.2 percent of exports and the paper and paper products industry follows with about 6 percent of exports.

Purchases by the federal government, logically a part of exports, are dominated by a very large purchase from the aircraft industry. The federal govern-

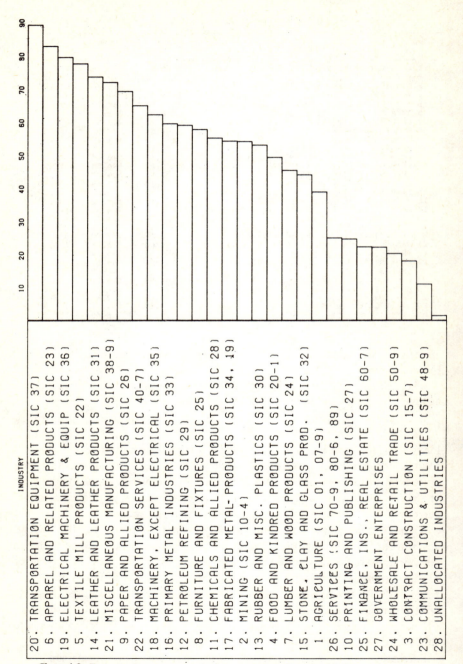

Chart 4.2a Export sales as a percent of gross output, Georgia, 1970.

Table 4.2b Exports by industries as a percent of total exports in Georgia, 1970.

INDUSTRY	FEDERAL GOVERNMENT (DEFENSE)	GOVERNMENT (OTHER)	PRIVATE EXPORTS	TOTAL EXPORTS
1 AGRICULTURE (SIC 01, 07-9)	.02	3.48	3.50	3.71
2 MINING (SIC 10-4)	.21	.00	.73	.69
3 CONTRACT CONSTRUCTION (SIC 15-7)	2.46	2.44	2.50	2.95
4 FOOD AND KINDRED PRODUCTS (SIC 20-1)	.14	.11	7.96	7.27
5 TEXTILE MILL PRODUCTS (SIC 22)	.03	.00	20.33	18.49
6 APPAREL AND RELATED PRODUCTS (SIC 23)	.08	.02	5.85	5.33
7 LUMBER AND WOOD PRODUCTS (SIC 24)	.01	.00	1.57	1.43
8 FURNITURE AND FIXTURES (SIC 25)	.02	.02	.95	.87
9 PAPER AND ALLIED PRODUCTS (SIC 26)	.02	.02	5.98	5.44
10 PRINTING AND PUBLISHING (SIC 27)	.15	.00	.58	.54
11 CHEMICALS AND ALLIED PRODUCTS (SIC 28)	.68	.07	2.70	2.55
12 PETROLEUM REFINING (SIC 29)	.45	.03	.14	.19
13 RUBBER AND MISC. PLASTICS (SIC 30)	.12	.01	.91	.84
14 LEATHER AND LEATHER PRODUCTS (SIC 31)	.00	.00	.41	.37
15 STONE, CLAY AND GLASS PROD. (SIC 32)	.03	.00	1.21	1.11
16 PRIMARY METAL INDUSTRIES (SIC 33)	.13	.00	1.20	1.10
17 FABRICATED METAL PRODUCTS (SIC 34, 19)	.35	.02	1.97	1.84
18 MACHINERY, EXCEPT ELECTRICAL (SIC 35)	.49	.08	1.80	1.71
19 ELECTRICAL MACHINERY & EQUIP (SIC 36)	.53	.07	1.95	1.85
20 TRANSPORTATION EQUIPMENT (SIC 37)	43.96	.20	9.70	14.34
21 MISCELLANEOUS MANUFACTURING (SIC 38-9)	.05	.02	1.11	1.02
22 TRANSPORTATION SERVICES (SIC 40-7)	.92	.11	5.98	5.57
23 COMMUNICATIONS & UTILITIES (SIC 48-9)	.44	.04	.95	.92
24 WHOLESALE AND RETAIL TRADE (SIC 50-9)	.48	.10	6.89	6.34
25 FINANCE, INS., REAL ESTATE (SIC 60-7)	.07	6.91	5.59	6.13
26 SERVICES (SIC 70-9, 80-6, 89)	2.61	1.00	6.92	6.77
27 GOVERNMENT ENTERPRISES	.07	.17	.63	.61
28 UNALLOCATED INDUSTRIES	.06	.14	.00	.03
29 TOTAL LOCAL PURCHASES	54.57	15.08	100.00	100.00
30 HOUSEHOLDS	45.43	65.49		
31 CAPITAL RESIDUAL	.00	.00		
32 CITY AND COUNTY GOVERNMENT	.00	2.02		
33 STATE GOVERNMENT	.00	17.41		
34 FEDERAL GOVERNMENT	.00	.00		
35 IMPORTS	.00	.00		
36 TOTAL PURCHASES	100.00	100.00		

ment also purchases a substantial amount from finance, insurance, and real estate and from construction.

One complicating factor in this approach to identifying the export base of the state lies in the large sales by the supporting industries to outsiders. Transportation services, trade, the finance, insurance, and real estate industry, and services all make large sales out of state. The sales by transportation services and trade are to a large extent connected to the sales of basic products to which these margins are attached, but they are also associated with Atlanta's position as a central distribution and trade point in the Southeast. Sales by the service industry include trade accommodations, personal services, and business services. Many of these are also related to Atlanta's position in the Southeast.

A third approach is through calculation of both direct and indirect exports. The discussion in this section has taken into account direct exports alone. But indirect exports, such as the export of chickens through the food and related products (meat products) industry or of wire through the fabricated metal products industry, are also important. A discussion of this approach is reserved for Chapter 7, where a 'skyline' or 'self-sufficiency' analysis is presented.

4.2.3 Local final demand

One of the interesting revelations of the input-output study is the relatively small amount of local products consumed by local consumers, which are defined as households, local governments, and state government. Only 29.2 percent of total local production is consumed by local final users. As Chart 4.2b points out, the industries producing the most for local consumption are limited in market area by transportation problems. Construction, trade, services, food products, and communications and utilities lead the list, all selling products which must be produced close to the point of consumption. Construction is obvious as a local sales leader. The trade industry is associated with each transaction by other industries in that it is the channel through which other products reach their consumers. The food products industry contains such market-dominated industries as the dairy products industry and the soft drink industry.

Chart 4.2c is included to point out the relative importance of local final demand and exports in total final demand. The cross-hatched part of each bar is exports, with the remainder being local final demand.

4.3 FINAL PAYMENTS

The final-payments quadrant is identical in size to the final-demand quadrant. It is the ultimate destination of the monies through which the demands of final users are expressed in the economy. We look here at the two largest and most stable components of the quadrant, payments to households and payments for imported intermediate products. Households provide 33 percent of the total inputs of Georgia industries, with payments taking the form of personal income, the largest share of which is wages and salaries. Of the total inputs of Georgia industries, 22 percent comes from outside the state. Of the remainder, 8 percent is for depreciation, retained earnings, and other capital-associated expenses, 4 percent is paid in federal taxes, 2 percent goes to the state government, and 1 percent goes to local governments.

4.3.1 Importing industries

Imports into the state are an important part of the input-output model. They are made in exchange for money payments which represent leakages from the economic system. Imports are expressed in the transactions table as a single row which contains the sums of columns in the imports tables. In the transactions table, then, we examine the industries purchasing imported products; we look

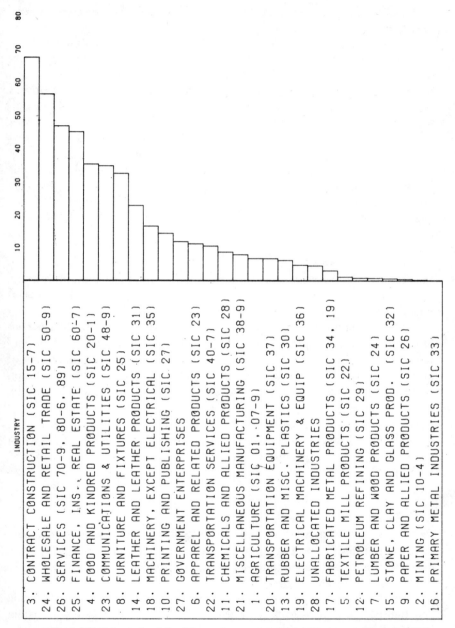

Chart 4.2b Sales to local final demand as a percent of gross output, Georgia, 1970.

at the paths through which leaks in money flows occur, but we do not pursue the causes of the leaks.

Chart 4.3a shows imports as a percent of total inputs of Georgia industries. The unallocated industry leads the list because of its composition. It records purchases and sales of office supplies, travel and business entertainment, and scrap goods. Georgia produces kraft paper, not bond paper, and her citizens travel on many travel lines, frequently to and from business destinations outside the state. Imports by the textile industry reflect raw-material and fiber needs. The large imports by the primary metal industries show the absence of aluminum and copper refineries in Georgia. The imports by transportation equipment can be explained by the functioning of aircraft and automobile producers in relative isolation from the remainder of the industry; they are primarily users of labor. The petroleum refining industry imports crude materials and processed oils for use in producing asphalt and lubricants. And so on. Each industry imports materials from outside the state.

4.3.2 Imported products

Imports may also be viewed as row sums from the imports tables. In this way, we examine the types of products (or the industries producing the products) imported into Georgia.

Table 4.3a reports the industries producing imported products. The table has been constructed to include imports by both Georgia industries and final consumers in Georgia (who buy 37 percent of all imports). The most imports are of products in the following industries: food and kindred products; transportation equipment; chemicals and allied products; finance, insurance, and real estate; and agriculture.

We have also calculated imports as a percent of total sales of each product in the state. This part of the table shows opportunities for import substitution in the state, providing, of course, that conditions are favorable for production in the state.

4.3.3 Household payments

Over 75 percent of personal income originates in private industry, with almost 69 percent of this $11.943 billion being wages and salaries. The remainder takes the form of property income, proprietors' income, other labor income, and wages and salaries of government enterprises.

Chart 4.3b shows payments to households as a percent of total inputs. Trade and transportation services top the list largely due to their nature as margin industries. Their 'output' is valued as the markup over producers' prices and a substantial part of this markup is in wages and salaries. The finance, insurance, and real estate industry maintains its high position because a large part of

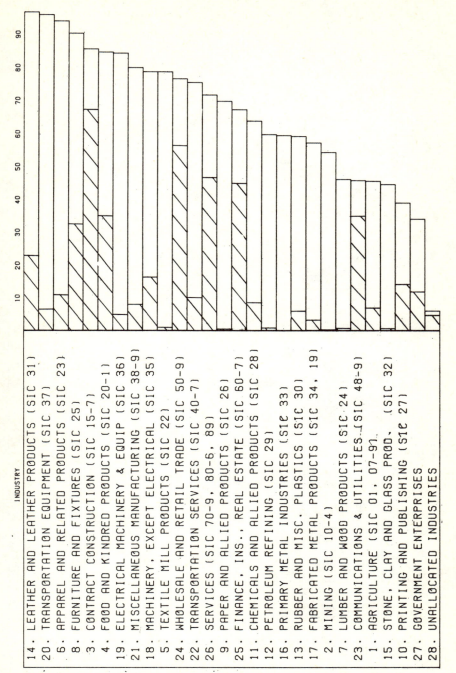

Chart 4.2c Sales to total final demand as a percent of gross output, Georgia, 1970.

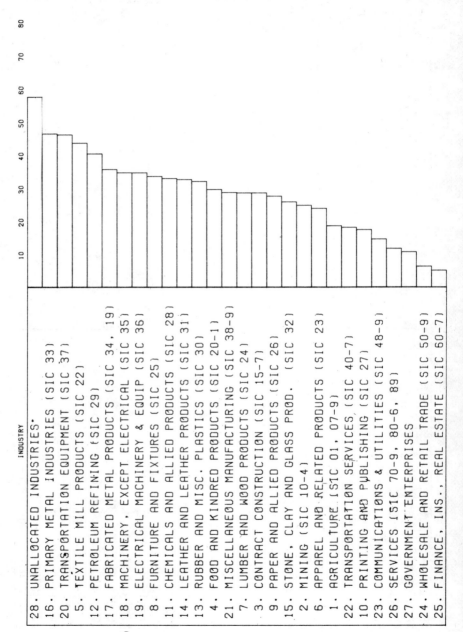

Chart 4.3a Imports as a percent of total inputs, Georgia, 1970.

Table 4.3a Imports, classified by producing industry, Georgia, 1970.

| PRODUCING INDUSTRY | IMPORTS | --PERCENT OF-- | |
		SALES	IMPORTS
1 AGRICULTURE (SIC 01, 07-9)	684.32	43.14	5.65
2 MINING (SIC 10-4)	29.77	24.83	.25
3 CONTRACT CONSTRUCTION (SIC 15-7)	195.74	8.67	1.62
4 FOOD AND KINDRED PRODUCTS (SIC 20-1)	1361.96	54.12	11.24
5 TEXTILE MILL PRODUCTS (SIC 22)	755.32	47.80	6.23
6 APPAREL AND RELATED PRODUCTS (SIC 23)	405.67	70.39	3.35
7 LUMBER AND WOOD PRODUCTS (SIC 24)	233.84	46.76	1.93
8 FURNITURE AND FIXTURES (SIC 25)	99.94	50.41	.82
9 PAPER AND ALLIED PRODUCTS (SIC 26)	411.07	52.46	3.39
10 PRINTING AND PUBLISHING (SIC 27)	134.40	34.36	1.11
11 CHEMICALS AND ALLIED PRODUCTS (SIC 28)	948.15	74.72	7.83
12 PETROLEUM REFINING (SIC 29)	490.50	96.03	4.05
13 RUBBER AND MISC. PLASTICS (SIC 30)	184.57	61.56	1.52
14 LEATHER AND LEATHER PRODUCTS (SIC 31)	97.34	82.62	.80
15 STONE, CLAY AND GLASS PROD. (SIC 32)	160.65	42.49	1.33
16 PRIMARY METAL INDUSTRIES (SIC 33)	507.32	81.35	4.19
17 FABRICATED METAL PRODUCTS (SIC 34, 19)	446.38	65.07	3.68
18 MACHINERY, EXCEPT ELECTRICAL (SIC 35)	521.42	76.47	4.30
19 ELECTRICAL MACHINERY & EQUIP (SIC 36)	508.09	87.32	4.19
20 TRANSPORTATION EQUIPMENT (SIC 37)	1177.99	81.36	9.72
21 MISCELLANEOUS MANUFACTURING (SIC 38-9)	298.15	82.96	2.46
22 TRANSPORTATION SERVICES (SIC 40-7)	530.34	53.35	4.38
23 COMMUNICATIONS & UTILITIES (SIC 48-9)	148.11	11.52	1.22
24 WHOLESALE AND RETAIL TRADE (SIC 50-9)	91.61	2.33	.76
25 FINANCE, INS., REAL ESTATE (SIC 60-7)	870.11	20.88	7.18
26 SERVICES (SIC 70-9, 80-6, 89)	682.26	17.88	5.63
27 GOVERNMENT ENTERPRISES	7.49	2.22	.06
28 UNALLOCATED INDUSTRIES	134.11	30.74	1.11
29 TOTAL LOCAL PURCHASES	12116.62	37.36	100.00

property income is channeled through it. Government enterprises, printing and publishing, and apparel are labor-intensive. Generally, in fact, service-related industries are at the top of the distribution due to their labor-intensive operations, and basic industries are at the bottom of the distribution due to their high output-labor ratios.

4.4 INTERINDUSTRY TRANSACTIONS

Of the parts of the Georgia input-output table, the interindustry quadrant is the largest in size, or number of cells, but it is also the smallest in dollar terms, recording only $9.967 billion in transactions. Out of total purchases and payments made by industries, only 28 percent are from local industries. Nevertheless, this is the most important part of a transactions table in input-output analysis; it is the quadrant through which the interactions between industries are traced. These interactions are reviewed in detail in Chapter 5 after the logic underlying the multiplier concept has been more fully developed.

Chart 4.4a records total local purchases by industries as a percent of total inputs. The food and kindred products industry leads the list because of the relatively high value of agricultural inputs, which cannot easily be transported

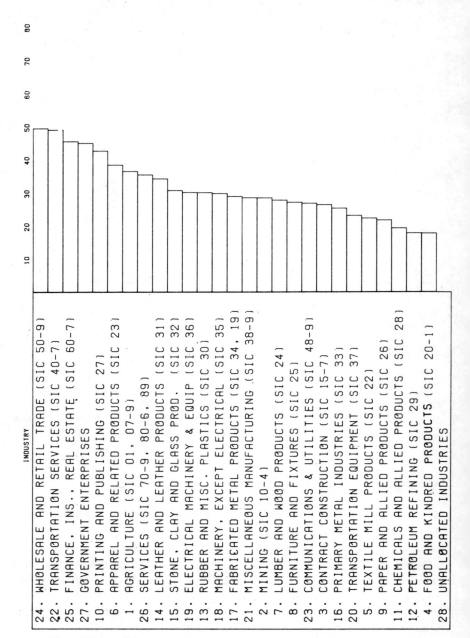

Chart 4.3b Payments to households as a percent of total inputs, Georgia, 1970.

long distances for processing. Only a few industries purchase a third or more of their total inputs from other local producers. Notice that many of the producers of 'hard' products appear near the bottom of the chart. Transportation equipment, trade, leather products, primary metal, etc., purchase very small amounts of their inputs from other local industries.

4.5 INCOME AND PRODUCT ACCOUNTS FOR GEORGIA, 1970

The input-output table embodies not only measures of gross state product but also a summary set of social, or income and product, accounts for the state. Like the input-output table itself, these accounts are part of a double-entry accounting system for the economy. In the same way that a businessman uses his accounts to develop a consolidated income statement for his firm, the economist uses income and product accounts to measure the performance of the economy and to compare the behavior of parts of the economy with other standards.

Table 4.5a is a transactions table for Georgia rearranged to emphasize Quadrant IV, the sector in which social accounts are traced. This social-accounts table completely eliminates the flows of intermediate products through the production quadrant and suppresses the details of the other quadrants. It emphasizes 1. the total final payments to resource owners for their contributions to production, 2. the aggregate demand for final products, and 3. the transfers which take place between primary units of the economy.

We have slightly rearranged the table. The row showing purchases from nonlocal industries (imports) has been moved above the final-payments rows. A row for transfers to households has been added to account for nonproductive money transfers to persons. And the one row for other payments in Table 2.2a has been expanded into four to show the details of final payments and transfers.

Six accounts are outlined in the table. The receipts side of the household account is shown in the household-income and household-transfers rows, which total to be personal income; the payments side is detailed in the household-expenditures column. The saving and investment account is shown in the capital-residual row (retained earnings, depreciation, savings) and the investment column. Local, state, and federal government accounts are shown in their rows and columns. And the rest-of-the-world account is shown in the row labeled 'purchases from nonlocal industry' and the column 'net exports.' By placing these accounts into one matrix, we gain both economy in presentation and a feeling for their commonality.

GSP may be measured in two ways, the incomes approach and the expenditures approach. Let us start with the expenditures approach.

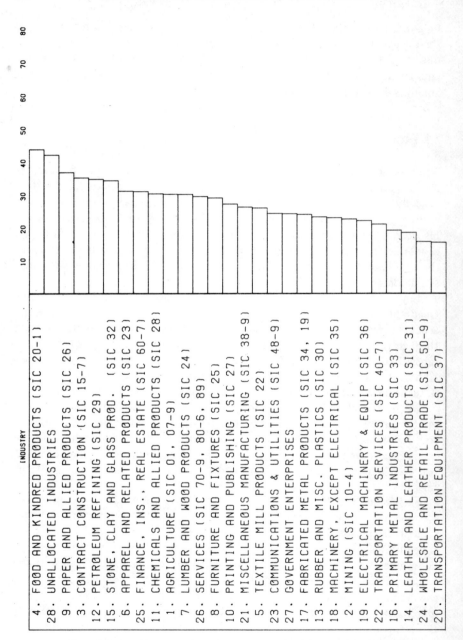

Chart 4.4a Total local purchases as a percent of total inputs, Georgia, 1970.

Table 4.5a Income and product accounts for Georgia, 1970.

Account making payment \ Account receiving payment	Sales to processing sectors	Household expenditures	Private investment	Expenditures of governments				Net exports	Total final demand	Total receipts
				Local	State	Federal, defense	Federal, other			
Purchases from local processors	8,527.3	8,199.3	1,400.4	460.9	432.3	1,057.0	353.9	14,091.3	25,995.1	34,522.3
Purchases from nonlocal industry	8,159.2	3,777.8	802.1	138.8	115.8	-	-	-12,993.8	-8,159.2	0
Total purchases from industry	16,686.5	11,977.1	2,202.5	599.7	548.1	1,057.0	353.9	-	17,835.9	34,522.3
Household income	11,882.6	99.7	-	790.7	372.7	671.0	689.3	-	2,623.3	14,506.0
Total purchases of goods and services	30,008.4	12,076.8	2,202.5	1,390.4	920.8	1,728.0	1,043.2	1,097.5	20,459.2	50,467.6
Household transfers	61.0	-	-	51.3	190.7	209.0	848.0	-	1,299.0	1,360.0
Capital residual	3,019.1	871.6	-	-	-	-	-	-1,688.2	-816.6	2,202.5
Local government income	480.3	377.9	-	-	445.9	-	47.3	112.4	983.5	1,063.8
State government income	858.8	341.9	-	22.1	-	-	408.8	-55.2	773.0	1,576.4
Federal government income	1,533.9	2,197.8	-	-	19.1	-	-	533.5	2,750.4	4,284.3
External transfers	-	-	-	-	-	-	-	-	-	-
Total outlay	34,522.3	15,866.0	2,202.5	1,463.8	1,576.4	1,937.0	2,347.3	0	25,393.0	61,354.6

Using expenditures, we define GSP as state output in terms of market value through the expenditures of final consumers. This approach accounts for the final demand for Georgia's product by four groups of consumers: households, investors, governments, and private units outside the state economy. In Table 4.5a, GSP is seen as total purchases of goods and services for final consumption, $20,459 million. In 1970, this was 2.1 percent of GNP. In comparison with expenditures for GNP, Georgia spends less of her gross product on personal consumption (59.0 percent in contrast to 62.9 percent for the nation), less on private investment (10.7, 13.5), and less on local and state government (11.3, 12.2); she makes up for this in terms of federal defense expenditures (8.4, 7.5), other federal expenditures (5.0, 3.6), and net private exports (5.3, 0.4).

Using the incomes approach, we can arrive at a similar GSP by adding the 'income receipts' of the various accounts. The major receipt is earned household or personal income, which is comprised of wages and salaries, other labor income, proprietors' income, and property incomes. Including business transfer payments (primarily bad debts) and social security contributions, this amounts to $14,567 million, or 71.2 percent of GSP; the corresponding national figure is 75.2 percent. The 'capital residual,' or gross business saving, of processors is $3,019 million and comprises 14.8 percent of GSP, which corresponds to 9.4 percent in the nation. The capital-residual row of Table 4.5a includes two transfers worth noting: one is personal savings; the other is a negative entry of $1,688 million in the exports column. This 'export' accounts for the surpluses and deficits of the various governments and the outside world. Much of it represents flows of retained earnings and capital consumption allowances to the nonresident owners of branch plants in Georgia.

The third receipt to be added to GSP is local government income from the processing sector. At $480 million, this figure accounts for 2.3 percent of GSP. The next largest income of local governments in Georgia is a set of intergovernmental transfers from the state government (much of which is offset by a similar transfer from the federal government to the state). The deficits of local governments are shown as an 'export' (primarily bonds) worth $112.4 million.

The fourth receipt to be counted as part of GSP is state government income from the processing sector of $859 million. Combined state and local revenues from industrial sources are 6.5 percent of GSP, compared to 8.5 percent on the national level. Note that the state had a surplus in 1970 of $55 million, entered as a negative value in the exports column.

The final receipt to be included in GSP is federal government income from the processing sectors. Totaling $1,534 million, this is 7.5 percent of GSP. This compares with 6.9 percent on the national level. Notice that the federal government still spent $534 million more in Georgia than it received in taxes, accounted for largely through defense expenditures.

In sum, total receipts and payments by each of the six final sectors in the economy were $25,393 million. This figure is $4,934 million in excess of GSP. Where Quadrant II shows intermediate transactions in the processing sector, the transfers quadrant records duplicative transactions in the social or political sector.

4.6 SUMMARY

A state input-output table accounts for flows of monies through the state, showing details regarding consumer behavior, the technology of production, incomes, and social transfers. A careful analysis of relationships recorded in these quadrants can provide to the regional planner many clues as to the character of his domain.

The transfers quadrant of a table can be slightly modified to show the details presented in the more traditional income and product accounts. The social accounts are useful in two ways. One is in comparisons between economies; a brief contrast of the Georgia and U. S. economies has been sketched here and Georgia has been found to be strong in trade and government and slightly below the national pattern in manufacturing and services. The other way is in comparisons over time. But to show performance over time, social accounts and input-output tables must be constructed on a regular basis by state agencies.

NOTES

1. For a discussion of the conceptual basis, application, limitations, and criticims of economic-base theory, see Charles M. Tiebout (1962), Walter Isard (1960), ch. 6), and Richardson (1969, ch. 10). A simple application of an economic-base multiplier in Georgia may be found in Davidson and Schaffer (1973).
2. While this point is made in Chapter 2, a further discussion of the mathematical similarity of economic-base models to regional input-output models may be found in Billings (1969) and Garnick (1970).
3. The distorting effect of aggregation really became clear when we compared Chart 4.2a with a corresponding chart for our more detailed 50-industry model. In the 50-industry version, the aircraft industry was the top exporter, followed by floor coverings, motor vehicles, electric transmission equipment, other transportation equipment, and then, finally, apparel, which is the second largest exporter in the 28-industry tables under review. Floor coverings, primarily tufted carpets, is hidden within textile mill products in the fourth position in Chart 4.2a. These observations emphasize the importance of detailed information when briefing decision-makers. The reduced version of the Georgia Economic Model, used here primarily to conserve space, obviously is not as useful as the more detailed version.

5. Economic multipliers for Georgia industries

5.1 INTRODUCTION

As noted in Chapter 2, the Georgia Economic Model can be treated as a multiplier model to trace the effects of changes in demand on economic activity in the state. After explaining the multiplier concept in simple graphic terms and outlining the mathematics of the multiplier system, this chapter presents employment, household-income, and government-income multipliers for Georgia and explores the contributions of Georgia industries to income and output.

5.2 THE MULTIPLIER CONCEPT

5.2.1 A general discussion
When used to trace individual changes in final demand through the economy over short periods of time, an input-output model can be called an impact model, or a multiplier model. A total-requirements table for the aggregated 6-industry model was presented in Table 2.5b. This table shows the direct, indirect, and induced changes in industry outputs required to deliver units to final demand. A table of this type is the key to all of the multipliers developed in this study.

To better understand the meaning of a total-requirements table, and the multipliers derived from it, let us trace through Table 2.5b the flow of outputs induced by a $100 purchase from the manufacturing sector. The result of this step-by-step tracing is illustrated in Figure 5.2a. First, $100 enters the state economy through manufacturing. To produce output worth $100, firms in manufacturing purchase inputs from other industries in the economy. According to column three in Table 2.5a, the direct-requirements table, $4.20 goes to agriculture and mining, $0.30 goes to construction, an additional $9.80 goes to other firms in manufacturing, $3.70 goes to trade, $6.10 goes to services, and $26.10 is paid to households in wages and salaries. Capacity permitting, each of these industries must expand its output to accommodate this additional production load. Thus, in producing additional output valued at $4.20, firms in agriculture and mining buy output worth $0.46 (10.9 percent of $4.20) from others in this sector, $0.03 (0.8 percent of $4.20) from construction, $0.36 (8.5 percent of $4.20) from manufacturing, and so on, for a total of $2.72. At the same time, each of the other industries is purchasing the additional inputs required to produce the output requested of them. The results are summarized in Figure 5.2a as the third round of purchases. Other purchases follow in succeeding rounds, each smaller as money flows out of the interindustry sector into the hands of the owners of primary inputs (excluding labor), into government coffers, and for the purchase of imported materials. This chain of purchases continues for all industries until the economy is again in equilibrium. The initial $100 purchase from manufacturing has led to the production of additional output by the entire state economy valued at $219, as shown in Figure 5.2a. Notice that if the value of additional output is summed through round six, most of the effect of the initial purchase has already been realized: $210 has been spent at this point. The total-requirements table just counts the rounds of spending to infinity and adds them up. The total appears in Table 2.5b as a column sum, and is called an 'output multiplier.'

As explained mathematically in the next section, each of the multipliers in the remainder of this chapter is a variation on this theme.

5.2.2 Mathematical formulations

At this point, it would be helpful to reduce the input-output model to more concise mathematical terms. Our state economy may be defined in terms of the following equation system:

$$\sum_{j=1}^{s} x_{ij} + \sum_{f=1}^{t} y_{if} + e_i = x_i, \quad (i = 1, 2, 3, \ldots s) \tag{5.1}$$

where

x_{ij} = sales of regional industry i to regional industry j,

y_{if} = sales of regional industry i to regional final demand sector f,

e_i = export sales of regional industry i,

x_i = total sales of regional industry i,

s = the dimension of the input-output matrix (for the Georgia Economic Model, $s = 28$), and

t = the number of final-demand sectors excluding exports (for the Georgia Economic Model, $t = 6$).

Similarly, the state economy may be defined in terms of purchases as:

$$\sum_{i=1}^{s} x_{ij} + \sum_{p=1}^{t} v_{pj} + \sum_{i=1}^{s} m_{ij} + \sum_{k=1}^{r} n_{kj} = x_j, \quad (j = 1, 2, 3, \ldots s) \tag{5.2}$$

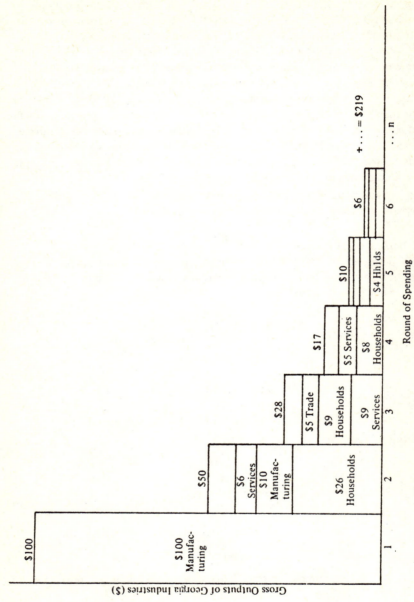

Figure 5.2a The multiplier effect of a $100 sale to final demand by the Georgia manufacturing sector.

where

v_{pj} = value added by final-payment sector p in industry j,

m_{ij} = imports by industry j of the products competitive to industry i,

r = the number of noncompetitive industries outside the regional system, and

n_{kj} = imports by industry j of the products of noncompetitive industry k.

The system is solved by assuming a constant production relation such that

$$x_{ij} = a_{ij} \cdot x_j ,$$ (5.3)

where $a_{ij} = x_{ij}/x_j$, and substituting (5.3) into (5.1):

$$\sum_{j=1}^{s} a_{ij} \cdot x_j + \sum_{f=1}^{t} y_{if} + e_i = x_i , \quad (i = 1, 2, 3, \ldots s)$$ (5.4)

In matrix notation, (5.4) can be represented as

$$A \cdot X + Y + E = X .$$ (5.5)

As is well known, the solution to this system is

$$(I - A)^{-1} \cdot (Y + E) = X .$$

For ease in exposition, we identify $(I - A)^{-1}$ as B, so that b_{ij} represents the direct and indirect purchases from industry i by industry j in satisfying one additional unit of final demand.

As pointed out in section 2.5, the A matrix is frequently augmented; A is closed with respect to households by the addition of the household row (v_{1j}, $j = 1, 2, 3, \ldots s + 1$) and the household column ($y_{i1}, i = 1, 2, 3, \ldots s$) to the regional transactions matrix (the x_{ij}'s) before dividing by X, a vector of gross outputs now extended to include x_{s+1}, personal income. When this is done, the elements of the direct-requirements matrix are designated $_2a_{ij}$ and the elements of the corresponding inverse are designated $_2b_{ij}$. These $_2b_{ij}$ represent the direct, indirect, and induced purchases from industry i by industry j in satisfying one additional unit of final demand (now y_{if}, for $f = 2, 3, \ldots t$, and e_j).

We have computed three types of multipliers: output multipliers, employment multipliers, and income multipliers. In relating changes in final demand to changes in their describing variables, these multipliers are common in interpretation. We outline below their evolution.

Output multipliers are merely the sums of columns in the inverse matrices, showing increases in outputs per dollar increase in final demand. The 'simple' output multiplier for industry j is the sum of cells in column j of the simple inverse:

$$_1z_j = \sum_{i=1}^{s} b_{ij} \,. \tag{5.7}$$

The 'total' output multiplier for industry j is the sum of cells in column j of the second, or augmented, inverse:

$$_2z_j = \sum_{i=1}^{s+1} {}_2b_{ij} \,. \tag{5.8}$$

The meanings attached here to 'simple' and 'total' apply throughout this discussion.[1]

Employment multipliers are derived from output multipliers simply by converting from an output to an employment base. The simple employment multiplier for industry j is derived as

$$_3z_j = \sum_{i=1}^{s} b_{ij} \cdot \frac{w_i}{x_i} \,, \tag{5.9}$$

and the total employment multiplier as

$$_4z_j = \sum_{i=1}^{s+1} {}_2b_{ij} \cdot \frac{w_i}{x_i} \,, \tag{5.10}$$

where w_i is employment in industry i. (In this study, we have used 'covered' employment as provided by the Georgia Department of Labor.)[2]

In constructing government-income multipliers, we simply substitute government-income coefficients for the employment-output ratios above.[3]

The government-income multipliers for industry j are derived as presented below:

Government	Simple multiplier	Total multiplier (5.11-16)
Local governments	$_5z_j = \sum_{i=1}^{s} b_{ij} \cdot \dfrac{v_{3i}}{x_i}$	$_6z_j = \sum_{i=1}^{s+1} {}_2b_{ij} \cdot \dfrac{v_{3i}}{x_i}$
State government	$_7z_j = \sum_{i=1}^{s} b_{ij} \cdot \dfrac{v_{4i}}{x_i}$	$_8z_j = \sum_{i=1}^{s+1} {}_2b_{ij} \cdot \dfrac{v_{4i}}{x_i}$
Federal government	$_9z_j = \sum_{i=1}^{s} b_{ij} \cdot \dfrac{v_{5i}}{x_i}$	$_{10}z_j = \sum_{i=1}^{s+1} {}_2b_{ij} \cdot \dfrac{v_{5i}}{x_i}$

'Income multiplier' is a term traditionally used to describe the additional household income in an economy attributable to a one-unit increase in household
income in the industry in question. We feel that this definition is awkward and
inconsistent with the approach taken in most interpretations. Therefore, we
have defined the 'household-income multiplier' for industry j to be the addition
to household incomes in the economy due to a one-unit increase in final
demand.[4] The simple household-income multiplier is derived as

$$_{11}z_j = \sum_{i=1}^{s} b_{ij} \cdot \frac{v_{1i}}{x_i} \, ,$$

and the total household-income multiplier as

$$_{12}z_j = \sum_{i=1}^{s+1} {}_2b_{ij} \cdot \frac{v_{1i}}{x_i} \, .$$

A glance at Table 5.4a and Table 4 of the Model will convince the reader that
these total multipliers are also found in the household row of the extended
inverse, that $_{12}z_j = {}_2b_{29,j}$.

In our discussion of household-income multipliers, we also present a table
showing income generated per dollar of final sales. In this table (5.4a), direct
income generated by industry j is simply the household-income coefficient,
$a_{29,j} = v_{1j}/x_j$; indirect income generated is the simple household-income
multiplier less direct income generated, or $_{11}z_j - a_{29,j}$; and induced income
generated is the total household-income multiplier less the simple one, or
$_{12}z_j - {}_{11}z_j$. Total income generated per unit of final sales is $_{12}z_j$, or the sum of
the above elements.

5.3 OUTPUT AND EMPLOYMENT MULTIPLIERS

Table 5.3a presents output and employment multipliers for industries in
Georgia. The simple multipliers should be interpreted as lower limits since they
exclude any of the effects induced by incomes circulating through households.
The total multipliers are based on an augmented inverse matrix as was discussed
in the previous section; they can be interpreted as upper limits and, we feel, are
reasonably close to the actual effects of changes in final demand.

Interestingly, the output multipliers are highest for the industries which we
generally have little power to influence and which do not export extensively.
Among these are finance, insurance, and real estate; services; government
enterprises; and printing and publishing. These industries are supporting
industries in Georgia. In contrast, the output multipliers are low for many
industries producing for export. Transportation equipment and textile mill
products are good examples; their positions on the list are probably due to the

Table 5.3a Employment and output multipliers, Georgia, 1970.

INDUSTRY	EMPLOYMENT MULTIPLIERS		OUTPUT MULTIPLIERS	
	SIMPLE	TOTAL	SIMPLE	TOTAL
1 AGRICULTURE (SIC 01, 07-9)	.09	.29	1.44	2.66
2 MINING (SIC 10-4)	.43	.58	1.31	2.25
3 CONTRACT CONSTRUCTION (SIC 15-7)	.54	.70	1.48	2.51
4 FOOD AND KINDRED PRODUCTS (SIC 20-1)	.33	.48	1.64	2.57
5 TEXTILE MILL PRODUCTS (SIC 22)	.40	.52	1.35	2.13
6 APPAREL AND RELATED PRODUCTS (SIC 23)	.91	1.11	1.42	2.63
7 LUMBER AND WOOD PRODUCTS (SIC 24)	.60	.76	1.43	2.42
8 FURNITURE AND FIXTURES (SIC 25)	.62	.78	1.40	2.35
9 PAPER AND ALLIED PRODUCTS (SIC 26)	.37	.51	1.53	2.42
10 PRINTING AND PUBLISHING (SIC 27)	.53	.74	1.40	2.70
11 CHEMICALS AND ALLIED PRODUCTS (SIC 28)	.36	.48	1.43	2.20
12 PETROLEUM REFINING (SIC 29)	.38	.50	1.48	2.28
13 RUBBER AND MISC. PLASTICS (SIC 30)	.44	.59	1.32	2.27
14 LEATHER AND LEATHER PRODUCTS (SIC 31)	.70	.86	1.26	2.27
15 STONE, CLAY AND GLASS PROD. (SIC 32)	.53	.71	1.47	2.56
16 PRIMARY METAL INDUSTRIES (SIC 33)	.32	.45	1.26	2.05
17 FABRICATED METAL PRODUCTS (SIC 34, 19)	.39	.53	1.32	2.25
18 MACHINERY, EXCEPT ELECTRICAL (SIC 35)	.42	.57	1.31	2.25
19 ELECTRICAL MACHINERY & EQUIP (SIC 36)	.41	.56	1.29	2.23
20 TRANSPORTATION EQUIPMENT (SIC 37)	.27	.39	1.21	1.92
21 MISCELLANEOUS MANUFACTURING (SIC 38-9)	.61	.77	1.36	2.31
22 TRANSPORTATION SERVICES (SIC 40-7)	.71	.93	1.29	2.71
23 COMMUNICATIONS & UTILITIES (SIC 48-9)	.39	.53	1.34	2.25
24 WHOLESALE AND RETAIL TRADE (SIC 50-9)	.77	.99	1.22	2.59
25 FINANCE, INS., REAL ESTATE (SIC 60-7)	.29	.53	1.44	2.94
26 SERVICES (SIC 70-9, 80-6, 89)	.55	.74	1.41	2.60
27 GOVERNMENT ENTERPRISES	.13	.34	1.35	2.69
28 UNALLOCATED INDUSTRIES	.23	.32	1.59	2.10
29 HOUSEHOLDS	.00	.38	.00	2.38

small amounts of local inputs, excepting labor, used in their production processes. As comparison of the simple and total output multipliers shows, a large labor input from the household sector can be important in increasing the multiplier for industries with low interindustry purchases in the economy.

Employment multipliers are output multipliers which have been converted to an employment base through the use of employee/output ratios. These multipliers are to be interpreted as showing the number of jobs created by a $10,000 export in their industry. The employment multiplier is highest in the apparel and related products industry and lowest in transportation equipment and government enterprises. Generally, the more labor-intensive an industry, the higher the multiplier.

An interesting aside involves the average output multiplier computed as the ratio of total output to exogenous final demand. The average simple multiplier is 1.38 when computed as total industry output divided by total final demand ($35,961.6M/$25,995.1M); it is 1.38 when computed as an average of simple multipliers. The average total multiplier is 2.48 when computed with the household sector treated as an industry ($44,160.9B/$17,795.8B); it is 2.40 when computed as an average of total multipliers.

5.4 HOUSEHOLD-INCOME MULTIPLIERS

The household-income multipliers shown in Table 5.4a relate changes in household income in the economy to changes in final demand. That is, each multiplier shows the total amount of household income that results from an additional dollar of sales to final demand by its industry. The multipliers are derived in three steps, which are represented by the first three columns in Table 5.4a.

The first column, showing the direct income created, is simply the wages and salaries, proprietors' income, etc., paid to households by an industry in producing additional goods or services worth one dollar for final sales. The indirect income represents the payments to households resulting from the purchase of goods and services from other industries necessary to produce the additonal output. The third column, or induced income, reports the income that is generated in the economy by households spending the additional income they receive from the increased sales to final demand.

The most meaningful column in Table 5.4a is the fourth one. This is the total income multiplier and shows the total changes in household income resulting from an additional dollar of sales to final demand for the various industries.

As with the output multipliers, the income multipliers are the highest for

Table 5.4a Income generated by final sales, Georgia, 1970.

INDUSTRY	INCOME CREATED PER DOLLAR OF FINAL SALES			
	DIRECT	INDIRECT	INDUCED	TOTAL
1 AGRICULTURE (SIC 01, 07-9)	.36	.15	.20	.71
2 MINING (SIC 10-4)	.28	.11	.15	.55
3 CONTRACT CONSTRUCTION (SIC 15-7)	.26	.17	.17	.60
4 FOOD AND KINDRED PRODUCTS (SIC 20-1)	.18	.21	.15	.54
5 TEXTILE MILL PRODUCTS (SIC 22)	.22	.11	.13	.46
6 APPAREL AND RELATED PRODUCTS (SIC 23)	.38	.12	.20	.70
7 LUMBER AND WOOD PRODUCTS (SIC 24)	.28	.14	.16	.58
8 FURNITURE AND FIXTURES (SIC 25)	.27	.13	.16	.56
9 PAPER AND ALLIED PRODUCTS (SIC 26)	.22	.15	.15	.52
10 PRINTING AND PUBLISHING (SIC 27)	.43	.12	.21	.76
11 CHEMICALS AND ALLIED PRODUCTS (SIC 28)	.19	.13	.13	.45
12 PETROLEUM REFINING (SIC 29)	.18	.16	.13	.47
13 RUBBER AND MISC. PLASTICS (SIC 30)	.30	.10	.16	.56
14 LEATHER AND LEATHER PRODUCTS (SIC 31)	.34	.08	.17	.59
15 STONE, CLAY AND GLASS PROD. (SIC 32)	.31	.15	.18	.64
16 PRIMARY METAL INDUSTRIES (SIC 33)	.25	.08	.13	.47
17 FABRICATED METAL PRODUCTS (SIC 34, 19)	.29	.10	.15	.54
18 MACHINERY, EXCEPT ELECTRICAL (SIC 35)	.30	.10	.15	.55
19 ELECTRICAL MACHINERY & EQUIP (SIC 36)	.30	.09	.15	.55
20 TRANSPORTATION EQUIPMENT (SIC 37)	.23	.07	.12	.42
21 MISCELLANEOUS MANUFACTURING (SIC 38-9)	.29	.12	.16	.56
22 TRANSPORTATION SERVICES (SIC 40-7)	.49	.11	.23	.83
23 COMMUNICATIONS & UTILITIES (SIC 48-9)	.27	.12	.15	.54
24 WHOLESALE AND RETAIL TRADE (SIC 50-9)	.49	.08	.22	.80
25 FINANCE, INS., REAL ESTATE (SIC 60-7)	.46	.17	.25	.87
26 SERVICES (SIC 70-9, 80-6, 89)	.35	.15	.20	.70
27 GOVERNMENT ENTERPRISES	.45	.11	.22	.79
28 UNALLOCATED INDUSTRIES	.00	.22	.08	.30
29 HOUSEHOLDS	.01		1.38	1.39

supporting industries and are relatively low for many export industries. However, among the manufacturing industries, relatively high multipliers are shown for apparel, printing and publishing, and stone, clay, and glass products. Relatively low multipliers are found for textile mill products, chemicals and chemical products, and transportation equipment. Attesting the relatively weak interindustry structure of the region are the high correlations between the direct-income coefficient, the induced-income coefficient, and the total income multiplier.

5.5 GOVERNMENT-INCOME MULTIPLIERS

Government-income multipliers provide an estimate of the range over which both local and state government revenues could be expected to rise for each dollar change in final demand for industries in Georgia.

Table 5.5a presents the simple and total multipliers for both local and state government. Except for agriculture and services on the local level and trade at the state level, the impact on government revenues of expanding sales to final demand does not vary substantially industry by industry and thus is not very interesting. The high state-income multiplier for trade is a result of our treatment of trade as a margin industry.

5.6 INDUSTRY CONTRIBUTIONS TO THE GEORGIA ECONOMY

Table 5.6a summarizes the contributions of each industry in the 28-sector model to the Georgia economy in terms of household income, local government revenues, state revenues, and total output in 1970. This table was produced by multiplying the final demands placed on each industry by the various (simple) multipliers reported in this chapter. A quick examination of the table indicates that the most important industries in the Georgia economy are contract construction; food and kindred products; textile mill products; trade; finance, insurance, and real estate; and services. Looking at the broad sectors of the economy, manufacturing is the most important contributor, followed by trade and services, contract construction, and agriculture.

A further examination of the table, however, reveals several points of concern. Most of the income, revenue, and output generated by the Georgia economy is produced in only a few industries. In fact, the six industries listed above account for over 67 percent of Georgia household income. It should be noted that only two of these eight industries are basic industries and both are facing difficulties in maintaining their present levels of production. It is obvious

Table 5.5a Government-income multipliers, Georgia, 1970.

INDUSTRY	CITY AND COUNTY SIMPLE	TOTAL	STATE SIMPLE	TOTAL
1 AGRICULTURE (SIC 01, 07-9)	.04	.06	.01	.04
2 MINING (SIC 10-4)	.01	.03	.01	.04
3 CONTRACT CONSTRUCTION (SIC 15-7)	.02	.03	.02	.05
4 FOOD AND KINDRED PRODUCTS (SIC 20-1)	.02	.03	.01	.04
5 TEXTILE MILL PRODUCTS (SIC 22)	.01	.02	.01	.04
6 APPAREL AND RELATED PRODUCTS (SIC 23)	.00	.02	.01	.05
7 LUMBER AND WOOD PRODUCTS (SIC 24)	.02	.04	.03	.06
8 FURNITURE AND FIXTURES (SIC 25)	.01	.03	.01	.04
9 PAPER AND ALLIED PRODUCTS (SIC 26)	.02	.03	.02	.04
10 PRINTING AND PUBLISHING (SIC 27)	.01	.03	.01	.05
11 CHEMICALS AND ALLIED PRODUCTS (SIC 28)	.02	.03	.02	.04
12 PETROLEUM REFINING (SIC 29)	.01	.03	.01	.04
13 RUBBER AND MISC. PLASTICS (SIC 30)	.01	.03	.01	.04
14 LEATHER AND LEATHER PRODUCTS (SIC 31)	.01	.02	.01	.04
15 STONE, CLAY AND GLASS PROD. (SIC 32)	.01	.03	.01	.04
16 PRIMARY METAL INDUSTRIES (SIC 33)	.01	.03	.01	.04
17 FABRICATED METAL PRODUCTS (SIC 34, 19)	.01	.03	.01	.04
18 MACHINERY, EXCEPT ELECTRICAL (SIC 35)	.01	.02	.01	.04
19 ELECTRICAL MACHINERY & EQUIP (SIC 36)	.01	.02	.01	.04
20 TRANSPORTATION EQUIPMENT (SIC 37)	.01	.02	.01	.04
21 MISCELLANEOUS MANUFACTURING (SIC 38-9)	.01	.03	.02	.05
22 TRANSPORTATION SERVICES (SIC 40-7)	.01	.03	.02	.06
23 COMMUNICATIONS & UTILITIES (SIC 48-9)	.04	.05	.01	.04
24 WHOLESALE AND RETAIL TRADE (SIC 50-9)	.02	.04	.13	.18
25 FINANCE, INS., REAL ESTATE (SIC 60-7)	.03	.06	.03	.07
26 SERVICES (SIC 70-9, 80-6, 89)	.03	.05	.02	.06
27 GOVERNMENT ENTERPRISES	.01	.03	.01	.05
28 UNALLOCATED INDUSTRIES	.01	.02	.01	.03
29 HOUSEHOLDS	.00	.04	.00	.07

that Georgia needs to encourage the expansion of other manufacturing industries if the economy is to be assured of future growth. (Chapter 7 discusses methods of selecting industries for expansion.)

Table 5.6a Contributions to personal income, city and county government incomes, and state government income by industry sales to final demand (including households), Georgia, 1970.

INDUSTRY	HOUSEHOLD ROW MULT	* FD	% TOT	CITY & COUNTY GOVT. MULT	* FD	% TOT	STATE GOVT. MULT	* FD	% TOT	OUTPUT MULT	* FD	% TOT
1 AGRICULTURE (SIC 01, 07-9)	.51	345.7	2.89	.04	26.5	5.53	.01	5.1	.59	1.44	974.3	2.72
2 MINING (SIC 10-4)	.39	42.1	.35	.01	1.6	.33	.01	1.2	.14	1.31	140.1	.39
3 CONTRACT CONSTRUCTION (SIC 15-7)	.43	933.6	7.82	.02	36.2	7.54	.02	43.1	5.02	1.48	3187.1	8.90
4 FOOD AND KINDRED PRODUCTS (SIC 20-1)	.39	755.3	6.32	.02	33.3	6.93	.01	23.9	2.78	1.64	3163.5	8.83
5 TEXTILE MILL PRODUCTS (SIC 22)	.33	956.7	8.01	.01	20.6	4.28	.01	35.6	4.15	1.35	3927.8	10.97
6 APPAREL AND RELATED PRODUCTS (SIC 23)	.51	474.3	3.97	.00	4.4	.91	.01	9.5	1.11	1.42	1335.3	3.73
7 LUMBER AND WOOD PRODUCTS (SIC 24)	.42	94.3	.79	.02	5.0	1.04	.03	7.2	.84	1.43	321.5	.90
8 FURNITURE AND FIXTURES (SIC 25)	.40	84.4	.71	.01	2.3	.48	.01	2.9	.33	1.40	294.0	.82
9 PAPER AND ALLIED PRODUCTS (SIC 26)	.37	315.4	2.64	.02	15.6	3.25	.01	14.3	1.67	1.53	1299.4	3.63
10 PRINTING AND PUBLISHING (SIC 27)	.55	72.8	.61	.01	1.5	.31	.02	1.6	.19	1.43	185.8	.52
11 CHEMICALS AND ALLIED PRODUCTS (SIC 28)	.32	148.0	1.24	.02	7.6	1.57	.02	7.2	.84	1.43	654.2	1.83
12 PETROLEUM REFINING (SIC 29)	.34	9.9	.08	.01	.4	.08	.02	.4	.05	1.48	43.8	.12
13 RUBBER AND MISC. PLASTICS (SIC 30)	.40	58.2	.49	.01	2.0	.42	.01	2.1	.25	1.32	192.3	.54
14 LEATHER AND LEATHER PRODUCTS (SIC 31)	.43	32.0	.27	.01	.6	.12	.01	1.0	.12	1.26	94.4	.26
15 STONE, CLAY AND GLASS PROD. (SIC 32)	.46	80.2	.67	.01	2.4	.50	.01	1.9	.22	1.47	255.0	.71
16 PRIMARY METAL INDUSTRIES (SIC 33)	.33	57.3	.48	.01	2.3	.48	.01	1.9	.22	1.26	215.7	.60
17 FABRICATED METAL PRODUCTS (SIC 34, 19)	.39	117.2	.98	.01	3.6	.74	.01	3.6	.42	1.32	396.5	1.11
18 MACHINERY, EXCEPT ELECTRICAL (SIC 35)	.40	132.5	1.11	.01	3.6	.61	.01	3.9	.46	1.31	438.0	1.22
19 ELECTRICAL MACHINERY & EQUIP (SIC 36)	.39	120.0	1.00	.01	3.1	.65	.01	3.3	.39	1.29	392.8	1.10
20 TRANSPORTATION EQUIPMENT (SIC 37)	.30	715.0	5.99	.01	13.3	2.76	.01	32.3	3.76	1.21	2886.5	8.06
21 MISCELLANEOUS MANUFACTURING (SIC 38-9)	.40	70.4	.59	.01	2.4	.50	.01	2.9	.34	1.36	238.4	.67
22 TRANSPORTATION SERVICES (SIC 40-7)	.60	599.5	5.02	.01	10.5	2.18	.02	18.3	2.13	1.29	1290.4	3.60
23 COMMUNICATIONS & UTILITIES (SIC 48-9)	.38	226.1	1.89	.04	23.5	4.89	.01	6.3	.74	1.34	785.7	2.19
24 WHOLESALE AND RETAIL TRADE (SIC 50-9)	.57	2120.2	17.75	.02	63.2	13.17	.13	495.3	57.67	1.22	4509.7	12.59
25 FINANCE, INS., REAL ESTATE (SIC 60-7)	.63	1793.4	15.02	.03	97.8	20.36	.03	72.7	8.47	1.44	4129.3	11.53
26 SERVICES (SIC 70-9, 80-6, 89)	.50	1503.6	12.59	.03	97.0	20.19	.02	60.2	7.01	1.41	4242.7	11.85
27 GOVERNMENT ENTERPRISES	.56	81.6	.68	.01	.8	.16	.02	.8	.09	1.35	194.8	.54
28 UNALLOCATED INDUSTRIES	.22	3.9	.03	.01	.1	.03	.01	.2	.02	1.59	28.9	.08
		11943.7	100.00		480.3	100.00		858.8	100.00		35817.8	100.00

NOTES

1. Multipliers dominate input-output literature. All input-output study reports have included an inverse, usually two as in this book, and too many have ended simply with a set of multipliers. As a result, much of this chapter is common to the literature. We have left the common path on two points; the major one is discussed in footnote 2 while the other is a matter of terminology.

   This change has been to use the terms 'simple' and 'total' rather than 'type I' and 'type II' to respectively describe multipliers derived from inverses excluding and including the household sector. The 'type' designation started with Moore and Petersen (1955) and has persisted to this day. But we prefer more descriptive terms.

2. The multiplier formulations used in this study are also based on linear and homogeneous relationships between output and the variables, income(s) and employment. As pointed out by Moore and Petersen (1955, p. 376) and by Hirsch (1959, p. 364) this assumption leads to an overstatement of income and employment effects. An ingenious solution to the problem for income is described in the Boulder study by Miernyk (1967, pp. 104-16). This approach requires development of local consumption functions disaggregated by income class, a chore which we were unable to perform due to resource limitations.

3. Our government-income multipliers follow ideas developed by Bahl and Shellhammer (1969).

4. The notion of an income multiplier as first introduced to the regional literature by Moore and Petersen (1955) was used to describe additional household income attributable to a unit change in household income in the industry in question. This definition is far removed from the exogenous changes which precipitate additional income changes, and it forces its user to unnecessary trouble in determining, e.g., the importance of an industry to its community. We have therefore switched to the definition used in the text. Although a similar concept appeared in Moore and Petersen and, in fact, is used here in Table 5.4a, our point is that the label is confusing. We first saw this concept discussed as 'income coefficients' in the Mississippi study by Carden and Whittington (1964) and used the term to distinguish our multiplier from the one seen in the literature as late as 1973. The Texas study (Grubb, 1973, vol. I, p. 108-11) included a table of income multipliers quite similar to those in Moore and Petersen, in Hirsch (1959), and repeated in the old but still popular standard introduction by Miernyk (1965).

   Davis (1968, p. 33) makes the importance of this distinction clear. Two old-style income multipliers may have exactly the same values but may differ substantially in terms of income change per unit change in final demand. He suggests that an emphasis on absolute changes, as here, rather than on relative changes, as in Moore and Petersen, be made to avoid confusion. The caution was also expressed by Miernyk (1967, p. 101) in his Boulder study, which reported old-style income multipliers.

6. Economic projections

A major use of input-output models is for making long-term projections.[1] We begin our discussion of this use of the Georgia Economic Model with comments on the various techniques available for projecting economic activity. While brief, it sets the scene. Then we outline the projection model in more detail, commenting on the assumptions and techniques used in its construction and on the way in which we have estimated final-demand and productivity changes for use in the projections. Third, we present and discuss our baseline projections for 1980 and we compare these projections with other projections for the same period. And fourth, we allocate our projections to the eight trade regions of Georgia.

6.2 TYPES OF PROJECTIONS

Of the several means of projecting regional activity, four are common: 1. straight-line extrapolation, 2. shift-share projections, 3. aggregate econometric projections, and 4. input-output projections.

Straight-line extrapolations are both easy and naïve. Growth rates over a recent period for industries in the economy are assumed to apply in the future. This technique obviously suffers: it ignores resource restrictions, can lead to negative predicted values in some cases and to absurdly high predicted values in others, and is based on an assumption that what has occurred in the past will continue to happen in the future. In spite of these shortcomings, we make limited use of it in the projections presented in the market analyses in Chapter 9. It is a simple means for handling a large number of calculations, does not vary depending upon factors unknown to the observer, and is easy to understand.

Shift-share projections represent an improvement on the straight-line method. Shift-share analysis divides growth in a regional industry into two parts: 1. the national growth rate; and 2. the regional-share component, or the difference between the regional industry growth rate and the national industry growth rate. In analyzing growth in an economy's employment, these parts are used to divide employment (income) growth for the region into three categories: 1. that associated with national growth, 2. that associated with industry mix in the region, and 3. that associated with characteristics peculiar to the region.

In projecting industry employment, several variations on the shift-share method are possible. Generally, they involve projecting industry growth at some national rate and adjusting this growth with a factor reflecting the regional-share component in a shift-share analysis of the previous period. With the assistance of Charles F. Floyd of the University of Georgia, we have made projections of employment in Georgia and the planning regions used in the Georgia Interindustry Study through 1980 using the shift-share technique. (See Appendix B.) We compare them with our projections later.

Aggregate econometric models are occasionally used in projecting economic activity. The equations used by state analysts in predicting tax revenues for the state of Georgia are typical of this family of models. They are designed to predict one quantity on the basis of a number of other observed quantities. Another example is the regional forecasting system modeled after the Wharton national econometric model and currently being used by the Bureau of Business and Economic Research at the University of Georgia. Generally, we can say that aggregate models are not competitive with input-output models. One is designed to predict or explain the behavior of a single variable or a small number of variables, while the other is designed to examine and project the behavior of the many components of the entire economic structure of an area.

Input-output models become projection models under a variety of assumptions. The models are especially designed for long-run projections of industry behavior. Our projection model is what might be called a 'basic' model. That is, it is an extension of the 1970 model without extensive sophistication. As we shall see, the simplicity of our model yields valuable results.

6.3 THE PROJECTION MODEL

6.3.1 Review of basic techniques
As pointed out in section 2.6.3, the solution to the set of equations describing the input-output system of an economy forms the basis for a projection model. This solution is expressed as

$$x' = (I - a)^{-1} y' \, ,$$

where x' is a vector or column of the gross outputs of industries in the economy in some future year, a is the direct-requirements matrix, $(I - a)^{-1}$ is the inverse, or total-requirements, matrix, and y' is the vector of final demands for goods in the economy in the future year under consideration.

If we assume that the direct-requirements matrix remains reasonably stable, we simply need to estimate values for the y' vector to be able to make consistent estimates of the future gross outputs of industries in the economy.

Why bother to estimate final demand for goods produced in the state in order to estimate gross outputs? The number of values to be estimated is the same and, on the surface, it appears difficult to estimate either set of values. The answer is fairly easy. First, estimates of industry growth rates are fairly easy to obtain in national statistics and provide a convenient starting point for estimating change in final demand. And second, estimates of future gross outputs for Georgia industries made independently of each other can be highly inconsistent. If we start with estimates of final demands which are reasonable, the input-output system forces us to calculate estimates of future gross outputs which are consistent with expected relationships and needs within the economy.

Our objective is to produce good and consistent estimates of the future structure of the economy with the least additional information.

6.3.2 Construction of the model

In constructing the projection model, we have slightly altered the 28-industry input-output model. Our primary modification has been to close the model with respect not only to the household sector but also to the private-investment and the state- and local-government sectors. That is, we have treated these sectors, which are traditionally part of final demand, as industries, and have assumed that their expenditures are reasonably dependent on their incomes. This step has left us with two final-demand sectors, the federal government and private exports. These two sectors are clearly exogenous to the Georgia economic system; there is no way to say that expenditures by the federal government in Georgia are related to federal revenues in the state, and there is no way to say that the purchases by industries outside the state are dependent on the sum of such purchases.

Since we are interested in basic projections, we have not altered the direct-requirements matrix to reflect changes in technology or changes in trade patterns. Speculations as to these changes are difficult to make, especially in the numbers required to make any difference in the projections, and are probably no more reliable than an assumption that no important changes take place.[2] This is especially true if we are looking for the minimum or baseline projections of activities.

But in estimating employment in 1980, we have attempted to account for trends in productivity growth rates. We have modified the ratios of employment to gross outputs in 1970 by expected productivity growth rates computed for national industries.

The result is a basic projection model which takes, as data, the direct-requirements table for Georgia, estimates of final demands for Georgia products computed from national growth patterns, and estimates of productivity growth. It yields, as outputs, estimates of the gross outputs and employment of industries in Georgia.

6.3.3 Basic assumptions

It might be useful to list some of the assumptions made in using our model. We have assumed 1. that no basic changes take place in the input requirements of Georgia industries, 2. that no changes occur in the trade patterns of Georgia industries, 3. that the demands for Georgia products keep pace with national demands, and 4. that no major changes in industry mix occur. These are fairly stringent assumptions; they cast our projections in the role of *baseline projections*, providing a yardstick against which to measure the success of development activities. The extent to which changes in employment between 1970 and 1980 exceed our projections will measure the success of the Georgia Department of Industry and Trade, the area planning and development commissions, and the various other public and private development agencies in promoting Georgia's economic future.

6.4 BASELINE PROJECTIONS OF THE GEORGIA ECONOMY, 1980

6.4.1 Estimates of growth in exogenous demands and productivity

As noted in the previous section, the projection model estimates 1980 outputs of Georgia industries on the basis of expected changes in demands by the federal government and by industries and consumers outside of Georgia. The model then projects employment in Georgia on the basis of these estimated outputs and expected changes in the ratios of employment to output in 1980, or the reciprocals of the 1980 productivity ratios, for industries in Georgia.

Growth rates in exogenous demands and in labor productivity have been derived from projections by the Bureau of Labor Statistics. These national industry growth rates are derived from a set of input-output projections based on the 80-industry national model. We have weighted these growth rates in accordance with the industry pattern in Georgia and have thus estimated average growth rates for private exports of each of the 29 industries in Georgia.

These estimates are shown in Table 6.4a. High growth rates are expected in chemicals, miscellaneous manufacturing, rubber and plastics, and communications and utilities. Low growth rates are expected in leather and leather products, transportation equipment, agriculture, mining, and lumber and wood products. We have projected federal defense expenditures to decline at 1.5 percent annually, meaning that these expenditures in 1980 will be 86 percent of their 1970 level and that we assume Lockheed Aircraft Corporation will

Table 6.4a Estimates of annual growth in exogenous demands and labor productivity (in percent).

INDUSTRY	ANNUAL EXPORT GROWTH RATE	PRODUCTIVITY GROWTH RATE
AGRICULTURE [SIC 01, 07-9]	2.757	3.13
MINING [SIC 10-4]	3.112	4.60
CONTRACT CONSTRUCTION [SIC 15-7]	4.165	1.25
FOOD AND KINDRED PRODUCTS [SIC 20-1]	3.295	4.00
TEXTILE MILL PRODUCTS [SIC 22]	3.928	5.00
APPAREL AND RELATED PRODUCTS [SIC 23]	3.783	1.25
LUMBER AND WOOD PRODUCTS [SIC 24]	3.281	5.00
FURNITURE AND FIXTURES [SIC 25]	5.062	2.13
PAPER AND ALLIED PRODUCTS [SIC 26]	4.705	3.00
PRINTING AND PUBLISHING [SIC 27]	4.400	3.00
CHEMICALS AND ALLIED PRODUCTS [SIC 28]	5.523	4.00
PETROLEUM REFINING [SIC 29]	3.500	5.00
RUBBER AND MISC. PLASTICS [SIC 30]	6.300	3.00
LEATHER AND LEATHER PRODUCTS [SIC 31]	1.191	1.25
STONE, CLAY AND GLASS PROD. [SIC 32]	4.519	3.00
PRIMARY METAL INDUSTRIES [SIC 33]	3.950	3.00
FABRICATED METAL PRODUCTS [SIC 34, 19]	3.881	2.65
MACHINERY, EXCEPT ELECTRICAL [SIC 35]	4.514	2.33
ELECTRICAL MACHINERY + EQUIP [SIC 36]	5.094	4.04
TRANSPORTATION EQUIPMENT [SIC 37]	2.729	1.83
MISCELLANEOUS MANUFACTURING [SIC 38-9]	5.670	4.33
TRANSPORTATION SERVICES [SIC 40-7]	4.000	3.00
COMMUNICATIONS + UTILITIES [SIC 48-9]	6.505	3.75
WHOLESALE AND RETAIL TRADE [SIC 50-9]	4.700	3.00
FINANCE, INS., REAL ESTATE [SIC 60-7]	4.622	3.08
SERVICES [SIC 70-9, 80-6, 89]	5.233	2.07
FEDERAL GOVERNMENT ENTERPRISES	5.100	.00
STATE + LOCAL GOVERNMENT ENTERPRISES	5.500	.00
UNALLOCATED INDUSTRIES	3.868	.00
FEDERAL DEFENSE EXPENDITURES	-.015	
OTHER FEDERAL EXPENDITURES	.021	

probably remain in operation. We have projected other federal expenditures to increase at 2.1 percent of their 1970 level. Both federal expenditure patterns are assumed to have the same basic composition in 1980.

6.4.2 The aggregate projections

Table 6.4b reports aggregate changes in the Georgia economy which would result under our assumptions. The gross state product would grow at 4.0 percent annually. This is lower than the 4.3 percent growth rate in gross national product projected by the Bureau of Labor Statistics. Georgia's relatively low projected growth rate results from the dominant positions of slow-growth industries in Georgia.

With personal income growing at 3.7 percent and the population growing at 1.7 percent, per capita income grows at 2.0 percent annually. This is less than the 3.1 percent growth rate which is expected for the nation over the 1970-80 period and reflects not only a low growth rate in personal income but also a relatively high population growth rate. We have projected population as 2.65 times employment in 1980, based on estimates of the labor-force participation

Table 6.4b Aggregate projections of the Georgia economy, 1980.

VARIABLE	1970	1980	ANNUAL PER-CENT GROWTH
GROSS STATE PRODUCT ($ MILLIONS)	20459.	30182.	4.0
PERSONAL INCOME ($ MILLIONS)	15866.	22863.	3.7
PER CAPITA INCOME ($)	3457.	4224.	2.0
EMPLOYMENT	1728318.	2038115.	1.7
POPULATION	4589575.	5412247.	1.7

ratio in 1970. If we had followed national estimates, population would be projected at 4,971,012, or 2.43 times employment, and the rate of growth for per capita income would be 2.9 percent, much closer to the growth rate for the nation.

Employment (including estimates of agricultural employment and military employment) is estimated at 2,038,115 in 1980, growing at 1.66 percent annually. This estimate is lower than that of most projections. The Bureau of Economic Analysis projects Georgia employment at 2,209,900 and our shift-share projection places Georgia employment between 2,276,739 and 2,346,520. Both of these projections are optimistic, assuming that trends set in the last decade will continue in the future. Our estimate is a *baseline* estimate, showing employment which can be expected in 1980 if only national trends influence Georgia's economy. The influence of Georgia entrepreneurs and planning and development agencies has not been taken into account.

6.4.3 Industry projections
Table 6.4c presents projected outputs and employment in 1980, by industry. The ten industries with the highest output growth rates are, in order:

> Contract construction
> Miscellaneous manufacturing
> Furniture and fixtures
> Stone, clay, and glass products
> Rubber and miscellaneous plastics
> Machinery, except electrical
> Electrical machinery
> Chemicals and chemical products
> Fabricated metals
> Paper and allied products

Many of these are industries which pay substantial wages and salaries; yet they are relatively small among industries which employ Georgians. The ten largest contributors to employment in the 1970's are expected to be:

Contract construction
City and county governments
Wholesale and retail trade
Services
State government
Federal government
Apparel
Transportation services
Finance, insurance, and real estate
Machinery, except electrical

And many of these pay fairly low wages and salaries, contributing to low per capita incomes.

Due to productivity increases (and to the expected decline in federal defense expenditures), employment is expected to drop in textile mill products, food and kindred products, lumber and wood products, transportation equipment, mining, and petroleum refining.

Table 6.4c Projected baseline industry outputs and employment, Georgia, 1980 (outputs in millions of dollars, employment in number of employees).

| | GEORGIA OUTPUTS | | GA. EMPLOYMENT | |
	1970	1980	1970	1980
AGRICULTURE [SIC 01, 07-9]	1477.610	2029.535	72710.	73381
MINING [SIC 10-4]	196.565	298.160	6304.	6099
CONTRACT CONSTRUCTION [SIC 15-7]	2519.575	4903.776	84875.	145892.
FOOD AND KINDRED PRODUCTS [STC 20-1]	2281.214	3213.706	47276.	44993.
TEXTILE MILL PRODUCTS [SIC 22]	3690.639	5425.393	110548.	99767.
APPAREL AND RELATED PRODUCTS [SIC 23]	997.556	1445.557	67174.	85970.
LUMBER AND WOOD PRODUCTS [SIC 24]	487.956	744.197	22348.	20924.
FURNITURE AND FIXTURES [SIC 25]	232.911	394.304	10976.	15050.
PAPER AND ALLIED PRODUCTS [STC 26]	1215.425	1907.113	24883.	29052.
PRINTING AND PUBLISHING [SIC 27]	341.004	511.856	14164.	15820.
CHEMICALS AND ALLIED PRODUCTS [STC 28]	716.413	1156.617	15516.	16923.
PETROLEUM REFINING [SIC 29]	49.490	74.120	1019.	937.
RUBBER AND MISC. PLASTICS [STC 30]	245.645	415.235	8074.	10156.
LEATHER AND LEATHER PRODUCTS [SIC 31]	77.844	94.174	4667.	4986.
STONE, CLAY AND GLASS PROD. [SIC 32]	389.017	657.795	14068.	17700.
PRIMARY METAL INDUSTRIES [SIC 33]	287.496	423.143	6734.	7375.
FABRICATED METAL PRODUCTS [STC 34, 19]	524.138	824.936	17373.	21050.
MACHINERY, EXCEPT ELECTRICAL [SIC 35]	425.458	715.259	13440.	17946.
ELECTRICAL MACHINERY + EQUIP [SIC 36]	360.887	589.159	11213.	12319.
TRANSPORTATION EQUIPMENT [SIC 37]	2492.129	2962.367	49663.	49243.
MISCELLANEOUS MANUFACTURING [SIC 38-9]	219.256	372.673	7153.	7957.
TRANSPORTATION SERVICES [SIC 40-7]	1327.270	1980.549	79849.	88659.
COMMUNICATIONS + UTILITIES [STC 48-9]	1280.511	1969.174	37732.	40154.
WHOLESALE AND RETAIL TRADE [SIC 50-9]	4820.279	7379.581	340753.	388174.
FINANCE, INS., REAL ESTATE [SIC 60-7]	4247.452	6287.692	75189.	82181.
SERVICES [SIC 70-9, 80-6, 89]	4182.537	6326.404	173085.	213302.
FEDERAL GOVERNMENT ENTERPRISES	220.344	338.847	19408.	29846.
STATE + LOCAL GOVERNMENT ENTERPRISES	204.635	311.630	10407.	15848.
UNALLOCATED INDUSTRIES	306.514	461.567	0.	0.
HOUSEHOLDS	15866.004	22863.257	0.	0.
CAPITAL RESIDUAL	2202.509	5788.630	0.	0.
CITY AND COUNTY GOVERNMENT	1463.800	1992.359	151483.	206182.
STATE GOVERNMENT	1576.441	2332.284	61142.	90457.
FEDERAL GOVERNMENT	4284.305	4554.817	169092.	179769.
TOTAL	61210.828	91745.866	1728318.	2038115.

6.4.4 Allocation of employment projections to trade regions

Using the allocation of industry employment to the eight trade regions (Chart 6.4a) developed in our shift-share projections, we have distributed changes in industry employment among the regions of Georgia.[3] Table 6.4d reports annual growth rates in employment in each region. (See Appendix B for a discussion of the shift-share method. Table 6.4d is derived from 'B' projections for each region based on tables similar to Table B.3a.)

According to the baseline projections, Region VI, with Augusta as its principal city, will grow the most rapidly over this decade, followed by Region II (Atlanta) and Region III (Gainesville-Athens). In the Augusta region, growth will be led by furniture and fixtures, machinery, paper, construction, and chemicals. In the Atlanta region, the faster-growing sectors should be construction, government activities, and services. In the Gainesville-Athens region, the leading sectors are construction, rubber products, the several metal and machinery industries, and printing and publishing.

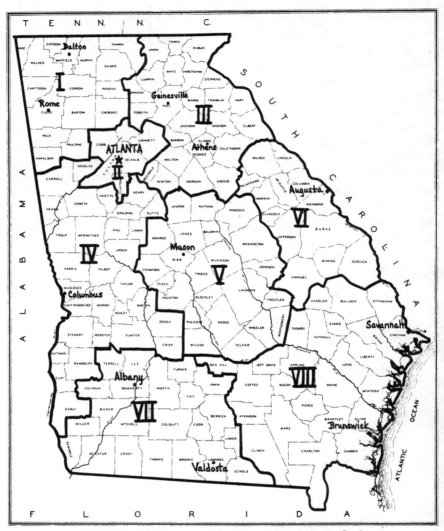

Figure 6.4a Trade regions of the Georgia Interindustry Study.

Table 6.4d Annual growth in projected baseline employment in Georgia, by industry and region,1970-80 (in percent).

Industry	I	II	III	IV	V	VI	VII	VIII
AGRICULTURE [SIC 01, 07-9]	3.04	1.29	3.25	-4.36	-3.32	-4.50	-2.13	3.64
MINING [SIC 10-4]	-4.74	1.29	1.37	-21.11	-.02	4.17	.11	6.28
CONTRACT CONSTRUCTION [SIC 15-7]	6.56	6.20	4.87	5.05	4.07	6.48	5.34	3.64
FOOD AND KINDRED PRODUCTS [SIC 20-1]	-.32	-.44	.90	-1.40	-2.09	.48	-.78	-.99
TEXTILE MILL PRODUCTS [SIC 22]	.58	-3.77	-1.42	-3.67	.21	-.08	1.11	5.23
APPAREL AND RELATED PRODUCTS [SIC 23]	1.94	.84	2.04	2.45	3.39	.67	4.14	5.06
LUMBER AND WOOD PRODUCTS [SIC 24]	-11.37	3.78	-.32	-6.48	.63	-3.97	.32	.14
FURNITURE AND FIXTURES [SIC 25]	1.97	1.07	1.73	5.81	2.60	9.75	8.49	1.78
PAPER AND ALLIED PRODUCTS [SIC 26]	1.13	2.80	2.01	4.54	-1.32	6.01	3.55	-.63
PRINTING AND PUBLISHING [SIC 27]	.38	1.25	3.11	2.27	-.23	.29	-1.61	-.91
CHEMICALS AND ALLIED PRODUCTS [SIC 28]	5.94	1.94	-2.13	1.51	2.72	5.58	1.06	-10.81
PETROLEUM REFINING [SIC 29]	.00	3.54	.00	.00	-.76	.00	.00	-3.04
RUBBER AND MISC. PLASTICS [SIC 30]	3.21	2.54	4.35	-3.69	-.86	1.15	4.36	4.38
LEATHER AND LEATHER PRODUCTS [SIC 31]	6.29	-1.15	2.00	-1.15	.00	.00	.00	.93
STONE, CLAY AND GLASS PROD. [SIC 32]	2.29	3.00	.96	3.10	.64	2.93	2.09	2.99
PRIMARY METAL INDUSTRIES [SIC 33]	-4.39	-1.57	4.77	2.56	-100.00	-100.00	4.17	5.93
FABRICATED METAL PRODUCTS [SIC 34, 19]	3.74	1.04	3.33	.80	3.47	1.70	.14	2.67
MACHINERY, EXCEPT ELECTRICAL [SIC 35]	3.57	1.44	3.13	-1.55	3.70	8.31	6.51	.25
ELECTRICAL MACHINERY + EQUIP [SIC 36]	-.75	.81	2.47	-3.34	1.91	-10.76	5.63	5.50
TRANSPORTATION EQUIPMENT [SIC 37]	-.08	-.76	2.34	3.05	2.29	1.57	4.55	-.29
MISCELLANEOUS MANUFACTURING [SIC 38-9]	-24.50	-2.24	1.70	3.58	4.89	-4.17	6.69	2.91
TRANSPORTATION SERVICES [SIC 40-7]	-.83	1.92	-.49	.23	-5.88	.81	-.94	.22
COMMUNICATIONS + UTILITIES [SIC 48-9]	.67	.77	1.57	1.11	.93	.95	.72	-2.80
WHOLESALE AND RETAIL TRADE [SIC 50-9]	1.21	1.80	1.57	.72	.59	2.12	.71	-.03
FINANCE, INS., REAL ESTATE [SIC 60-7]	.89	.64	2.50	1.79	2.11	.39	1.58	-.58
SERVICES [SIC 70-9, 80-6, 89]	1.96	3.12	1.92	1.32	.45	1.20	1.92	1.32
FEDERAL GOVERNMENT ENTERPRISES	2.72	4.34	2.71	5.56	2.37	7.24	-7.46	-2.30
STATE + LOCAL GOVERNMENT ENTERPRISES	4.32	4.33	4.33	4.30	4.28	4.28	4.27	4.26
UNALLOCATED INDUSTRIES	.00	.00	.00	.00	.00	.00	.00	.00
HOUSEHOLDS	.00	.00	.00	.00	.00	.00	.00	.00
CAPITAL RESIDUAL	.00	.00	.00	.00	.00	.00	.00	.00
CITY AND COUNTY GOVERNMENT	3.16	3.16	3.17	3.13	3.11	3.11	3.10	3.10
STATE GOVERNMENT	4.02	4.03	4.03	3.99	3.98	3.98	3.96	3.96
FEDERAL GOVERNMENT	.50	1.27	.44	.14	.07	1.79	-.34	-.43
TOTAL	1.74	2.00	1.92	.80	1.37	2.35	1.50	1.21

NOTES

1. While input-output studies typically conclude with multiplier computations and impact analyses, projections have become increasingly evident, with models such as those for Washington (Beyers, *et al.*, 1970; Bourque, 1971; and Tiebout, 1969), Kansas (Emerson), and West Virginia (Miernyk, *et al.*, 1970) seeing extensive use. The rise of strong projection models can be attributed to both experience and larger budgets. Readers are referred to the above references for developments beyond the elementary stage presented here.
   Evidence of the dominance of forecasting uses (and associated problems) can be seen in the fact that Richardson devotes 32 percent of one applications section of his input-output text (1972) to regional forecasting. This is almost twice the space allocated to any other application, and 15 percent of the entire book.

2. The problems associated with projecting coefficients are almost overwhelming. But of these problems, detecting potential changes in technology has attracted the most attention; the most common method being to identify 'best-practice establishments,' which are leaders in their industries, for use in constructing coefficients at some future time. Miernyk, *et al.* (1970) provides the best exposition of this technique. Probably the most important, the problem of changes in trade patterns has not been approached extensively in the literature. Price changes and consequent input substitutions are normally ignored; input-output analyses are phrased in 'real' terms specifically to avoid such issues. Another major cause of coefficient changes is changes in industry mix; shifts in the composition of an aggregated industry could cause substantial changes in regional coefficients. All of these problems make alterations in the direct-requirements matrix particularly difficult when the analyst is faced with a limited budget.

3. This method was also used in the Kansas study (Emerson).

7. Economic intelligence

7.1 THE STRATEGY OF DEVELOPMENT AND INPUT-OUTPUT ANALYSIS

As Georgia has industrialized and grown in population and employment needs, numerous public and private agencies have been created to aid in the 'development' of the state. Typical of these agencies are the Georgia Department of Industry and Trade, the Office of Planning and Budget, the Area Planning and Development Commissions, Georgia Tech's Industrial Development Division, the University of Georgia's Institute for Community and Area Development, and many others among the chambers, utilities, banks, and foundations of the state. Generally, their purposes have been to generate better employment opportunities, higher incomes, and a better life for residents of Georgia. Often, pressed for time and hampered by inadequate financing, these agencies have been forced to act without a strategy in pursuit of their goals.

Now, however, some of these development agencies are actively forming a strategy for development. This Georgia Interindustry Study, in fact, was initiated by the Department of Industry and Trade and the Office of Planning and Budget in an attempt to establish a strong information system for the state. It is a means for gathering and organizing information, or intelligence, about the economy as a basis for forming a development strategy.

A frequent question asked by development agencies is: what economic activities should we encourage in the state? This chapter examines that question in the light of our study.

Obviously, all industries are not equally desirable in terms of potential contributions to Georgia incomes. Some industries, for example, may be capital-intensive and employ relatively few workers. Others may not be compatible with the resources of the Georgia economy, and therefore may have few linkages with other local industries. It is important that planning and development agencies in Georgia use selection criteria which will ensure that major promotional efforts, prime industrial sites, and other resources are allocated to the industries that will provide the most income for Georgia residents.

This chapter uses the data developed in the input-output study to examine the question of which industries should be encouraged in Georgia. This examination is made with the help of a self-sufficiency analysis and a set of income-per-employee indices.

7.2 A SELF-SUFFICIENCY ANALYSIS

One approach to answering the question of which economic activities to encourage in Georgia is through examining the structure of the economy and identifying apparent 'missing links' or 'bottlenecks.' This approach is a 'supply' approach and involves an evaluation of the level of 'self-sufficiency' of each industry in the 28-industry input-output model.

Although total self-sufficiency (*i.e.* zero imports) should clearly not be a goal of an economic development program, greater self-sufficiency often might be. That is, if an economy has 'missing links' in an industry or family of industries, then the opportunities in that economy for generating employment and income are lessened. Two illustrations of industrial development activities based on this concept should make the point clear.

In 1959, the Industrial Development Division of Georgia Tech released a report documenting the market for tin cans in the Southeast. This documentation could well have been based on an input-output table if one had existed at the time. Georgia and most of the Southeast were being served by plants outside the area. Shortly after the study was completed, Crown Cork and Seal announced their intention to establish a plant in Georgia; American Can followed Crown Cork and Seal into Georgia to help in filling the production gap in the Southeast. The missing link in a family of food-processing activities had been filled.

A second illustration involves the efforts by the Georgia Department of Industry and Trade leading to the location in Georgia of a plant producing olefin fibers for the carpet industry. This plant filled a major gap in our floor-covering industry, since almost all of the fibers used in producing carpets were imported from outside the state.

Both the can and the fiber plants are economically feasible in Georgia. By adding them to the industry structure of the state, Georgia not only relieves some of the potential cost pressures associated with imports but also generates additional employment and income opportunities for its citizens.

A skyline or self-sufficiency chart helps to illustrate the approach of this section.[1] Chart 7.2a graphically portrays the status of each of the 28 industries in the Georgia Economic Model. Each vertical bar in the chart contains three elements: a block representing self-sufficiency output, a block representing direct and indirect exports by an industry, and a block representing direct and indirect imports of the products of the industry. As shown in Figure 7.2a, these elements are combined to produce an industry 'skyline' for Georgia, showing the gross outputs of each industry in relation to a 'self-sufficiency horizon.'

Self-sufficiency output is represented by that part of the bar for an industry lying below the 100 percent self-sufficiency line. It is defined for each of Georgia's 28 industries as the outputs necessary to completely satisfy the direct

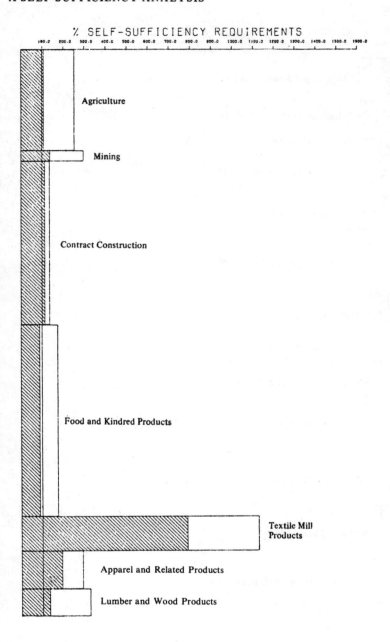

Chart 7.2a Skyline chart, Georgia, 1970.

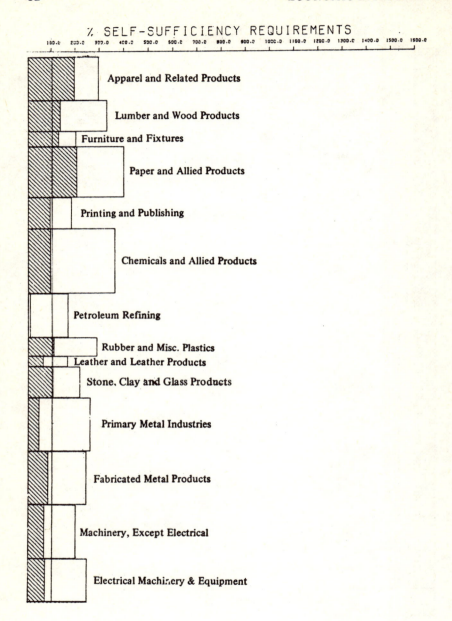

Chart 7.2a Skyline chart, Georgia, 1970 (continued).

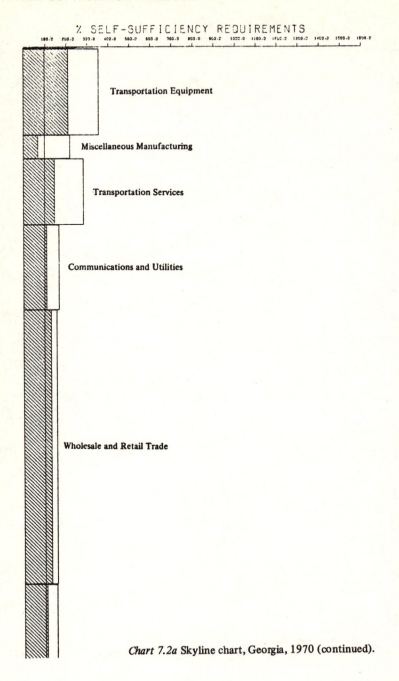

Chart 7.2a Skyline chart, Georgia, 1970 (continued).

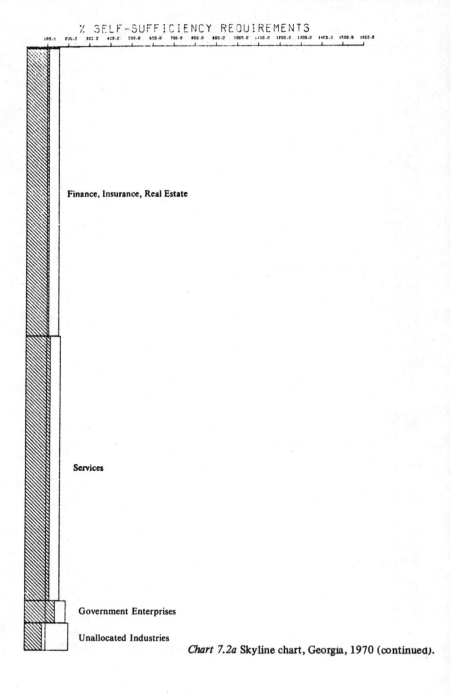

% SELF-SUFFICIENCY REQUIREMENTS

Finance, Insurance, Real Estate

Services

Government Enterprises

Unallocated Industries

Chart 7.2a Skyline chart, Georgia, 1970 (continued).

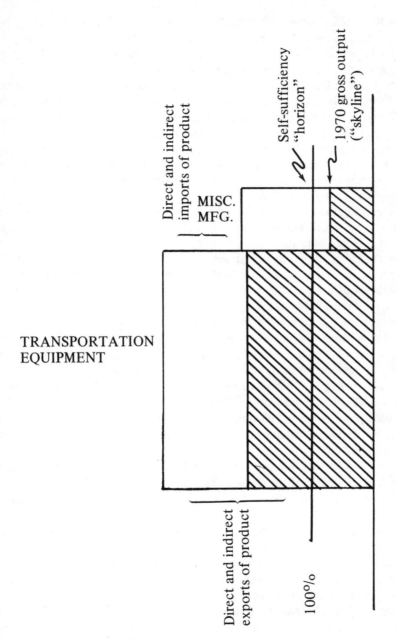

Figure 7.2a Illustrative interpretation of skyline chart.

and indirect requirements of domestic final-demand sectors (expenditures by households, for private investment, and by state and local governments). If Georgia imported and exported nothing, industries in the state would have to produce at self-sufficiency levels to satisfy domestic needs.

Direct and indirect exports are represented by the remainder of the bar for an industry. This value is defined as the production required by an industry to satisfy export demand for its products. Export demand is the remainder of final demand, or federal government expenditures and private exports.

Direct and indirect imports are represented by the unshaded area at the top of each bar. This value is defined as the imports of products of each industry which are required in excess of local production to satisfy all direct and indirect requirements for these products.

The gross output of each industry is represented by the shaded area in each bar. Industries which are more than self-sufficient have gross outputs in excess of self-sufficiency outputs.

A scanning of the skyline chart shows several prominent points. One is the strength of the Georgia economy in the textile, apparel, and paper industries. The families of industries comprising these major groups are strong and inter-related; they form important parts of Georgia's economic base.

Another interesting point is the bar representing transportation equipment. It is almost alone in the section of the chart showing durable goods, and it point to a weak corner in Georgia's economy.[2] The durable-goods industries in Georgia are associated more with imports than with exports; investigations of these industries in detail should turn up many import-substitution possibilities which are feasible and practical for the state.

A final point concerns the various service industries. Their relative strength can be attributed to Atlanta's position as a major trade center of the Southeastern United States.

Table 7.2a reports the data represented in the skyline chart to permit a better understanding of the absolute magnitudes of the outputs, imports, and exports discussed above. Compared with Table 4.3a, which shows the direct imports of products into the state, this data can yield information of interest to development agencies. Georgia has several industries (e.g. fabric mills, paper products, and finance, insurance, and real estate) whose outputs are more than sufficient to meet all of the demands of other Georgia producers for their products. Yet, products of these same industries also comprise a large percentage of the products imported by local industries. This indicates a need to investigate such industries, to determine the products normally associated with them which Georgia industries are not now producing but should be encouraged to produce. In some cases, only a strong promotional effort may be necessary to encourage a diversification and strengthening of the Georgia economy.

Table 7.2a Self-sufficiency output, direct and indirect exports and imports, and gross output for industries in Georgia, 1970 (in millions of dollars).

INDUSTRY	SELF-SUF-FICIENCY OUTPUT	DIRECT AND INDIRECT EXPORTS	IMPORTS	GROSS OUTPUTS	GROSS OUTPUT AS PERCENT OF SELF-SUFFICIENCY
1 AGRICULTURE (SIC 01, 07-9)	1375.590	2110.63	2010.03	1477.61	107.42
2 MINING (SIC 10-4)	143.339	280.94	227.83	196.57	137.13
3 CONTRACT CONSTRUCTION (SIC 15-7)	2235.170	787.11	502.91	2519.57	112.72
4 FOOD AND KINDRED PRODUCTS (SIC 20-1)	2592.040	1899.34	2211.65	2281.21	88.01
5 TEXTILE MILL PRODUCTS (SIC 22)	469.198	4811.62	1597.24	3690.64	786.59
6 APPAREL AND RELATED PRODUCTS (SIC 23)	519.604	990.55	512.64	997.56	191.98
7 LUMBER AND WOOD PRODUCTS (SIC 24)	765.076	820.38	697.72	487.96	133.66
8 FURNITURE AND FIXTURES (SIC 25)	183.726	178.99	129.81	232.91	126.77
9 PAPER AND ALLIED PRODUCTS (SIC 26)	601.349	1772.23	1159.21	1215.43	202.12
10 PRINTING AND PUBLISHING (SIC 27)	373.320	295.76	328.88	341.00	91.34
11 CHEMICALS AND ALLIED PRODUCTS (SIC 28)	768.179	1982.81	2036.28	716.41	93.26
12 PETROLEUM REFINING (SIC 29)	527.510	344.97	823.23	49.49	9.38
13 RUBBER AND MISC. PLASTICS (SIC 30)	227.903	418.89	401.37	245.64	107.78
14 LEATHER AND LEATHER PRODUCTS (SIC 31)	125.122	79.35	126.65	77.84	62.21
15 STONE, CLAY AND GLASS PROD. (SIC 32)	371.717	423.30	406.11	389.02	104.65
16 PRIMARY METAL INDUSTRIES (SIC 33)	637.607	1000.18	1356.70	287.50	45.09
17 FABRICATED METAL PRODUCTS (SIC 34, 19)	628.257	880.93	985.35	524.14	83.43
18 MACHINERY, EXCEPT ELECTRICAL (SIC 35)	639.789	617.63	832.16	425.46	66.50
19 ELECTRICAL MACHINERY & EQUIP (SIC 36)	505.825	726.63	871.80	360.89	71.35
20 TRANSPORTATION EQUIPMENT (SIC 37)	1169.541	3012.33	1689.99	2492.13	213.09
21 MISCELLANEOUS MANUFACTURING (SIC 38-9)	316.742	383.23	481.06	219.26	69.22
22 TRANSPORTATION SERVICES (SIC 40-7)	901.544	1669.95	1246.11	1327.27	147.22
23 COMMUNICATIONS & UTILITIES (SIC 48-9)	1170.240	791.43	681.55	1280.51	109.42
24 WHOLESALE AND RETAIL TRADE (SIC 50-9)	3689.350	2099.32	969.41	4820.28	130.65
25 FINANCE, INS., REAL ESTATE (SIC 60-7)	3921.534	2175.53	1850.29	4247.45	108.31
26 SERVICES (SIC 70-9, 80-6, 89)	3586.345	2299.49	1704.64	4182.54	116.62
27 GOVERNMENT ENTERPRISES	296.160	278.17	149.46	424.98	143.50
28 UNALLOCATED INDUSTRIES	369.195	398.33	466.03	306.51	83.02

Thus, the self-sufficiency analysis indicates areas in which state development and promotional efforts may be focused to Georgia's advantage.

As will be discussed in the next section, this is not to say that self-sufficient industries should be ignored. Rather, the industries representing missing links in the economy may be given priorities in the allocation of funds in order to avoid bottlenecks in production.

7.3 INCOME-PER-EMPLOYEE INDEX

An alternative approach to determining which economic activities to encourage in Georgia is through the use of an index of income generated per employee.[3] Such an index is presented in Table 7.3a. It is the ratio of the total income multiplier to the

Table 7.3a Indices of income generated per employee (direct, indirect, and induced), Georgia, 1970 (in tens of thousands of dollars).

INDUSTRY	INDEX
1 AGRICULTURE (SIC 01, 07-9)	.95
2 MINING (SIC 10-4)	.92
3 CONTRACT CONSTRUCTION (SIC 15-7)	.84
4 FOOD AND KINDRED PRODUCTS (SIC 20-1)	.91
5 TEXTILE MILL PRODUCTS (SIC 22)	.85
6 APPAREL AND RELATED PRODUCTS (SIC 23)	.62
7 LUMBER AND WOOD PRODUCTS (SIC 24)	.71
8 FURNITURE AND FIXTURES (SIC 25)	.70
9 PAPER AND ALLIED PRODUCTS (SIC 26)	.97
10 PRINTING AND PUBLISHING (SIC 27)	1.00
11 CHEMICALS AND ALLIED PRODUCTS (SIC 28)	.91
12 PETROLEUM REFINING (SIC 29)	.90
13 RUBBER AND MISC. PLASTICS (SIC 30)	.92
14 LEATHER AND LEATHER PRODUCTS (SIC 31)	.67
15 STONE, CLAY AND GLASS PROD. (SIC 32)	.88
16 PRIMARY METAL INDUSTRIES (SIC 33)	1.01
17 FABRICATED METAL PRODUCTS (SIC 34, 19)	.99
18 MACHINERY, EXCEPT ELECTRICAL (SIC 35)	.94
19 ELECTRICAL MACHINERY & EQUIP (SIC 36)	.96
20 TRANSPORTATION EQUIPMENT (SIC 37)	1.05
21 MISCELLANEOUS MANUFACTURING (SIC 38-9)	.71
22 TRANSPORTATION SERVICES (SIC 40-7)	.86
23 COMMUNICATIONS & UTILITIES (SIC 48-9)	.93
24 WHOLESALE AND RETAIL TRADE (SIC 50-9)	.78
25 FINANCE, INS., REAL ESTATE (SIC 60-7)	1.59
26 SERVICES (SIC 70-9, 80-6, 89)	.91
27 GOVERNMENT ENTERPRISES	.93
28 UNALLOCATED INDUSTRIES	.90
29 HOUSEHOLDS	.96

total employment multiplier for an industry and should be interpreted as the income generated (direct, indirect, and induced) per additional employee in each of the industries.[4] The index, we should stress, deals with total personal income generated throughout the economy and not just the wages and salaries paid per employee in the various industries.

In 1970, $11,213 million in personal income was created by a nonagricultural, nongovernmental labor force of 1,244,076 for an average income generated of $9,093. Thus, index values greater than $9,100 show industries which clearly contribute to higher income per capita in the state. Industries such as transportation equipment, primary metals, pulp and paper, and electrical equipment clearly tend to raise per capita income in Georgia. On the other hand, industries such as apparel, leather and leather products, and furniture and fixtures may add less to personal income per employee than others.

This is not to say that industries with low indices will lower per capita incomes in Georgia. They create jobs, sometimes many jobs, and if located in a high-unemployment area, they may contribute substantially to per capita income by providing second jobs in families.

7.4 SYNTHESIS

The self-sufficiency analysis and the income-per-employee index are complementary approaches to determining which economic activities should be encouraged in Georgia. The self-sufficiency analysis identifies the industries in which increased outputs would strengthen the structure of the economy. and create stronger interindustry linkages. The index permits a priority ranking of these industries for the allocation of development funds. For example, from the self-sufficiency analysis, expanded outputs are signaled for both the machinery and the leather products industries. However, the income-per-employee index shows that the machinery industry ($9,400) will generate the most personal income per job and should receive priority in the allocation of development efforts. In addition, the index provides a means for ranking presently self-sufficient industries as to income-generating potential.

It should be apparent that neither of these approaches provides a method for evaluating industries not presently located in the state. However, the development simulator presented in Chapter 8 was developed specifically for this purpose.

7.A MATHEMATICAL APPENDIX ON SKYLINE CHARTS

The self-sufficiency chart is drawn from computations involving an inverse based on the Georgia total-flows matrix. The total-flows matrix, with elements written as x_{ij}^T, is computed by adding the regional-transactions matrix (x), the competitive-imports matrix (m), and the noncompetitive-imports matrix (n). To facilitate this addition, the noncompetitive industries have been identified with their most comparable industries in Georgia and aggregated to form a 28-industry matrix. Elements in the total-flows matrix, then, are

$$x_{ij}^T = x_{ij} + m_{ij} + n_{ij} .$$

Proceeding, we compute a comparable direct-requirements matrix with elements

$$a_{ij}^T = \frac{x_{ij}^T}{x_j} .$$

The solution to the total-flows model, then, can be written as

$$B^T = (I - A^T)^{-1} .$$

Domestic final demand for each industry i is computed as

$$dy_i = \sum_{f=1}^{4} y_{if} + \sum_{f=1}^{4} {}_m y_{if} + \sum_{f=1}^{4} {}_n y_{if},$$

where f counts through domestic final-demand sectors (personal consumption expenditures, net private investment, and the state and local government categories), ${}_m y_{if}$ denotes a competitive import by final-demand sector f of the product of industry i, and ${}_n y_{if}$ denotes a noncompetitive import. Export demand is redefined as the remainder

$$e_i' = e_i + \sum_{f=5}^{6} y_{if},$$

where f counts federal government expenditures on defense and on civil matters.

With these variables we can examine self-sufficiency in Georgia. The output of industry i required for the state to be 100 percent self-sufficient is

$${}_s x_i = \sum_{j=1}^{s} dy_j \cdot b_{ij}^T .$$

The direct and indirect imports of the products of industry i into Georgia are

$${}_s m_i = \sum_{j=1}^{s} b_{ij}^T \cdot \left[\sum_{k=1}^{s} m_{ik} + \sum_{k=1}^{s} n_{ik} + \sum_{f=1}^{t} {}_m y_{if} + \sum_{f=1}^{t} {}_n y_{if} \right].$$

The direct and indirect exports of the products of industry i from Georgia are

$$_se_i = b_{ij}^T \cdot e_i \ .$$

The self-sufficiency chart, as explained in the text, is plotted from these values.

NOTES

1. The self-sufficiency analysis is patterned after a similar analysis in the Mississippi study by Carden and Whittington (1964), the only regional application of this tool with which we are familiar. We also benefited from a description by Leontief (1963). Obviously, the concept of self-sufficiency is deficient in many ways and skyline charts can easily be misinterpreted by the unwary reader.
A mathematical formulation is appended to this chapter. A skyline chart does not prescribe steps to development, and it does not set self-sufficiency as a goal; rather it simply provides a focus for orderly discussion. Carden and Whittington make this clear in a creative interpretation of their Mississippi study; the interested reader is referred to them.
2. As noted earlier, there are disadvantages to working with an aggregated table. This is particularly true in this chapter, which represents that part of an interindustry study in which the analyst is searching for suggestions to pass on to the planner regarding potential new activities. The strength of the 'transportation equipment' industry resides largely with the aircraft and mobile-home industries, as a look at our earlier 50-industry skyline chart would show. And not all durable-goods industries are deficit industries; the aggregation has concealed Georgia's strength in electric transmission equipment, for example.
3. Our 'income-per-employee index' was developed out of frustration in our attempts at using conventional multipliers in identifying industries to promote in the state. The literature is filled with discussions of multipliers as powerful analytic tools, yet they are grossly inadequate in the face of a sponsor's skepticism. More than just area-income expansion or job creation is involved in formulating a development strategy, and our index is intended to at least hint at per-capita income as a major concern in outlining a strategy. Many other factors are involved, of course, and our purpose is simply to place the Georgia Economic Model and its interindustry relationships in the context of development planning.
4. In the terms used in section 5.2.2, the income-per-employee index may be expressed as

$$I/E = \frac{12^{z_j}}{4^{z_j}}$$

We also computed the index using simple income and employment multipliers, but the results were not significantly different from those reported here.

8. Impact analysis

8.1 TYPES OF SHORT-RUN CHANGES

As indicated earlier (2.6), an input-output model is commonly used to answer questions regarding the economic impact of changes on the economy. Long-term changes in the final demand for goods produced in Georgia are treated in Chapter 6, which makes baseline forecasts of industry outputs in 1980. Short-term changes may take three forms. One is a simple change in final demand, *e.g.* a $1,000,000 change in sales by the carpet industry to buyers outside the state. The effect of this kind of change can be examined through the multipliers presented in Chapter 5.

The second type of short-run change is a change in trade patterns. Technically, changes in trade patterns require that changes be made in the direct-requirements matrix and that the total-requirements table be recomputed before the effects of these changes can be properly evaluated. Practically, however, this involves more expertise than is assumed of users of this model. We discuss a reasonable means of approximating the effects of trade-pattern changes using the existing tables.

The third type of short-run change is the introduction of a new plant or industry into the state. This involves a change in the internal structure of the input-output model. Our development simulator provides a means for making this change and examining the effects of a potential change on incomes and outputs in the state.

8.2 TRADE-PATTERN ANALYSIS

Technically, the proper way in which to analyze the effect of a change in the trade pattern of an industry in Georgia is to change the direct-requirements matrix to reflect the changes which we wish to examine. This is easily seen if we recall the solution to the input-output system as expressed in 2.6.3. In determining the effect of changes in final demand (y_i') on gross output (x_i'), we multiply the inverse matrix by the new final-demand vector to get the new gross-output vector:

$$x' = {}^{\cdot}(I - a)^{-1} y'.$$

The direct-requirements matrix is expressed as a in this formula. As pointed out earlier (2.6.2), each a_{ij} in this table is the product of a technical production coefficient, p_{ij}, and a regional trade coefficient, t_{ij}. The technical production coefficient is the proportion of total inputs purchased from industry i by industry j, and the regional trade coefficient is the proportion of this purchase made in the state.

In a proper trade-pattern analysis, we would be attempting to demonstrate the effect of changes in some of the t_{ij} in the regional trade coefficient matrix, t. And we should consequently change the matrix t to reflect these changes and so change the a matrix. Although this procedure is simple, a tracing of the effect of such changes requires high familiarity with the model itself as well as with the computing procedures needed to insert the changes into the system.

An alternative solution available to the analyst without computing assistance ignores this technical problem to yield an acceptable first approximation to the effect of trade-pattern changes. We suggest the following. Say we have estimated the trade changes which might take place as the result of, e.g., a marketing conference or a 'Buy Georgia' campaign by some particular industry. We sum these expected trade changes in dollar terms to show the additional sales expected in Georgia. We then multiply the additional sales expected in each industry by the output multiplier (or whichever multiplier series we desire) of the selling industry. The result is an approximation of the impact of the trade-pattern change. In effect, we introduce changes in final demand corresponding to the expected changes in local sales. The estimated impact is conservative in that we have ignored the indirect effects on production in the selling industries themselves.

8.3 DEVELOPMENT SIMULATORS

8.3.1 Introduction

While the general list of multipliers discussed earlier (5.3.5) has been estimated for each of the 28 industries in the published Georgia model, specific interest may center on some of the more detailed industries defined in the working tables. This concern may be satisfied with what we call 'development simulators.'

A simulator is a set of procedures designed to add another industry to the published data and to examine its characteristics as part of the economy. The idea is not new, although the techniques outlined here, to our knowledge, are innovative. Our interest in establishing these procedures was piqued by a reading of Tiebout's suggestion (1967) that rows and columns representing a firm could be inserted into national and regional tables for further analysis. We then designed our procedures after studying impact analysis in Bangor (Clark and Coupe, 1967), Clinton County (Gamble and Raphael, 1965), New Mexico (Lindberg, 1966b), Washington (Bourque, 1971), and West Virginia (Miernyk, 1971). Miernyk's work was especially useful and his careful analyses should be read by serious analysts. We should note that, unlike Miernyk's meticulously tailored simulations, our development simulators are 'turn-key' devices. They have been designed to make the most of minimum information; like all short cuts, they yield results which should be interpreted carefully, with one eye on our strong assumptions and the other on available information. Hopefully, they would stimulate more detailed investigations.

The simulators work in two ways. One is to isolate a detailed industry which already operates in Georgia but which is normally defined as part of an aggregated industry in the published table. We call this version a 'new-plant simulator.' The other way is to introduce a row and a column representing an industry not previously existing in the state. This approach is labeled the 'new-industry simulator.'

8.3.2 New-plant simulator

The new-plant simulator is actually a reorganization of the published table. We simply specify that the aggregation of industries in the detailed working table be expanded from 28 to 29 industries. The 29th industry is the one in which the new plant is classified. In addition, we specify the size of plant which we are considering as an addition to the state's economy. The model is developed as usual. Since little benefit accrues from the printouts of the completely revised model, we print only a couple of check tables in addition to the special simulator table.

This special simulator table is shown here in Figure 8.3a. Our example covers the addition of a $5,000,000 additional output in the veneer and plywood industry. Figure 8.3a shows the computer printout recording computed changes in the Georgia economy resulting from the additional plant (or expansion of existing capacity) in terms of industry outputs, employment, personal income, city and county government revenue, and state government revenue. The development of each of the five total multipliers for the new plant can be seen in the table. Column 1, for example, reports each of the summed elements used in computing the total output multiplier times $5,000,000. The sum of the column is the total output multiplier times $5,000,000. Each of the last four columns in the table shows the application of the various multipliers discussed in Chapter 5 to estimating the impact of a new plant on the state's economy.

8.3.3 New-industry simulator

While the new-plant simulator is merely a twist on the aggregation procedure, the new-industry simulator is more complex. In this case, the industry does not

Changes in the Georgia economy resulting from an additional $ 5.000 million plant in the veneer and plywood industry (millions of dollars)

INDUSTRY	OUTPUT VALUE	PERCENT	NUMBER OF EMPLOYEES	PERSONAL INCOME	CITY & COUNTY REVENUE	STATE REVENUE
	--- C H A N G E D U E T O N E W P L A N T I N ---					
AGRICULTURE (SIC01, 07-9)	.2		0.	.1	.0	.0
MINING (SIC 10-4)	.0		0.	.0	.0	.0
CONTRACT CONSTRUCTION (SIC 15-7)	.6		0.	.1	.0	.0
FOOD AND KINDRED PRODUCTS (SIC 20-1)	.3		5.	.0	.0	.0
TEXTILE MILL PRODUCTS (SIC 22)	.0		1.	.0	.0	.0
APPAREL AND RELATED PRODUCTS (SIC 23)	.0		2.	.0	.0	.0
LUMBER AND WOOD PRODUCTS (SIC 24)	.7		33.	.2	.3	.0
FURNITURE AND FIXTURES (SIC 25)	.0		1.	.0	.0	.0
PAPER AND ALLIED PRODUCTS (SIC 26)	.0		1.	.0	.0	.0
PRINTING AND PUBLISHING (SIC 27)	.0		2.	.0	.0	.0
CHEMICALS AND ALLIED PRODUCTS (SIC 28)	.1		1.	.0	.0	.0
PETROLEUM REFINING (SIC 29)	.0		0.	.0	.0	.0
RUBBER AND MISC. PLASTICS (SIC 30)	.0		0.	.0	.0	.0
LEATHER AND LEATHER PRODUCTS (SIC 31)	.0		1.	.0	.0	.0
STONE, CLAY AND GLASS PROD. (SIC 32)	.0		1.	.0	.0	.0
PRIMARY METAL INDUSTRIES (SIC 33)	.0		0.	.0	.0	.0
FABRICATED METAL PRODUCTS (SIC 34, 19)	.0		1.	.0	.0	.0
MACHINERY, EXCEPT ELECTRICAL (SIC 35)	.0		1.	.0	.0	.0
ELECTRICAL MACHINERY & EQUIP (SIC 36)	.0		0.	.0	.0	.0
TRANSPORTATION EQUIPMENT (SIC 37)	.1		0.	.0	.0	.0
MISCELLANEOUS MANUFACTURING (SIC 38-9)	.0		0.	.0	.0	.0
TRANSPORTATION SERVICES (SIC 40-7)	.2		10.	.1	.0	.0
COMMUNICATIONS & UTILITIES (SIC 48-9)	.3		8.	.1	.0	.0
WHOLESALE AND RETAIL TRADE (SIC 50-9)	1.0		70.	.5	.0	.1
FINANCE, INS., REAL ESTATE (SIC 60-7)	.8		14.	.4	.0	.0
SERVICES (SIC 70-9, 80-6, 89)	.8		32.	.3	.0	.0
GOVERNMENT ENTERPRISES	.1		0.	.0	.0	.0
UNALLOCATED INDUSTRIES	.1		0.	.0	.0	.0
VENEER AND PLYWOOD	5.3	12.2	318.	2.0	.0	.0
HOUSEHOLDS	4.2		0.	.0	.1	.1
CAPITAL RESIDUAL	.7		0.	.0	.0	.0
CITY AND COUNTY GOVERNMENT	.3		0.	.2	.1	.0
STATE GOVERNMENT	.3		0.	.1	.1	.0
TOTAL	16.0	12.8	503.	4.2	.3	.3

Figure 8.3a Illustration of the development simulator.

presently exist in the state, so a row of potential sales and a column of probable purchases must be constructed for it. We use the noncompetitive-imports matrix as the basis for the sales row and a technology matrix based on the national input-output table as the basis for the purchases column.

The noncompetitive-imports row for the new industry is moved up into the local-industry matrix. The column of national input-output coefficients for the new industry is multiplied by the expected gross output of the new industry and is moved over into the local-industry matrix. We then apply a modified supply-demand pool technique to estimating the regional trade patterns associated with the industry. If it produces more than is needed of its product in the state, we satisfy local demands and export the rest. If it supplies less than is demanded, we satisfy local demands to the extent possible and import the rest. We use average trade coefficients for each of its suppliers as first estimates of trade coefficients which we then apply to cell values in the column for the new industry. We then aggregate to 29 industries, calculate direct requirements, invert, and multiply back through by the total final-demand vector less households to obtain estimates of gross outputs of industries after the new industry is established in the state. Gross outputs of industries existing in 1970 are subtracted from these newly estimated gross outputs and these changes in gross outputs are used to construct the simulator table, which is identical in format to the table for the new-plant simulator.

8.4 ANALYSIS OF PUBLIC PROJECTS: A DEVELOPMENT HIGHWAY

A somewhat different form of impact analysis can be seen in an examination of the economic impact of a potential development highway in North Georgia (Schaffer, 1974).[1] In this case, insertion of new rows and columns into the transactions matrix is inappropriate, since a highway is a public good; its effect, outside of the construction impact, is indirect, being felt through final-demand changes and through its stimulation of industrial growth.

To localize the impact of the potential highway, we constructed a 10-county substate model using a modification of the procedures outlined in Chapter 3. We started with the Georgia transactions table, constructed a first estimate using the supply-demand pool procedure, and, after a series of interviews with businessmen and planners, used the selected-values method to construct a model of the study area.

To provide a no-highway alternative against which to measure our impact estimates, we used shift-share projections of area employment to produce benchmark projections for 1980 and 1990. We converted these to output estimates using ratios of output to employment and of productivity change, and then developed future input-output tables for the area based on these estimates and the area direct-requirements matrix. From these tables, we obtained estimates of gross regional product in the area for 1980 and 1990, assuming no development highways.

For each of five highway alternatives, we developed three expenditure vectors: 1. sales out of region, 2. sales to transient buyers, and 3. sales to partial residents. Sales to out-of-region buyers are primarily export sales due to highway-related expansion of manufacturing activities, but they also include 'sales' of community labor, valued as net commuting income. These sales estimates were based on a review of industrial expansion along similar development highways as well as the regional-share components of our earlier projections.

Sales to transient buyers are primarily sales to tourists and campers expected to use the scenic mountain area more intensively as a result of the highway. Sales to partial residents are expenditures by second-home owners attracted to the area from nearby Atlanta.

The above expenditures are classified in such categories as: highway construction expenditures; expenditures for second-home construction, support, and taxes; tourist expenditures; and changes in income from industrial expansion. To be traced through an input-output model, many of these expenditures by category must be transformed into purchases by industry. This transformation includes a shift from purchasers' to producers' prices and identification of local versus imported purchases. To show the importance of the consumption 'bridges' mentioned in section 3.3, it is constructive to review the transformation in its algebraic formulation (as taken from Schaffer, 1974, pp. 14-15):

To explain the adjustment, we define the following variables:

$C_{kh} = $ Expenditure in category k associated with highway h. Only two categories are included in this matrix: second-household expenditures and tourist expenditures. Items in this matrix must be distributed to more than one industry. There are 10 highway alternatives, 5 each in 1980 and 1990.

$D_{ik} = $ Proportional distribution of expenditures classified by category among the region's industries, or sectors, i. There are 33 sectors: the 29 normally defined industries plus households, capital residual, local government, and state government. This allows us to trace expenditures through all parts of the economy. The distribution is in producers' prices since the trade margins have all been allocated to the trade sector. Generally this matrix is based on the personal consumption data associated with the U.S. input-output study, although some distributions are self-evident.

L_i =   Ratio of local purchases to total purchases from industry i. Since the
expenditures affected are all household-related, we calculate the ratio
from data derived from the household column of the input-output
table.

M_{ih} =   Miscellaneous expenditures in sector i associated with highway h. This
matrix includes entries in row 3 for second-home construction, row 30
for commuting income, and row 32 for second-home taxes associated with highway alternatives.

G_{ih} =   Growth expected in manufacturing industry i associated with highway
h. This growth is expressed in the same dollar units used in the C
matrix.

E_{ih} =   Expenditures in industry i associated with highway h.

The computation is fairly simple:

$$E_{ih} = L_i \left(\sum_k D_{ik} \cdot C_{kh} \right) + M_{ih} + G_{ih}.$$

The first term on the right is the local expenditures made with industry i in
association with highway alternative h. The L_i permits us to trace only
expenditures made with local industries through the model while the summed
element in parentheses converts expenditures by category to expenditures by
industry. The second term on the right covers expenditures already designated
by sector and the third term is an estimate of industrial expansion by industry.
To project the potential economic impact of the five alternative highway
corridors on the region, we first determined the direct effect of each alternative
(E_{ih}) and then traced this impact through the regional model to obtain
comparative statistics. The model was defined in exactly the same terms as used
in Chapter 6. The regional production coefficients were modified slightly
(reduced) in the 1980 and 1990 models to account for production (under the
no-highway alternative) short of additional expected needs in agriculture (1990
only), transportation services, and trade. The adjustment was necessary because
of a relatively slow projected growth compared to local needs in these three
industries. The coefficient changes were minor, however, and reflect a
reasonable compatibility of shift-share and input-output techniques.

Projection of gross outputs was according to common practice. We post-multiplied the inverse of the input-output model by the vectors of changes in final demand (E_{ih}), obtaining

$$_n\Delta x_i = (I - _n a)^{-1} \cdot E_{ih},$$

where the prescript indicates the year.

Then we reconstructed the input-output tables by alternative and year. Multiplication of elements in the direct-requirements matrix $(_n a_{ij})$ by total sector outputs $(_n x_j)$, which are calculated as 1970 outputs $(_0 x_j)$ plus changes in outputs $(_n \Delta x_j)$, yielded transactions in the interindustry and final-payments quadrants of the tables. Assuming that federal expenditures would be the same as projected for the no-highway alternative and calculating exports as a residual, we were able to project input-output tables for each alternative and year. From these tables we derived projections of gross regional product, personal income, saving and investment, and local government revenues.

A final step is estimating employment, which is simple. We divide changes in industry outputs by output-per-employee ratios modified for expected productivity change. Adding these changes to 1970 employment yielded estimates of employment and completed the statistics required to compare the economic impact of the various alternatives. These economic effects were then distributed according to land-use allocation models developed for other parts of the overall study.

NOTES

1. This project was part of a study performed by Interplan, Inc., for the Appalachian Regional Commission and the Georgia Department of Transportation (GDOT). While the complete report is available for review at GDOT, the procedures for the economic study are outlined in Schaffer (1974). Of the authors, Schaffer, Floyd, and Hamby were associated with the highway study.

9. A market information system for Georgia

Showing the sales and purchase patterns of industries in an economy, an input-output table is an excellent base for a market information system. This chapter presents the tables for a sample market analysis produced from the Georgia Economic Model.[1]

In an attempt to more clearly delineate markets, the Georgia market information system organizes data from the state input-output tables in a less complex form than the transactions table. Rows in the state table and in the competitive-imports table are used to identify sales patterns in the state. Columns in these tables are used to identify purchase patterns. Similar tables present projections to 1980 of these sales and purchases. Two other tables present sales and purchase patterns for the Southeast as derived from an input-output table approximated for Georgia and the five contiguous states.

The chapter closes with a review of sources and computations for our tables.

9.2 A SAMPLE MARKET ANALYSIS

The following text is derived from the material designed to accompany each market analysis released to the public. It briefly describes the analysis and is followed by copies of the printed tables. Tables are included for only one of the analyses derived from the 28-industry input-output tables. The tables available for 105 more detailed industries are similar but do not include data for the Southeast. Figure 9.2a is a sample market analysis derived from the 28-industry Georgia Economic Model.[2]

A basic component of the Georgia information system is the interindustry transactions table, or input-output table. As noted earlier, the table delineates in its columns purchases by industries and consuming sectors from 28 other industries in and outside the state. In its rows, the table shows sales by industries in the state to 28 other industries in the state and to seven consuming sectors. An 'imports table' of similar format shows sales by industries outside the state to Georgia's industries and consumers.

To make the system more useful as a source of market information, we also constructed a similar model of the Southeast, including Georgia and the five

SUMMARY OF THE MARKETS IN GEORGIA AND THE SOUTHEAST FOR THE
PAPER PRODUCTS EXC CONTAINERS (SIC 264)   INDUSTRY

1.   TOTAL SALES IN GEORGIA, 1970

PURCHASES BY FIRMS IN GEORGIA ARE ESTIMATED AT $ 403.9 MILLIONS FOR
PRODUCTS OF THIS INDUSTRY IN 1970.   55.7% OF TOTAL SALES ARE PRODUCED
BY FIRMS LOCATED WITHIN THE STATE, LEAVING 44.3% OR $ 179.0 MILLIONS
PRODUCED BY OUT-OF-STATE PRODUCERS.

2.   TOTAL PRODUCTION IN GEORGIA, 1970

FIRMS IN GEORGIA PRODUCED OUTPUT VALUED AT $ 224.9 MILLIONS IN 1970
SELLING ABOUT 76.3% WITHIN THE STATE.   36 ESTABLISHMENTS,
EMPLOYING APPROXIMATELY 7210 WORKERS, PRODUCED GOODS IN GEORGIA
IN 1970 *; THIS COMPARES WITH   27 ESTABLISHMENTS WITH 5988
EMPLOYEES IN 1964.

3.   MARKET GROWTH IN GEORGIA, 1964-70, AND PROJECTIONS TO 1980

THE MARKET FOR THIS INDUSTRY HAS GROWN AT AN AVERAGE ANNUAL RATE OF
2.7%.   IF GROWTH CONTINUES AT THIS RATE, THE MARKET WILL REACH
$ 553.8 MILLIONS BY 1980.

4.   INDUSTRY GROWTH, 1964-70, AND PROJECTION TO 1980

THE INDUSTRY HAS GROWN AT AN AVERAGE ANNUAL RATE OF   2.8%.   IF
GROWTH CONTINUES AT THIS RATE AND OTHER CONDITIONS REMAIN THE SAME,
GEORGIA PRODUCERS WILL BE CAPABLE OF SERVING 52.1% OF THE
PROJECTED MARKET IN 1980.

5.   TOTAL SALES IN THE SOUTHEAST, 1970

PURCHASES BY FIRMS IN THE SOUTHEAST ARE ESTIMATED AT $ 1067.0 MILLIONS
IN 1970.   85.3% OF TOTAL SALES COULD BE SUPPLIED BY SOUTHEASTERN
PRODUCERS. (THIS LEAVES AT LEAST 14.7% TO BE SUPPLIED BY OUTSIDE
PRODUCERS.)

6.   TOTAL PRODUCTION IN THE SOUTHEAST, 1970

FIRMS IN THE SOUTHEAST PRODUCED OUTPUT WITH VALUE ESTIMATED AT
$ 909.8 MILLIONS IN 1970. THIS REPRESENTS APPROXIMATELY   187
ESTABLISHMENTS EMPLOYING ABOUT   25514 WORKERS.

*   NUMBER OF ESTABLISHMENTS IN GEORGIA, IN 1970, BY EMPLOYMENT-SIZE CLASS
ESTIMATED FROM COUNTY BUSINESS PATTERNS AND LOCAL EMPLOYMENT DATA.

EMPLOYEES	NUMBER OF UNITS
1-3	3
4-7	2
8-19	2
20-49	9
50-99	6
100-249	5
250-499	5
500 OR MORE	4

Figure 9.2a A sample market analysis.

Table 1. Summary of sales in Georgia in 1970 by the paper products exc containers (sic 264) industry (millions of dollars)

PURCHASER OR USER GA. INDUSTRY	TOTAL SALES		SALES BY GA. PRODUCERS		SALES BY OTHER PRODUCERS	
	VALUE	PERCENT	VALUE	PERCENT	VALUE	PERCENT
AGRICULTURE (SIC 01, 07-9)	.7	.2	.1	.1	.7	.2
MINING (SIC 10-4)	.7	.2	.0	.0	.7	.2
CONTRACT CONSTRUCTION (SIC 15-7)	9.1	2.2	6.7	1.7	2.3	.6
FOOD AND KINDRED PRODUCTS (SIC 20-1)	26.3	6.4	1.6	.4	24.7	6.2
TEXTILE MILL PRODUCTS (SIC 22)	59.7	13.0	6.7	1.7	53.2	13.1
APPAREL AND RELATED PRODUCTS (SIC 23)	1.3	.3	.8	.2	.5	.1
LUMBER AND WOOD PRODUCTS (SIC 24)	1.3	.3	.4	.1	.9	.2
FURNITURE AND FIXTURES (SIC 25)	.2	.0	.1	.0	.1	.0
PAPER AND ALLIED PRODUCTS (SIC 26)	10.5	2.6	8.0	2.0	2.5	.6
PRINTING AND PUBLISHING (SIC 27)	3.2	.8	3.0	.7	.2	.0
CHEMICALS AND ALLIED PRODUCTS (SIC 28)	8.4	2.1	.8	.3	7.6	2.0
PETROLEUM REFINING (SIC 29)	2.6	.7	2.1	.5	.5	.1
RUBBER AND MISC. PLASTICS (SIC 30)	1.4	.3	1.1	.3	.3	.1
LEATHER AND LEATHER PRODUCTS (SIC 31)	.1	.0	.0	.0	.1	.1
STONE, CLAY AND GLASS PROD. (SIC 32)	4.4	1.1	.5	.1	3.9	1.0
PRIMARY METAL INDUSTRIES (SIC 33)	.5	.1	.0	.0	.3	.1
FABRICATED METAL PRODUCTS (SIC 34, 19)	1.6	.4	.5	.1	1.1	.3
MACHINERY, EXCEPT ELECTRICAL (SIC 35)	.4	.1	.2	.1	.1	.1
ELECTRICAL MACHINERY & EQUIP (SIC 36)	1.8	.5	.4	.1	1.4	.3
TRANSPORTATION EQUIPMENT (SIC 37)	4.2	1.0	3.4	.8	.9	.3
MISCELLANEOUS MANUFACTURING (SIC 38-9)	.6	.2	.5	.1	.2	.0
TRANSPORTATION SERVICES (SIC 40-7)	.3	.1	.1	.0	.3	.1
COMMUNICATIONS & UTILITIES (SIC 48-9)	.6	.1	.3	.1	.2	.1
WHOLESALE AND RETAIL TRADE (SIC 50-9)	20.6	5.1	3.0	.8	17.5	4.3
FINANCE, INS., REAL ESTATE (SIC 60-7)	3.1	.8	1.5	.4	1.5	.4
SERVICES (SIC 70-9, 80-9, 89)	8.1	2.0	1.3	.3	6.8	1.7
GOVERNMENT ENTERPRISES	.6	.2	.2	.1	.4	.1
UNALLOCATED INDUSTRIES	14.8	3.7	1.0	.3	13.7	3.4
TOTAL LOCAL INDUSTRY SALES	187.2	46.3	44.7	11.1	142.5	35.3
FINAL USERS						
GEORGIA HOUSEHOLD CONSUMERS	37.4	9.3	1.8	.4	35.6	8.8
GEORGIA PRIVATE INVESTMENT	.6	.0	.0	.0	.0	.0
GEORGIA LOCAL GOVERNMENT	.6	.1	.1	.0	.5	.1
GEORGIA STATE GOVERNMENT	.2	.1	.1	.0	.4	.1
FEDERAL GOVERNMENT, DEFENSE	.2	.1	.2	.0	.0	.0
FEDERAL GOVERNMENT, OTHER	.2	.0	.2	.0	.0	.0
PRIVATE USERS OUTSIDE GEORGIA	177.7	44.0	177.7	44.0	.0	.0
TOTAL FINAL SALES	216.7	53.7	180.2	44.6	36.5	9.0
TOTAL SALES	403.9	100.0	224.9	55.7	179.0	44.3

Figure 9.2a A sample market analysis (continued)

Table 2. Summary of purchases and payments in Georgia in 1970 by the paper products exc containers (sic 264) industry (millions of dollars)

PRODUCER OF GOOD OR SERVICE GA. INDUSTRY	TOTAL PURCHASES		PURCHASES FROM GA. PRODUCERS		PURCHASES FROM OTHER PRODUCERS	
	VALUE	PERCENT	VALUE	PERCENT	VALUE	PERCENT
AGRICULTURE (SIC01, 07-9)	.0	.0	.0	.0	.0	.0
MINING (SIC 10-4)	.8	.4	.8	.4	.0	.0
CONTRACT CONSTRUCTION (SIC 15-7)	1.6	.7	1.6	.7	.0	.0
FOOD AND KINDRED PRODUCTS (SIC 20-1)	1.4	.6	1.3	.6	.1	.0
TEXTILE MILL PRODUCTS (SIC 22)	.8	.3	.4	.1	.4	.2
APPAREL AND RELATED PRODUCTS (SIC 23)	.9	.4	.8	.4	.1	.1
LUMBER AND WOOD PRODUCTS (SIC 24)	12.9	5.7	12.8	5.7	.2	.1
FURNITURE AND FIXTURES (SIC 25)	.0	.0	.0	.0	.0	.0
PAPER AND ALLIED PRODUCTS (SIC 26)	74.2	33.0	48.3	21.5	25.8	9.5
PRINTING AND PUBLISHING (SIC 27)	3.4	1.5	2.5	1.1	1.0	.4
CHEMICALS AND ALLIED PRODUCTS (SIC 28)	15.8	7.0	4.9	2.2	10.8	4.8
PETROLEUM REFINING (SIC 29)	1.8	.8	.1	.1	1.7	.7
RUBBER AND MISC. PLASTICS (SIC 30)	5.6	2.5	3.8	1.7	1.7	.8
LEATHER AND LEATHER PRODUCTS (SIC 31)	.5	.0	.0	.0	.0	.0
STONE, CLAY AND GLASS PROD. (SIC 32)	.6	.2	.0	.0	.4	.2
PRIMARY METAL INDUSTRIES (SIC 33)	1.2	.5	.5	.2	.1	.1
FABRICATED METAL PRODUCTS (SIC 34, 19)	.6	.3	.3	.1	1.0	.4
MACHINERY, EXCEPT ELECTRICAL (SIC 35)	.7	.3	.0	.0	.6	.3
ELECTRICAL MACHINERY & EQUIP (SIC 36)	.0	.0	.0	.0	.6	.3
TRANSPORTATION EQUIPMENT (SIC 37)	.4	.2	.0	.0	.0	.0
MISCELLANEOUS MANUFACTURING (SIC 38-9)	.4	.2	.3	.2	.0	.0
TRANSPORTATION SERVICES (SIC 40-7)	4.6	2.0	2.0	.9	2.6	1.2
COMMUNICATIONS & UTILITIES (SIC 48-9)	8.1	3.6	8.0	3.5	.1	.1
WHOLESALE AND RETAIL TRADE (SIC 50-9)	5.8	2.6	5.6	2.5	.2	.1
FINANCE, INS., REAL ESTATE (SIC 60-7)	3.1	1.4	2.1	.9	1.0	.5
SERVICES (SIC 70-9, 80-6, 89)	4.2	1.9	3.0	1.3	1.3	.5
GOVERNMENT ENTERPRISES	.2	.1	.2	.1	.0	.0
UNALLOCATED INDUSTRIES	2.7	1.2	1.7	.8	.9	.4
TOTAL LOCAL INDUSTRY PURCHASES	151.8	67.5	101.1	44.9	50.7	22.6
PRIMARY INPUTS						
GEORGIA HOUSEHOLDS	45.9	20.4	45.9	20.4	.0	.0
CAPITAL OWNERSHIP	11.3	5.0	11.3	5.0	.0	.0
GEORGIA LOCAL GOVERNMENTS	1.3	.6	1.3	.6	.0	.0
GEORGIA STATE GOVERNMENT	1.2	.5	1.2	.5	.0	.0
FEDERAL GOVERNMENT	10.7	4.8	10.7	4.8	.0	.0
TOTAL FINAL PAYMENTS	70.4	31.3	70.4	31.3	.0	.0
NON-COMPETITIVE IMPORTS	2.6	1.2	.0	.0	2.6	1.2
TOTAL PURCHASES AND PAYMENTS	224.9	100.0	171.5	76.3	53.4	23.7

Figure 9.2a A sample market analysis (continued).

Table 3. Summary of sales in Georgia in 1980 by the paper products exc containers (sic 264) industry (millions of dollars)

PURCHASER OR USER GA. INDUSTRY	TOTAL SALES		SALES BY GA. PRODUCERS		SALES BY OTHER PRODUCERS	
	VALUE	PERCENT	VALUE	PERCENT	VALUE	PERCENT
AGRICULTURE (SIC 01, 07-9)	1.1	.2	.1	.0	1.1	.2
MINING (SIC 10-4)	.9	.2	.1	.0	.9	.2
CONTRACT CONSTRUCTION (SIC 15-7)	13.0	2.3	8.6	1.6	4.4	.8
FOOD AND KINDRED PRODUCTS (SIC 20-1)	26.9	4.9	1.6	.2	25.4	4.6
TEXTILE MILL PRODUCTS (SIC 22)	103.3	18.7	8.5	1.6	94.8	17.1
APPAREL AND RELATED PRODUCTS (SIC 23)	1.7	.3	.9	.2	.7	.1
LUMBER AND WOOD PRODUCTS (SIC 24)	1.0	.2	.3	.1	.7	.1
FURNITURE AND FIXTURES (SIC 25)	.2	.0	.1	.0	.7	.1
PAPER AND ALLIED PRODUCTS (SIC 26)	13.5	2.5	9.0	1.7	4.4	.8
PRINTING AND PUBLISHING (SIC 27)	4.5	.8	3.8	.7	.7	.1
CHEMICALS AND ALLIED PRODUCTS (SIC 28)	11.2	2.0	1.0	.2	10.1	1.8
PETROLEUM REFINING (SIC 29)	3.6	.7	2.6	.5	1.0	.2
RUBBER AND MISC. PLASTICS (SIC 30)	2.7	.5	1.8	.3	.8	.1
LEATHER AND LEATHER PRODUCTS (SIC 31)	.1	.0	.0	.0	.1	.0
STONE, CLAY AND GLASS PROD. (SIC 32)	5.5	1.0	.6	.1	4.9	.9
PRIMARY METAL INDUSTRIES (SIC 33)	.8	.1	.0	.0	.8	.1
FABRICATED METAL PRODUCTS (SIC 34, 19)	2.1	.4	.6	.1	1.4	.3
MACHINERY, EXCEPT ELECTRICAL (SIC 35)	.5	.1	.3	.1	.2	.0
ELECTRICAL MACHINERY & EQUIP (SIC 36)	2.9	.5	.6	.1	2.4	.4
TRANSPORTATION EQUIPMENT (SIC 37)	8.3	1.5	6.3	1.1	2.1	.4
MISCELLANEOUS MANUFACTURING (SIC 38-9)	1.0	.2	.6	.1	.4	.1
TRANSPORTATION SERVICES (SIC 40-7)	.5	.1	.2	.0	.3	.1
COMMUNICATIONS & UTILITIES (SIC 48-9)	.9	.2	.4	.1	.5	.1
WHOLESALE AND RETAIL TRADE (SIC 50-9)	29.8	5.4	3.9	.7	25.8	4.7
FINANCE, INS., REAL ESTATE (SIC 60-7)	4.3	.8	1.9	.3	2.3	.4
SERVICES (SIC 70-9, 80-6, 89)	13.5	2.4	1.9	.3	11.6	2.1
GOVERNMENT ENTERPRISES	.8	.2	.3	.1	.6	.1
UNALLOCATED INDUSTRIES	14.8	2.7	.9	.2	13.8	2.5
TOTAL LOCAL INDUSTRY SALES	269.5	48.7	57.1	10.3	212.4	38.3
FINAL USERS						
GEORGIA HOUSEHOLD CONSUMERS	53.7	9.7	2.3	.4	51.4	9.3
GEORGIA PRIVATE INVESTMENT	.0	.0	.0	.0	.0	.0
GEORGIA LOCAL GOVERNMENTS	1.0	.2	.2	.0	.8	.1
GEORGIA STATE GOVERNMENT	1.0	.2	.2	.0	.8	.1
FEDERAL GOVERNMENT, DEFENSE	.3	.1	.3	.1	.0	.0
FEDERAL GOVERNMENT, OTHER	.3	.1	.3	.1	.0	.0
PRIVATE USERS OUTSIDE GEORGIA	227.9	41.2	227.9	41.2	.0	.0
TOTAL FINAL SALES	284.4	51.3	231.3	41.8	53.1	9.6
TOTAL SALES	553.8	100.0	288.4	52.1	265.4	47.9

Figure 9.2a A sample market analysis (continued).

Table 4. Summary of purchases and payments in Georgia in 1980 by the paper products exc containers (sic 264) industry (millions of dollars)

PRODUCER OF GOOD OR SERVICE GA. INDUSTRY	TOTAL PURCHASES		PURCHASES FROM GA. PRODUCERS		PURCHASES FROM OTHER PRODUCERS	
	VALUE	PERCENT	VALUE	PERCENT	VALUE	PERCENT
AGRICULTURE (SIC01, 07-9)	.0	.0	.0	.0	.0	.0
MINING (SIC 10-4)	1.0	.4	1.0	.4	.0	.0
CONTRACT CONSTRUCTION (SIC 15-7)	2.1	.7	2.0	.7	.1	.0
FOOD AND KINDRED PRODUCTS (SIC 20-1)	1.7	.6	1.6	.6	.1	.0
TEXTILE MILL PRODUCTS (SIC 22)	1.0	.3	.5	.1	.5	.2
APPAREL AND RELATED PRODUCTS (SIC 23)	1.2	.4	1.0	.4	.2	.1
LUMBER AND WOOD PRODUCTS (SIC 24)	16.6	5.7	16.4	5.7	.2	.1
FURNITURE AND FIXTURES (SIC 25)	.0	.0	.0	.0	.0	.0
PAPER AND ALLIED PRODUCTS (SIC 26)	95.1	33.0	62.0	21.5	33.0	11.5
PRINTING AND PUBLISHING (SIC 27)	4.4	1.5	3.2	1.1	1.2	.4
CHEMICALS AND ALLIED PRODUCTS (SIC 28)	20.2	7.0	6.3	2.2	13.9	4.8
PETROLEUM REFINING (SIC 29)	2.3	.8	.2	.1	2.1	.7
RUBBER AND MISC. PLASTICS (SIC 30)	7.1	2.5	4.9	1.7	2.2	.8
LEATHER AND LEATHER PRODUCTS (SIC 31)	.0	.0	.0	.0	.0	.0
STONE, CLAY AND GLASS PROD. (SIC 32)	.6	.2	.0	.0	.6	.2
PRIMARY METAL INDUSTRIES (SIC 33)	.8	.3	.6	.2	.2	.1
FABRICATED METAL PRODUCTS (SIC 34, 19)	1.6	.5	.3	.1	1.2	.4
MACHINERY, EXCEPT ELECTRICAL (SIC 35)	.8	.3	.0	.0	.8	.3
ELECTRICAL MACHINERY & EQUIP (SIC 36)	.9	.3	.0	.0	.8	.3
TRANSPORTATION EQUIPMENT (SIC 37)	.0	.0	.0	.0	.0	.0
MISCELLANEOUS MANUFACTURING (SIC 38-9)	.5	.2	.4	.2	.0	.0
TRANSPORTATION SERVICES (SIC 40-7)	5.9	2.0	2.6	.9	3.3	1.2
COMMUNICATIONS & UTILITIES (SIC 48-9)	10.4	3.6	10.2	3.5	.2	.1
WHOLESALE AND RETAIL TRADE (SIC 50-9)	7.4	2.6	7.2	2.5	.2	.1
FINANCE, INS., REAL ESTATE (SIC 60-7)	4.0	1.4	2.6	.9	1.3	.5
SERVICES (SIC 70-9, 80-9, 89)	5.5	1.9	3.9	1.3	1.6	.5
GOVERNMENT ENTERPRISES	.2	.1	.2	.1	.0	.0
UNALLOCATED INDUSTRIES	3.4	1.2	2.2	.8	1.2	.4
TOTAL LOCAL INDUSTRY PURCHASES	194.7	67.5	129.6	44.9	65.0	22.6
PRIMARY INPUTS						
GEORGIA HOUSEHOLDS	58.9	20.4	58.9	20.4	.0	.0
CAPITAL OWNERSHIP	14.5	5.0	14.5	5.0	.0	.0
GEORGIA LOCAL GOVERNMENTS	1.7	.6	1.7	.6	.0	.0
GEORGIA STATE GOVERNMENT	1.5	.5	1.5	.5	.0	.0
FEDERAL GOVERNMENT	13.8	4.8	13.8	4.8	.0	.0
TOTAL FINAL PAYMENTS	90.3	31.3	90.3	31.3	.0	.0
NON-COMPETITIVE IMPORTS	3.4	1.2	.0	.0	3.4	1.2
TOTAL PURCHASES AND PAYMENTS	288.4	100.0	220.0	76.3	68.4	23.7

Figure 9.2a A sample market analysis (continued).

Table 5. Summary of sales in the southeast in 1970 by the paper products exc containers (sic 264) industry (millions of dollars)

PURCHASER OR USER SOUTHEASTERN INDUSTRY	TOTAL SALES		SALES BY S.E. PRODUCERS		SALES BY OTHER PRODUCERS	
	VALUE	PERCENT	VALUE	PERCENT	VALUE	PERCENT
AGRICULTURE (SIC01, 07-9)	2.4	.2	2.2	.2	.2	.0
MINING (SIC 10-4)	2.9	.3	2.5	.2	.4	.0
CONTRACT CONSTRUCTION (SIC 15-7)	51.4	4.8	50.0	4.7	1.5	.1
FOOD AND KINDRED PRODUCTS (SIC 20-1)	125.7	11.8	115.4	10.8	10.3	.9
TEXTILE MILL PRODUCTS (SIC 22)	122.0	11.5	110.8	10.4	11.4	1.1
APPAREL AND RELATED PRODUCTS (SIC 23)	7.2	.7	5.4	.5	1.8	.2
LUMBER AND WOOD PRODUCTS (SIC 24)	2.8	.3	2.2	.2	.6	.1
FURNITURE AND FIXTURES (SIC 25)	1.3	.1	.7	.1	.6	.1
PAPER AND ALLIED PRODUCTS (SIC 26)	38.9	3.6	38.2	3.5	.7	.1
PRINTING AND PUBLISHING (SIC 27)	16.8	1.6	15.9	1.5	1.0	.1
CHEMICALS AND ALLIED PRODUCTS (SIC 28)	56.1	5.3	51.4	4.8	4.8	.5
PETROLEUM REFINING (SIC 29)	12.4	1.2	12.4	1.2	.0	.0
RUBBER AND MISC. PLASTICS (SIC 30)	6.5	.6	6.2	.6	.4	.0
LEATHER AND LEATHER PRODUCTS (SIC 31)	.6	.1	.5	.0	.2	.0
STONE, CLAY AND GLASS PROD. (SIC 32)	13.8	1.3	12.5	1.2	1.4	.1
PRIMARY METAL INDUSTRIES (SIC 33)	1.8	.1	1.4	.1	.5	.0
FABRICATED METAL PRODUCTS (SIC 34, 19)	7.5	.7	6.7	.6	.9	.1
MACHINERY, EXCEPT ELECTRICAL (SIC 35)	2.5	.2	1.8	.1	.7	.1
ELECTRICAL MACHINERY & EQUIP (SIC 36)	15.6	1.4	13.9	1.3	1.7	.2
TRANSPORTATION EQUIPMENT (SIC 37)	9.0	.8	8.2	.7	.7	.1
MISCELLANEOUS MANUFACTURING (SIC 38-9)	4.3	.5	3.5	.3	.8	.1
TRANSPORTATION SERVICES (SIC 40-7)	1.4	.1	.9	.1	.5	.0
COMMUNICATIONS & UTILITIES (SIC 48-9)	2.9	.3	1.9	.2	1.0	.1
WHOLESALE AND RETAIL TRADE (SIC 50-9)	112.4	10.5	97.7	9.2	14.7	1.4
FINANCE, INS., REAL ESTATE (SIC 60-7)	11.8	1.1	8.0	.7	3.8	.4
SERVICES (SIC 70-9, 80-6, 89)	31.3	3.0	23.5	2.3	7.8	.7
GOVERNMENT ENTERPRISES	2.5	.2	1.5	.1	1.0	.1
UNALLOCATED INDUSTRIES	102.7	9.6	94.7	8.9	8.0	.7
TOTAL LOCAL INDUSTRY SALES	767.3	71.9	689.9	64.7	77.3	7.2
FINAL USERS						
SOUTHEASTERN HOUSEHOLD CONSUMERS	210.4	19.7	134.0	12.6	76.4	7.2
SOUTHEASTERN PRIVATE INVESTMENT	.0	.0	.0	.0	.0	.0
SOUTHEASTERN LOCAL GOVERNMENTS	3.9	.4	2.1	.2	1.8	.2
SOUTHEASTERN STATE GOVERNMENTS	3.8	.4	2.1	.2	1.7	.2
FEDERAL GOVERNMENT, DEFENSE	3.4	.3	3.4	.3	.0	.0
FEDERAL GOVERNMENT, OTHER	1.2	.1	1.2	.1	.0	.0
PRIVATE USERS OUTSIDE THE SOUTHEAST	77.0	7.2	77.0	7.2	.0	.0
TOTAL FINAL SALES	299.7	28.1	219.9	20.6	79.9	7.5
TOTAL SALES	1067.0	100.0	909.8	85.3	157.2	14.7

Figure 9.2a A sample market analysis (continued).

Table 6. Summary of purchases and payments in the southeast in 1970 by the paper products exc containers (sic 264) industry (millions of dollars)

PRODUCER OF GOOD OR SERVICE SOUTHEASTERN INDUSTRY	TOTAL PURCHASES		PURCHASES FROM S.E. PRODUCERS		PURCHASES FROM OTHER PRODUCERS	
	VALUE	PERCENT	VALUE	PERCENT	VALUE	PERCENT
AGRICULTURE (SIC01, 07-9)	.0	.0	.0	.0	.0	.0
MINING (SIC 10-4)	3.1	.4	2.7	.3	.4	.0
CONTRACT CONSTRUCTION (SIC 15-7)	1.7	.2	1.7	.2	.0	.0
FOOD AND KINDRED PRODUCTS (SIC 20-1)	2.9	.3	2.8	.3	.1	.0
TEXTILE MILL PRODUCTS (SIC 22)	5.3	.6	4.5	.5	.8	.1
APPAREL AND RELATED PRODUCTS (SIC 23)	4.7	.5	4.7	.5	.0	.0
LUMBER AND WOOD PRODUCTS (SIC 24)	30.5	3.4	30.2	3.3	.3	.0
FURNITURE AND FIXTURES (SIC 25)	.0	.0	.0	.0	.0	.0
PAPER AND ALLIED PRODUCTS (SIC 26)	294.9	32.5	272.8	30.0	22.2	2.4
PRINTING AND PUBLISHING (SIC 27)	13.7	1.5	13.6	1.5	.1	.0
CHEMICALS AND ALLIED PRODUCTS (SIC 28)	31.2	3.5	30.6	3.4	.6	.1
PETROLEUM REFINING (SIC 29)	5.1	.6	.3	.0	4.9	.5
RUBBER AND MISC. PLASTICS (SIC 30)	21.9	2.4	20.5	2.3	1.4	.2
LEATHER AND LEATHER PRODUCTS (SIC 31)	.1	.0	.1	.0	.0	.0
STONE, CLAY AND GLASS PROJ. (SIC 32)	1.5	.2	1.0	.1	.4	.0
PRIMARY METAL INDUSTRIES (SIC 33)	3.7	.4	3.7	.4	.0	.0
FABRICATED METAL PRODUCTS (SIC 34, 19)	1.5	.2	.8	.1	.7	.1
MACHINERY, EXCEPT ELECTRICAL (SIC 35)	.9	.1	.4	.0	.5	.0
ELECTRICAL MACHINERY & EQUIP (SIC 36)	1.4	.2	.7	.1	.8	.1
TRANSPORTATION EQUIPMENT (SIC 37)	.1	.0	.1	.0	.0	.0
MISCELLANEOUS MANUFACTURING (SIC 38-9)	1.4	.2	1.4	.2	.1	.0
TRANSPORTATION SERVICES (SIC 40-7)	17.4	1.9	17.2	1.9	.2	.0
COMMUNICATIONS & UTILITIES (SIC 48-9)	9.2	1.0	8.6	.9	.6	.1
WHOLESALE AND RETAIL TRADE (SIC 50-9)	24.6	2.7	24.6	2.7	.0	.0
FINANCE, INS., REAL ESTATE (SIC 60-7)	12.2	1.3	11.5	1.3	.7	.1
SERVICES (SIC 70-9, 80-6, 89)	17.6	1.9	16.5	1.8	1.1	.1
GOVERNMENT ENTERPRISES	.7	.1	.7	.0	.0	.0
UNALLOCATED INDUSTRIES	11.6	1.3	10.3	1.1	1.3	.1
TOTAL LOCAL INDUSTRY PURCHASES	519.0	57.0	481.7	52.9	37.3	4.1
VALUE ADDED	385.8	42.4	385.8	42.4	.0	.0
NON-COMPETITIVE IMPORTS	5.1	.6	.0	.0	5.1	.6
TOTAL PURCHASES AND PAYMENTS	909.8	100.0	867.4	95.3	42.4	4.7

Figure 9.2a A sample market analysis (continued).

contiguous states. Only published data was used in the Southern model. While these tables are printed in the same formats as for Georgia tables, their interpretation is different. Since trade patterns have not been determined in detail, 'sales outside the region' represent surplus production in the Southeast. In the same way, 'imports from outside the region' represent deficit production by local supplying industries.

Projections of market size in 1980 are also made for the Georgia model. These projections of market· transactions, industry by industry, are based on recent growth rates for Georgia industries.

The tables included in the market analysis are reviewed briefly below. These tables are all available for the 28- and 50-industry classification used in the published tables of the Georgia Economic Model. Tables 1 through 4 are also available for 140 selected industries.

Summary. This table summarizes the remaining tables, showing the size of the market for the industry in Georgia and in the Southeast. In addition, it presents data from *County Business Patterns* showing approximate employment and number of establishments in the industry in Georgia. It is intended to be a management briefing sheet, with the remaining tables providing details, if required.

Table 1. This table shows sales in Georgia in 1970, estimating sales by in-state and out-of-state producers to industries and final consumers in Georgia. It permits the analyst to identify industries in which major customers in Georgia may be found.

Table 2. This table estimates the purchases from other industries and the payments required to produce the output of this industry in Georgia. Review of this table yields insight into the sources of materials in the state.

Table 3. Using linear projections of sales to other industries based on employment growth in these industries from 1964 to 1970, this table estimates sales in Georgia in 1980. Not allowing for import substitution, it conservatively projects local sales to grow at no more than the projected rates.

Table 4. Assuming that industries in the state will continue to grow in proportion to employment growth from 1964 to 1970, this table projects Table 2 to 1980.

Table 5. Similar in format to Table 1, this table estimates sales in 1970 in Georgia and the adjoining states of South Carolina, North Carolina, Tennessee, Alabama, and Florida.

Table 6. Table 6 is similar in format to Table 2 and estimates purchases and payments in the Southeast.

9.3 SOURCES OF DATA AND COMPUTATIONS FOR MARKET ANALYSES

The following notes are intended to amplify the above summary descriptions for the serious reader, showing how each item in the analysis is derived.

Table 1. This table shows sales in Georgia in 1970 in six columns. These columns are derived directly from the Georgia transactions table.

Column 1 is the row for the industry in the total transactions table, showing sales of products by the subject industry to each of the other industries and final-user sectors in Georgia. Column 2 is a percentage version of column 1.

Column 3 is the row for the industry in the regional transactions table, showing sales by Georgia producers in the subject industry in the same format as column 1. Total sales in column 3 equals total purchases in column 1 of Table 2. Column 4 shows each sale in column 3 as percentages of total sales. The total for this column indicates how much of the total local market is served by Georgia producers.

Columns 5 and 6 are similar to columns 3 and 4 but are derived from the imports matrix. They show sales by producers in the subject industry but located outside the state, and then show these sales as percentages of total sales.

Column 1 is the sum of columns 3 and 5.

When a detailed market analysis is produced, as here, the values for a detailed industry are used, but they are aggregated to the 28-industry level for presentation. This means that the appropriate rows of the detailed worksheet tables are aggregated to the 28-industry level, while the columns remain at the detailed level. When a simple market analysis is compiled, the table is directly traceable to the 28-industry tables as published.

Table 2. Table 2 shows the purchase columns of the Georgia transactions tables and is derived directly from these tables. In format and interpretation, it is similar to Table 1 but treats purchases and payments instead of sales.

Column 1 presents total purchases and payments without regard for state of origin. Column 2 is a percentage version of column 1. This column shows the technology of production in the subject industry, identifying the pattern of inputs required to produce the gross output of the subject industry. Its total matches that of column 3 in Table 1.

Column 3 shows purchases by the subject industry from the industries within the state. It is derived directly from the regional transactions table and sums to be total purchases less imports. Column 4 is column 3 expressed as percentages of total purchases.

Column 5 shows purchases by the subject industry from industries located outside the state of Georgia. It is derived directly from the imports table. Column 6 is column 5 expressed in percent of total purchases.

For detailed analyses, data is taken from the unpublished detailed transactions table and aggregated to the 28-industry scheme. For simple market analyses, the data in Table 2 is derived directly from the published Georgia transactions tables.

Table 3. This table is a linear projection to 1980 of Table 1. It is not based on the projection model of the state as reported in Chapter 6. The projection model is experimental and subject to change and to various interpretations. Table 3 is based on simple, understandable assumptions and growth rates. While less finely tuned than other more sophisticated projections may be, it at least is subject to review and interpretation by the business analyst. We feel that this simplification is justified, since the analyst should rightly be suspicious of data manipulations which he cannot question or understand. This interpretation would not be possible if the complete model were used.

The calculations are simple. Projected sales in 1980 by industry i to sector j (PA_{ij}) are a product of sales in 1970 (A_{ij}) and a growth factor for sector j:

$$PA_{ij} = A_{ij} \cdot (1 + GR_j),$$

where GR_j is 10 times the average annual growth rate for industry j between 1964 and 1970. (Projected values are denoted throughout this section by the prefix 'P'.) With very few exceptions, this growth rate is calculated from industry employment reported in *County Business Patterns* with adjustments based on statistics reported by the Georgia Department of Labor. Growth rates for final-demand sectors are calculated from personal-income estimates.

If the subject industry i is projected to grow faster than the market for its products, then regional sales by industry i to sector j (RA_{ij}) can reasonably be assumed to grow at the projected rate,

$$PRA_{ij} = RA_{ij} \cdot (1 + GR_j).$$

Projected exports are computed as a residual,

$$PEX_i = X_i \cdot (1 + GR_i) - \sum_{j}^{n+k-1} PRA_{ij},$$

where X_i is the 1970 gross output of industry i, and n and k are the numbers of industries and final-demand sectors, respectively. In this fast-growth case, we assume that trade coefficients (or the proportions of total transactions in each cell originating in Georgia) do not exceed their 1970 values; this assumption controls the values of projected regional sales and forces a major change in projected exports. The assumption makes our estimates of coverage of local markets by local industries conservative.

If the subject industry i is projected to grow at a slower rate than that of the market for its products, then it is reasonable to assume that local sectors import more in 1980 from outside the state than they did in 1970. We assume that the subject industry continues to export from the state the same proportion of its output:

$$PEX_i = EX_i \, (1 + GR_i).$$

Sales to other sectors in Georgia by the subject industry are assumed to be in proportion to the 1970 sales pattern:

$$PRA_{ij} = \frac{RA_{ij} \cdot (1 + GR_j)}{\sum\limits_{j}^{n+k-1} RA_{ij}(1 + GR_j)} \cdot [X_i \cdot (1 + GR_i) - PEX_i].$$

In this slow-growth case, we assume that exports (or private sales outside the state) grow at the same rate as the subject industry; this assumption controls the value of projected exports and limits projected regional sales to values less than the upper limits computed in the fast-growth case. Imports are the residual here, not exports. As in the case above, our estimates of local market coverage by local industries are conservative.

Table 4. This table is a linear projection to 1980 of Table 2. It is constructed in a manner similar to that of Table 3, but the subject industry is now industry j, reflecting our interest in columns in the transactions tables.

Entries in column 1, the values of projected total purchases, are computed for industry j as

$$PA_{ij} = A_{ij} \cdot (1 + GR_j).$$

Column 2 is simply a percentage version as in Table 2.

Column 3 is computed dependent on differences in growth rates for the various industries. If the selling industry i is projected to grow faster than the subject industry j, then purchases from local industry i can be assumed to grow at the projected rate,

$$PRA_{ij} = RA_{ij} \cdot (1 + GR_j),$$

as can projected imports,

$$PM_{ij} = M_{ij} \cdot (1 + GR_j).$$

We assume that sales by Georgia industries do not increase beyond the proportions enjoyed in 1970.

If the selling industry i is projected to grow at a slower rate than that of the subject industry j, then projected regional purchases by industry j are

$$PRA_{ij} = \frac{RA_{ij} \cdot (1 + GR_j)}{\displaystyle\sum_{j}^{n+k-1} RA_{ij} \cdot (1 + GR_j)} \cdot (X_i - EX_i)(1 + GR_i).$$

Projected imports from other states are calculated as a residual:

$$PM_{ij} = PA_{ij} - PRA_{ij}.$$

Column 4, as in Table 2, shows purchases from Georgia producers as a percent of total purchases. Column 5 reports the imports, or purchases from producers outside Georgia, projected above, while column 7 is its percentage representation.

Table 5. Table 5 is similar to Table 1 but reports sales in the Southeast by the subject industry. The Southeast is defined as Georgia and the five adjoining states: South Carolina, North Carolina, Tennessee, Alabama, and Florida. We have constructed a model of the Southeast similar to the first estimate constructed for Georgia in the study. That is, it is a model with gross outputs based on employment ratios, with purchase patterns based on national relationships, and with 'exports' and 'imports' computed using the supply-demand pool technique discussed in Chapter 3. We assume local trade, where possible, and end up with what is properly called a 'balance-of-trade' model. No corrections based on interviews and survey results have been made. Because of this approximate nature of the Southeast model, we prefer that it be used in the simple 28-industry market analyses rather than in the detailed 140-industry analyses. In addition, the computer runs recovering detailed information are substantially longer than the simple runs, providing ample excuse for not displaying them in the more numerous detailed analysis series.

Because of the technique used in constructing the Southeast model, the imports, or 'sales by other producers', column will be in constant proportion (equal to or greater than zero) to the total sales column. We assume a relatively even sharing of locally produced sales across all local industries.

Table 6. Table 6 is similar to Table 2 in format and shows purchases and payments by the subject industry in the Southeast. The cautions expressed above still hold.

Total purchases are taken directly from the appropriate column in the total transactions table for the Southeast. Purchases from Georgia suppliers in industry i are derived as the lesser of

$$RA_{ij} = A_{ij} \text{ or}$$

$$RA_{ij} = A_{ij} \cdot \frac{X_i}{\sum\limits_{j}^{n+k-1} A_{ij}}.$$

The ratio in the last equation above reflects the 'balance of trade' of industry i, a selling industry. A ratio greater than one means that total output by industry i in the Southeast is greater than the total needs for the products of industry i. An 'export surplus' exists, so no imports are estimated. If the ratio is less than one, an 'import deficit' exists, so no exports are estimated.

In the 300-industry detailed worksheet table, each industry would show either a trade surplus, and so would export, or a trade deficit, and so would have its products imported. At the 140-industry level, where many industries have been combined, exports and imports may occur at the same time. This is especially the case at the 28-industry level of aggregation. While aggregation produces a table which looks normal, with all industries possibly exporting and all importing, there is no assurance that these values are correct. But by estimating our trade balances at the 300-industry level, we have gone a long way toward improving these estimates.

9.4 SUMMARY

One of the emphases of this volume has been the usefulness of regional input-output tables as the basis for an information system. A critical feature of a good information system is that it be accessible to potential users in an acceptable format. We feel that a presentation such as described here meets this criterion. Easily programmed, such a system makes an input-output study more than just an exercise to derive multipliers and provides the regional planner in a private-enterprise economy with another very useful tool.

NOTES

1. The literature frequently refers to the usefulness of input-output tables in identifying markets for businessmen. To make the tasks involved as simple as possible, we designed our 'instant market analysis.' Our intent has been to relieve the busy decision-maker of as many reading chores as possible; though a picture of simplicity to the economist, an input-output table is frequently overwhelming to a layman. We claim credit for designing the market information system with little assistance from the literature, but two references which stimulated us are Rapkin (1963) and Cleland (1959).
2. Market analyses released by the Georgia Department of Community Development were produced in a 50-industry format. Reduced tables are used here for consistency with the remainder of this book.

10. Conclusions and extensions

10.1 STUDY SUMMARY

This book has attempted to show the variety of results which may be derived from a simple regional input-output model. We should now briefly summarize the usefulness of the study.

10.1.1 Empirical results

As an accounting system, an input-output table permits the analyst to examine both the magnitude of an economy and its structure.

Georgia's gross state product. Analogous in concept to gross national product (GNP), the gross state product (GSP) of a state can be defined as 'the product of all economic units in the state' or as 'total production without duplication.' In 1970, Georgia's GSP was $20.459 billion, or 2.1 percent of GNP for the United States.

This total can be viewed in two ways: 1. as incomes received in payment for producing GSP, or 2. as expenditures to purchase the fruits of these labors. Of incomes received from producing sectors in Georgia, 71 percent went to households, 15 percent was retained as business savings and depreciation, and local, state, and federal governments respectively received 2, 4, and 8 percent. After taxes, the distribution shifted to become 57 percent for households, 15 percent as a capital residual, and 4, 6, and 18 percent for governments.

But expenditures are a different matter, for nonmarket transfers between economic units shift the balance again. Household expenditures were 59 percent of GSP, private investment expenditures were 11 percent, and local, state, and federal government expenditures were 7, 4, and 14 percent, with the remaining 5 percent of GSP appearing as net exports to purchasers outside the state. When grants and defense expenditures are considered, the federal government spent over $533 million more than it received in Georgia; local governments incurred a deficit of $112 million; and the state government showed a surplus of $55 million.

Most of Georgia's GSP originated in the service, manufacturing, and trade industries, indicating Georgia's position as an industrialized state. The industrial origins of GSP for Georgia in 1970 and of GNP for the U.S. in 1966 are as follows:

Origin	Georgia, percent of GSP, 1970	U.S., percent of GNP, 1966
Agriculture and mining industries	4	5
Construction	4	6
Manufacturing industries	26	29
Transportation, communication, and utilities	8	8
Wholesale and retail trade	18	14
Service industries	26	27
Local government payrolls	4	*
State government payrolls	2	11
Federal government payrolls	7	*
Total	100	100

* Less than 0.5 percent

Georgia manufactures less than the nation as a whole but makes more of her income in trade and government activities, due largely to her central position in the Southeast.

Georgia's economic structure. The Georgia input-output table provides insight into the economic structure of the state, showing who buys Georgia products, who receives payments for goods produced in Georgia, and how production takes place.

Who buys Georgia products? In producing the gross state income of $20,459 million, economic units in Georgia produced output worth a total of $35,962 million. But 28 percent of this output was sold to other Georgia producers for further processing. Only 29 percent was purchased by Georgia households, while 43 percent was exported, or sold to producers and consumers outside the state.

While 16 out of the 28 industries sold over half of their outputs to purchasers outside the state, a large portion of Georgia's $14,091 million in exports was accounted for by a few major industries. The textile industry accounted for 20 percent of Georgia's exports, the transportation equipment industry for 10 percent, the food and kindred products industry for 8 percent, and the apparel and paper industries for 6 percent each.

From whom do Georgia producers buy? Of the purchases and payments involved in producing the gross outputs of Georgia industries, 28 percent was paid for purchases from other Georgia producers, 33 percent was paid to households in wages and salaries and other personal income, 8 percent went to depreciation and retained earnings and other capital-associated expenses, and 1, 2, and 4 percent were paid respectively to local, state, and federal governments. The remaining 23 percent was paid to producers outside of Georgia in return for goods and services not available in Georgia.

State government imported only 21 percent of its purchases from outside the state. Local governments imported 23 percent, the same as private producers; 31 percent of household purchases were produced outside the state; and 36 percent of investment expenditures were for equipment produced outside of Georgia.

10.1.2 Analytic results
The Georgia input-output table outlines the economy as it existed in 1970. Through a series of calculations, this accounting system can be converted into a model for use in analyzing economic change in the state. Short-run changes in industry sales and trade patterns are traced through a multiplier, or impact, model, while long-run changes are examined through a projection model.

Interindustry relationships. The Georgia Economic Model has been used to compute a series of multipliers measuring the effects of additional sales on output, employment, and income in the state.

Output multipliers are highest in Georgia among supporting industries which are not directly influenced by development activities and which do not export extensively: services, printing and publishing, and finance, insurance, and real estate are examples. (Many supporting industries such as transportation services and trade show high multipliers because their outputs are defined as gross operating margins which have a high labor content relative to other industries. High direct payments to households frequently lead to high multipliers because of large local expenditures by households in succeeding rounds of spending.) The multipliers are low for many industries producing for export. Transportation equipment and textiles are good examples of industries with low multipliers due primarily to the small amount of local inputs, excluding labor, used in their production processes. With interindustry flows traced through both industries and households, output multipliers range from 2.94 for services to 1.92 for transportation equipment.

Employment multipliers show the number of employees required per $10,000 in additional sales. They also are high for supporting industries but show wide range among manufacturing industries. The highest is in the apparel industry (1.11), well known for the high labor content of its products, while the lowest is in transportation equipment (0.39), which has few interindustry linkages in Georgia.

Income multipliers report the personal income generated per unit of additional sales. They range from a high of 0.87 in finance, insurance, and real estate to a low of 0.42 in transportation equipment. Much depends on the initial payments of income to households by an industry and on the circulation induced by this income. But indirect income from circulation through the industrial structure is also important, especially in the food and service industries.

Generally, the multipliers show that the linkage between industries in Georgia is weak, with much local circulation depending on the respending of income by households. Georgia industrialized late, with strong market channels already established by outside producers; much of the linkage present in a more mature economy remains to be developed.

Economic structure in 1980. An important use of the Georgia Economic Model is in projecting the future Georgia economy. With expected national growth rates and expected changes in labor productivity as controlling inputs, the Georgia projection model provides insight into Georgia's potential for growth. If Georgia industries responded only to national needs, Georgia's gross state product would grow at 4 percent annually, personal income at 3.7 percent, employment at 1.7 percent, and population at 1.5 percent. This growth pattern would yield a per capita income growth at 2.2 percent annually, considerably short of the expected 3.1 percent growth in national per capita income.

This potential slowness in growth of per capita income could be avoided in two ways. One is simply to create more jobs and to increase the proportion of the population which is working. An increase in the labor-force/population ratio to expected national levels in 1980 would raise Georgia's per capita income growth rate to 2.9 percent.

The other way is more difficult, for not only must more jobs be created, but they must be the right jobs in the right places. The industries which dominated Georgia in 1970 are expected to grow slowly during the decade; they are facing strong competition and many pay relatively low wages. To increase the rate of growth in per capita income will require a shift of Georgia's economic structure toward higher-income industries. This task requires continued efforts not only in promoting new industry but also in upgrading labor skills, in educating and assisting new entrepreneurs, in providing public services, and in carefully selecting industries to encourage in the state.

Selecting new industries. In selecting industries to encourage in Georgia, development agencies should be concerned with several things. One is activities in which the state has a clear comparative advantage (as in certain stone and clay products, floor coverings, and pulp and paper products). Many of these are resource-related or require special skills or groups of activities which have developed locally; they have energed because they are obvious. Another concern is the impact of new activities on the environment and on the social needs of the people. A third is the possibility of filling in missing links in the industrial structure and improving the flow of income within the state. And a fourth concern is the effect of new activities on per capita income.

A useful feature of the Georgia Economic Model is its ability to reveal both the direct and the indirect effects of changes in imports and exports. Thus, it can trace the importing of raw milk through the dairy products industry or the exporting of pulpwood through the paperboard container industry. An analysis of direct and indirect import and export patterns reveals that Georgia's strength lies in agriculture, textiles, apparel, lumber and wood products, and pulp and paper products. The state holds its own in supporting and service industries. The largest missing links are in petroleum production and in primary iron and steel, industries about which little can be done. Although strong in producing certain durable goods such as aircraft, mobile homes, and electrical transmission equipment, the state's deficiencies are primarily in durable-goods manufacturing. To round out the economy and to improve its industrial linkages, the state should encourage activities in this area.

Which export activities will yield the greatest increases in per capita income? In 1970, $11,213 million in personal income was associated with an industrial labor force of 1,244,076 for an average of $9,093 in personal income per worker. With the Georgia Economic Model, an index comparing income and employment generated per dollar of additional sales was computed to include both direct and indirect effects of new activities. Values greater than $9,093 show industries which clearly contribute to higher per capita income. Examples of these industries are found in the finance, insurance, and real estate, transportation equipment, primary metals, pulp and paper, and electrical machinery aggregations.

Simulating economic development. The Georgia Economic Model has been programmed to permit the simulation of economic change in the state. The 28-industry model can be modified to show the effects of a new plant or an entirely new industry on the economy. The analyst specifies the industry code and size of the new plant and the computing system responds by constructing a 29-industry model. containing the new industry. The printout shows the probable effects of the new activity on industry outputs, employment, personal income, and government revenues. The analyst can then use this information, modified as needed to fit the specific nature of the new plant, to make decisions as to the importance of the new activity and can identify ways to better integrate it into the Georgia economy.

When the analyst has time and resources, a more careful analysis can be made in the same format, using specific data for a potential new plant. In addition, public projects affecting the economy may be examined by tracing induced structural and final-demand changes through the model.

The market information system. To insure maximum use of the Georgia Economic Model as an economic information system, a series of programs have been carefully developed to print the information developed in the study in the form of market analyses. These analyses report sales and production in Georgia in 1970, expected markets and production in 1980, and summary sales and production figures for the Southeast in 1970. They assist in interpreting the transactions table and make its contents more accessible to the private planner.

10.2 EXTENSIONS OF THE BASIC REGIONAL MODEL

It is appropriate to note at the conclusion of our study what additions and improvements might be made to extend its usefulness while remaining within a reasonable budget and in the context of a single-state system. Outside of continued revisions and bi-annual updating, to insure reliability of the data reported in the table and to permit more current assessments of the state's economy, the system could be extended in three ways. Chart 10.2a conceptualizes a more complete regional system. This book represents completion of Phases I and II; the following brief comments outline the suggested extensions.

10.2.1 An area model system
We have already started a series of area models in the state, having constructed models of planning areas in Northeast Georgia and North Georgia. These models have been constructed as afterthoughts due to resource limitations for our original study. A properly organized and financed study program could collect the primary data required to construct both area and state models. Many planning functions have been relegated to the level of the 19 Area Planning and Development Commissions in Georgia. A united effort could result in substantial savings and a set of area tables which would be quite useful in both economic and environmental planning.

10.2.2 An extended projection model
The projection model developed here is rudimentary and could be improved substantially by appending a supplementary econometric model to forecast final-demand changes, which really are the key to the projections. Since the Georgia·economy is closely linked to national markets, the final-demand model would of necessity be tied to national forecasts as well as to indicators of regional competitive advantage.

A second improvement would be a means of providing for the effects of coefficient change and productivity change. Coefficient changes involve substitutions among inputs due to price changes, trade-pattern changes, technological change, and industry- or product-mix changes. All of these are important sources of change, and means for identifying them should be carefully explored. While Miernyk's best-practice analysis may handle part of this task, the serious problems of trade-pattern changes and industry-mix changes remain. Productivity change depends on substitutions in the final-payments sector between various categories of capital and labor inputs. Perhaps the easiest way to handle this kind of change is to modify the model to account for intensive and extensive labor-input changes as suggested by Tiebout (1969).

10.2.3 An economic-ecologic system

The final phase noted in Chart 10.2a is an economic-ecologic system. By this we do not propose a comprehensive, completely integrated system with intersectoral feedbacks as has been suggested by Isard (1972). Rather, we feel that the less costly approach of Laurent and Hite (1971) would satisfy most state needs. They construct an emissions matrix which is used to estimate pollutants as well as natural-resource requirements associated with changes in economic activity. This matrix could be amended to include energy use, land-use probabilities, and other estimates of interest to planners.

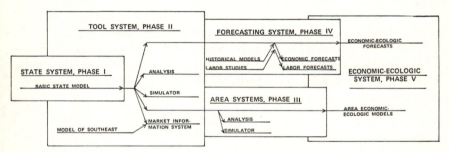

Chart 10.2a System organization for an extended regional input-output study.

10.3 CONCLUSION

Our primary purpose has been to confirm a recent remark by Harry Richardson (1973, p. 43) that '... regional input-output models do not deserve the bad press they have received in many quarters.' We have focused on the use of input-output analysis for regional planning in a free-enterprise system, hoping to show the versatility of our subject.

A. Income and product accounts for Georgia, 1970

As noted in Chapter 4, a set of income and product accounts is a normal by-product of an interindustry study. This appendix reproduces the accounts underlying the estimates of gross state product presented in Chapter 4 without further explanation, primarily to show the difference between the procedures required to produce these more traditional accounts and those now used in many states to construct GSP estimates. The latter are usually some variant of the 'Kendrick-Jaycox method,' which relies on fairly aggregated ratio computations to reduce national product estimates to the regional level. The best recent statement of this method was made by Niemi (1975), who used a modified Kendrick-Jaycox method to produce real GSP estimates for Southeastern states.

To our knowledge, the best and most detailed GSP accounts were produced for Hawaii by Y.C. Shang and his associates at the University of Hawaii (1967, 1970). We benefited substantially from a brief association with the Hawaii team and a long study of their procedures. The integration of the Hawaii accounts into an input-output study is shown in Schaffer, *et al.* (1972). These accounts follow most of the Hawaii conventions.

Personal or household account

RECEIPTS

Line	Sector making payment		Income	Transfers	Total
1	Local industries		11,882.6	61.0	11,943.6
2	Wage and salary disbursements	8,158.3			
3	Other labor income	552.0			
4	Proprietors' income	1,357.0			
5	Property income	1,637.7			
6	Business transfer payments	61.0			
7	Federal government enterprise	149.6			
8	State and local government enterprise	28.0			
9	Local households		99.7		99.7
10	Local governments		790.7	51.3	842.0
11	Wage and salary disbursements	771.2			
12	Retirement payments	14.8			
13	Direct relief payments	14.9			
14	Other transfer payments	21.6			
15	Interest paid to persons	19.5			
16	State government		372.7	190.7	563.4
17	Wage and salary disbursements	360.8			
18	Retirement payments	32.2			
19	Direct relief payments	149.1			
20	Other transfer payments	9.4			
21	Interest paid to persons	11.9			
22	Federal government, defense		671.0	209.0	880.0
23	Military pay	636.0			
24	Military reserve pay	35.0			
25	Veterans' benefits, retirement	209.0			
26	Federal government, other		689.3	848.0	1,537.3
27	Civilian pay	587.4			
28	Interest paid to persons	101.9			
29	Other transfer payments	848.0			
30	Total receipts from all sectors		14,506.0	1,360.0	15,866.0

PAYMENTS

Line	Sector receiving payment		Total
31	Industry, total purchases of goods and services		11,977.1
32	Local industry	8,199.3	
33	Nonlocal industry	3,777.8	
34	Households		99.7
35	Gross saving		871.6
36	Personal tax and nontax payments		2,917.6
37	Local governments	377.9	
38	State government	341.9	
39	Federal government	2,197.8	
40	Total payments to all sectors		15,866.0

Savings and investment account

	RECEIPTS			PAYMENTS	
Line	Sector making payment	Total	Line	Sector receiving payment	Total
1	Local industries	3,019.1	9	Industry, total purchases of goods and services	2,202.5
2	Local households	871.6	10	Local industry	1,400.4
3	Other saving:	-1,688.2	11	Nonlocal industry	802.1
4	Local governments	-112.4	12	Total	2,202.5
5	State government	55.2			
6	Federal government	-533.5			
7	Nonlocal private units	-1,097.5			
8	Total	2,202.5			

Local government account

	RECEIPTS			PAYMENTS	
Line	Sector making payment	Total	Line	Sector receiving payment	Total
1	Local industries	480.3	7	Industry, total purchases of goods and services	599.7
2	Local households	377.9	8	Local industry	460.9
3	State government	445.9	9	Nonlocal industry	138.8
4	Federal government	47.3	10	Households (income)	790.7
5	Gross deficit	112.4	11	Households (transfers)	51.3
6	Total	1,463.8	12	State government	22.1
			13	Total	1,463.8

State government account

RECEIPTS

Line	Sector making payment		Total
1	Local industries		858.8
2	Taxes	724.7	
3	Current charges and miscellaneous general revenue	55.7	
4	Trust earnings	40.7	
5	Unemployment contribution	37.8	
6	Local households		341.9
7	Taxes	216.6	
8	Current charges and miscellaneous general revenue	86.5	
9	Retirement contribution of local employees	38.7	
10	Local governments		22.1
11	Transfer payments	11.2	
12	Retirement contribution for covered employees	10.9	
13	Motor vehicle registration	*	
14	Federal government		408.8
15	Transfer payments	408.7	
16	Motor vehicle registration	*	
17	Gross saving		-55.2
18	Total receipts from all sectors		1,576.4

PAYMENTS

Line	Sector receiving payment		Total
19	Industry, total purchases of goods and services		548.1
20	Local industry	432.3	
21	Nonlocal industry	115.8	
22	Households (income)		372.7
23	Households (transfers)		190.7
24	Local governments (transfers)		445.9
25	Federal government		19.1
26	Total payments to all sectors		1,576.4

Federal government account

RECEIPTS

Line	Sector making payment	Total
1	Local industries	1,533.9
2	Local households	2,197.8
3	State government	19.1
4	External funds (deficit)	533.3
5	Total	4,284.3

PAYMENTS

Line	Sector receiving payment	Defense	Other	Total
6	Local industries	1,057.0	353.9	1,410.9
7	Household income	671.0	689.3	1,360.3
8	Household transfers	209.0	848.0	1,057.0
9	Local governments		47.3	47.3
10	State government		408.8	408.8
11	Total	1,937.0	2,347.3	4,284.3

Rest-of-world account

	RECEIPTS			PAYMENTS		
Line	Sector making payment	Total	Line	Sector receiving payment		Total
1	Local industries	8,159.2	7	Rest-of-world industries		14,091.3
2	Local households	3,777.8	8	Net government deficit		590.7
			9	Local governments (deficit)	112.4	
3	Private investment	802.1	10	State government (surplus)	-55.2	
			11	Federal government (deficit)	533.5	
4	Local governments	138.8				
			12	Nonlocal private sector		-1,688.2
5	State government	115.8	13	Net import surplus, Georgia	-1,097.6	
			14	Balance	-590.7	
6	Total	12,993.8				
			15	Total		12,993.8

NOTES ON PERSONAL OR HOUSEHOLD ACCOUNT:

Unless otherwise noted, the sources for estimates of household receipts are Robert B. Bertzfelder, 'Regional and State Income Gains in 1970,' *Survey of Current Business* (August 1971), 27-41, and the intermediate worksheets underlying the state income estimates reported by Bertzfelder. These worksheets were made available by Edwin J. Coleman, Chief, Economic Measurement Branch, Regional Economics Division, U.S. Department of Commerce.

Line 2: Reported nongovernment wage and salary disbursements less estimated disbursements by private households (line 9).

Line 3: Other labor income less military reserve pay.

Line 5: Reported property income less government interest.

Line 7: Wages and salaries paid by federal government enterprises were estimated from ES-202 data at $150 million (post office, $133.044 million, and other federal enterprises, $16.573 million).

Line 8: Expenditures for current operations by locally operated public utilities in Georgia were $76.1 million ($32.3 million for water supply systems and $43.8 million for other systems, *Government Finances in 1969-70*, p. 44). Assuming that expenditures for personal services were in proportion to national expenditures (.446 of current expenditures for water systems and .311 for electric utilities, *Government Finances in 1969-70*, p. 26) then expenditures by state local government enterprises for personal services were approximately $28 million ($14.406 million for water systems and $13.622 million for other systems).

Line 9: Wages received for personal services and private-household employment were reported at $294 million. Wage and salary disbursements by private households were assumed to be in proportion to receipts by the household industry in the 1963 national input-output table relative to value added in the personal services and household industries (OBE industries 72.02, 72.03, and 86.00); on this basis, wage payments by local households in Georgia were $99.692 million.

Line 11: The payroll of local governments is estimated at $799.240 million as that proportion of the calendar-year state and local government payroll ($1,160 million) which was paid over the fiscal year by local governments (.669, *Government Finances in 1969-70,* p. 51). This payroll less that for local government enterprise (line 8) is $771 million.

Line 12: Total state and local retirement payments ($47 million) less state retirement payments ($32.23 million, *State Government Finances in 1969-70,* p. 37 (fiscal-year estimate)).

Line 13: Total direct relief payments by state and local governments ($164 million) less cash assistance payments by state government ($149.106 million, *State Government Finances in 1969-70,* p. 31 (fiscal-year estimate)).

Line 14: Other state and local transfer payments ($31 million) less other state transfer payments as estimated on line 20.

Line 15: Government interest paid to individuals in Georgia is estimated as follows:
a. Interest on general debt of the U.S. Government is assumed to be paid in the state in proportion to personal income (in 1970, personal income in Georgia was 1.921 percent of U.S. personal income) and to be paid to individuals in proportion to their holdings (in 1970, individuals held 37.8 percent of privately held U.S. government securities *(Federal Reserve Bulletin* (August 1971), p. A44)). This interest amounts to $102 million (0.378 × 0.019 × $14,037 million, *Government Finances in 1969-70,* p. 17).
b. Interest on general debt of state and local governments in Georgia is reported as $31.6 million for state government and $51.6 million for local governments (*Government Finances in 1969-70,* p.35). We assume that local holdings of debt of other governments are balanced by holdings of Georgia public debt by outsiders. If individuals hold these securities in proportion to their national holdings, individuals in Georgia received $11.9 million from state government and $19.5 million from local governments.
c. These calculations and others are summarized as:

	Payments (in millions) by			
Payments in Georgia to:	*State government*	*Local governments*	*Federal government*	*Total*
Individuals (.378)	11.9	19.5	101.9	133.3
Banks (.259)	8.2	13.4	69.9	91.5
Insurance companies (.031)	1.0	1.6	8.4	11.0
Others (.322)	10.5	17.1	89.6	117.2
Total	31.6	51.6	269.8	353.0

Line 17: Total state and local government payroll ($1,160 million) less local government payrolls ($799 million).

Line 18: See line 12.

Line 19: See line 13.

Line 20: State expenditures for assistance and subsidies ($158.507 million) less cash assistance payments for fiscal year ($149.106 million) (*State Government Finances in 1969-70,* pp. 27, 31).

Line 21: See line 15.

Line 27: Total federal civilian pay ($737 million) less wage and salary disbursements by federal government enterprises ($150 million, line 7).

Line 28: See line 15.

Line 29: Total federal transfer payments less veterans' benefits.

Line 31: Computed from average personal consumption expenditures (PCE) for the United States and personal income estimates (PI) as follows:

$$\text{Ga. PCE} = \frac{\text{U.S. PCE} + \text{U.S. interest paid}}{\text{U.S. PI}} \times \text{Ga. PI} - \text{Household payments}$$

$$= ((615.8 + 16.9)/803.9) \times 15,345 - 100 = 11,977.089$$

(See *Survey of Current Business* (August, 1971), p. 11, and line 9 above.)

Lines 32, 33: Based on the *Georgia Interindustry Study*.

Line 34: See line 9 above.

Line 35: Computed as a residual.

Line 37: See local government account, line 2.

Line 38: See state government account, line 6.

Line 39: Computed from average personal tax and nontax payments (PTx) for the U.S. as follows:

$$\text{Ga. PTx} = \frac{\text{U.S. PTx}}{\text{U.S. PI}} \times \frac{(\text{Ga. social insurance/Ga. PI})}{(\text{U.S. social insurance/U.S. PI})} + \text{Ga. S.S. contributions}$$

$$= 15,345 \times (92.2/803.6) \times (.03395/.03484) + 482.267 = 2,197.838$$

The social-insurance factor above is used to reflect the lower incomes in Georgia relative to the nation. The personal social-insurance contribution includes a residual to insure consistency with published total personal income for Georgia and is equal to personal contributions for social insurance (521 million) less employee contributions to state and local retirement systems (38.733 million, from state government account, line 9).

NOTES ON SAVING AND INVESTMENT ACCOUNT:

Line 1: Based on the *Georgia Interindustry Study*.

Line 2: See household account, line 35.

Line 4: See rest-of-world account, line 9, or local government account, line 5.

Line 5: See rest-of world account, line 10, or state government account, line 17.

Line 6: See rest-of-world account, line 11, or federal government account, line 4.

Line 7: See rest-of-world account, line 13.

Line 9: Computed from data assembled for the *Georgia Interindustry Study* and from 'Interindustry Transactions in New Structures and Equipment, 1963,' (multilithed, U.S. Department of Commerce, Office of Business Economics, September 1971), called here the 'capital-formation matrix.' The capital-formation matrix (CF) shows purchases by the 80 two-digit OBE industries (columns) from the 102 producing industries and four categories of construction (rows). The producing industries correspond to those in the 367-industry OBE classification. This matrix is adjusted for price changes to 1970 (p_i) and multiplied by the ratio of industry gross outputs in Georgia in 1970 (GQ_j) to those in the U.S. in 1963 price-adjusted to 1970 (NQ_j) to yield estimates of purchases by Georgia industries of capital equipment and structures (GC_i). Their sum is gross private domestic investment in Georgia in 1970 (GC):

$$GC = \sum_{i}^{367} \sum_{j}^{80} P_i \cdot CF_{ij} \cdot GQ_j/NQ_j.$$

Line 10, 11: Based on the *Georgia Interindustry Study*.

NOTES ON LOCAL GOVERNMENT ACCOUNT

Line 1: Tax receipts and charges and miscellaneous general revenue (as reported in *Government Finances in 1969-70*, p. 31) are divided into industry and personal payments using the allocations of state and local property taxes in 1967 estimated in Advisory Commission on Intergovernmental Relations, *State-Local Finances and Suggested Legislation*, 1971 Edition (Government Printing Office, 1970), p. 149. For governments in Georgia in 1970, these divisions are as follows:

Item	Amount (in millions)
Local industries, total	480.3
Property taxes	237.5
Public utilities	46.0
Business motor vehicle	24.1
All other business	143.6
Agricultural	23.8
Other taxes	32.0
Charges and miscellaneous general revenue	210.8
Local households, total	377.9
Property taxes	196.3
Residential	152.3
Vacant lots	7.4
Motor vehicles	36.6
Other taxes	23.9
Charges and miscellaneous general revenue	157.7

Other taxes and charges and miscellaneous general revenue are assumed to be paid by business in proportion to property taxes (less motor-vehicle taxes) paid by business (57.2 percent).

Line 2: See line 1.

Line 3, 4: *Government Finances in 1969-70*, p. 31.

Line 5: Total general revenue less direct general expenditures and less transfer to state (*Government Finances in 1969-70*, pp. 31, 34).

Line 7: Calculated as a residual.

Lines 8. 9: Based on the *Georgia Interindustry Study.*

Lines 10, 11: Personal income worksheets (see household account, line 10).

Line 12: Payments to state government include (in $ millions): transfers from local governments of 11.241, retirement contributions by local governments of 10.869 (see *State Government Finance in 1970*, pp. 22, 25), and motor-vehicle registration fees of .007 (estimated by Motor Vehicle Unit, Georgia Department of Revenue).

NOTES ON STATE GOVERNMENT ACCOUNT

The major source of data for this account is U.S. Bureau of the Census, *State Government Finances in 1970*, Series GF70, No. 3 (Washington: U.S. Government Printing Office, 1971). Two problems should be noted. First, these estimates are on a fiscal-year basis. We have not adjusted them to a calendar-year base. And second, the estimates vary slightly from values reported in the *Report of the State Auditor of Georgia, 1970.* For consistency, we follow the Census publications in estimating all government accounts. The *State Audit* is used in estimating detail, but totals are based on *State Government Finances.*

Line 2: Estimates of taxes collected were derived from totals in *State Government Finances.* When the allocation to industry or household categories was in question, other sources were used: 1. property taxes were allocated as described in local government account, line 1; and 2. motor vehicle and title registration fees were allocated using figures obtained from the Georgia Department of Revenue. Since the totals reported in *State Government Finances* ($941,334,000) and *State Audit* ($947,945,000) differ, the allocations based on *State Audit* were adjusted to match the *State Government Finances* figure. In summary, taxes paid by industry in Georgia are classified in the *Georgia Interindustry Study* as follows:

Item		*Total (in thousands)*
Retail trade		336,167
General sales and gross receipts taxes	335,807	
Retail liquor licenses	360	
Wholesale trade		253,068
Selective sales taxes	253,002	
Wholesale liquor licenses	66	
Insurance taxes		21,905
Motor transportation		4,812
Distillers' taxes		23
Real estate transfer taxes		12
Taxes distributed among all industries		108,685
Corporate net income taxes	84,735	
Motor vehicles license tax	12,706	
Occupation and business licenses	6,350	
Other taxes	4,844	
Total		724,672

Line 3: Estimates of charges and miscellaneous general revenue were taken from *State Government Finances*. Current charges to agriculture, water terminals, and miscellaneous commercial activities were assigned to industry and charges for education and hospitals to households. Miscellaneous general revenue from sale of property, from interest earnings, and from royalties were assigned to industry. The remaining charges and miscellaneous general revenues were split in proportion to the totals assigned to industry and to households. In summary, current charges and miscellaneous general revenues collected from industries in Georgia are classified in the *Georgia Interindustry Study* as follows:

Item	Total (in thousands)
Water transport	7,653
Banking (interest earnings)	37,296
Distributed	10,795
Total	55,744

Line 4: State Government Finances, p. 25.

Line 5: State Government Finances, p. 26.

Line 7: Taxes paid by households were estimated from *State Government Finances* in a manner similar to that described for line 2 above. In summary, these payments include:

Item	Total (in thousands)
Personal income taxes	184,943
Motor vehicle registration	19,767
Death and gift taxes	5,642
Other taxes and licenses	6,279
Total	216,631

Line 8: Current charges and miscellaneous general revenue collected from households were estimated from *State Government Finances* as noted in line 3 above. In summary, they include:

Item	Total (in thousands)
Education charges	70,786
Hospital charges	9,275
Fines	477
Miscellaneous charges and revenue	6,000
Total	86,538

Line 9: State Government Finances, p. 25.

Line 11: State Government Finances, p. 22.

Line 12: State Government.Finances, p. 25.

Line 13: Motor vehicle registration fees paid by local governments were estimated at $7,000 from records of the Georgia Department of Revenue.

Line 15: State Government Finances, p. 21.

Line 16: Motor vehicle registration fees paid by the federal government were estimated at $24,000 from records of the Georgia Department of Revenue.

Line 17: Gross saving or surplus ($55,180,000) is computed as total revenue ($1,631,621,000) less total expenditures ($1,576,441,000). See *State Government Finances*, pp. 19, 28.

Line 19: Computed as a residual.

Line 20, 21: Based on the *Georgia Interindustry Study*.

Line 22: See household account, lines 17, 21.

Line 23: See household account, lines 18-21.

Line 24: Government Finances in 1969-70, p. 31.

Line 25: Total intergovernmental expenditures ($464,971,000) less transfers to local governments ($445,900,000). See line 24 and *State Government Finances*, p. 27.

NOTES ON FEDERAL GOVERNMENT ACCOUNT

Line 1: Computed from estimates provided by the Georgia Department of Revenue.

Line 2: See household account, line 39.

Line 3: See state government account, line 25.

Line 4: Computed as the difference between total expenditures ($4,284,305,000, from *Federal Outlays in Georgia, 1970*, p. 4) and total receipts in Georgia ($3,750,800,000).

Line 6: Defense expenditures with Georgia industries are computed as the sum of prime contracts as reported in Office of Economic Opportunity, *Federal Outlays in Georgia, 1970* (compiled for the Executive Office of the President, 1971), p. 1. Other expenditures with Georgia industries are computed as a residual.

Line 7: See household account, lines 22 and 26.

Line 8: See household account, lines 22 and 26.

Line 9: See local government account, line 14.

Line 10: See state government account, line 14.

NOTES ON REST-OF-WORLD ACCOUNT

Lines 1-6: Based on the *Georgia Interindustry Study*. These receipts by the rest of the world summarize the imports row of the Georgia interindustry flows table.

Line 7: Based on the *Georgia Interindustry Study*. This item is the value of gross exports by Georgia industries.

Line 9: See local government account, line 5.

Line 10: See state government account, line 17.

Line 11: See federal government account, line 4.

Line 13: Computed as the difference between imports and exports by Georgia industries, this item is the 'import surplus' of Georgia industries (a negative value) and the 'export surplus' of industries in the rest of the world.

Line 14: A balancing entry computed as the negative sum of lines 9-11.

B. Projections of employment growth in Georgia: A shift and share analysis

BY CHARLES F. FLOYD, PROFESSOR
DEPARTMENT OF REAL ESTATE
THE UNIVERSITY OF GEORGIA

B.1 INTRODUCTION

The shift and share method of regional analysis is a useful technique for comparing an area's economic growth performance to that experienced by the entire nation. This national basis of comparison eliminates the narrow view that often results from comparing the performance of a state or regional economy to some past period or to that of some closely linked geographical area. This appendix will discuss the methodology of the shift and share method as a technique for both analyzing past growth and projecting future growth, and will demonstrate its application by briefly analyzing the recent and projected growth of the Georgia economy.

B.2 SHIFT AND SHARE METHODOLOGY

Although the technique of shift and share analysis had its earliest roots in the work of David Creamer in the 1940's, its refinement resulted from the more recent work of Edgar S. Dunn, Jr. and Lowell D. Ashby.[1] Working with Census of Population data and under Ashby's direction, the Regional Economics Division of the Bureau of Economic Analysis utilized the method to analyze employment changes during the periods of 1940 to 1950 and 1950 to 1960 for each county in the United States.[2] The technique has also been used by many other researchers to analyze growth in various regions.[3]

The shift and share method's greatest virtue is its ability to place regional growth in a national perspective, eliminating the narrow view that often results from comparing the performance of a state or a regional economy to its own performance in some past period or to that of some closely linked geographical area.

Reference to Table B.2a for the United States and Table B.2b for Georgia will aid in understanding the shift and share analysis.[4] The first table shows that the total number of persons employed throughout the United States grew by 14,519,000 during the 1959 to 1970 period, an increase of 22.6 percent.

Tabel B.2a Employment and components of employment change, United States, 1950-1959 and 1959-1970.

| | EMPLOYMENT IN | | | COMPONENTS OF EMPLOYMENT CHANGE | | | | | | | | | |
| | | | | 1950 to 1959 | | | | | 1959 to 1970 | | | | |
	1950	1959	1970	Tot Ch	Natl Growth	Ind Mix	Reg Share	% Ch	Tot Ch	Natl Growth	Ind Mix	Reg Share	% Ch
Agriculture	6796	4866	3419	-1930	661	-2591	0	-3.6%	-1447	1101	-2548	0	-3.2%
Mining	965	756	664	-209	94	-303	0	-2.7%	-92	171	-263	0	-1.2%
Contract Cons.	3399	3634	4261	235	331	-96	0	0.7%	627	822	-195	0	1.5%
LOW WAGE MFG.	7674	7359	7869	-315	746	-1061	0	-0.5%	510	1665	-1155	0	0.6%
HIGH WAGE MFG.	7978	9647	11872	1669	775	894	0	2.1%	2225	2183	42	0	1.9%
Food Products	1928	1890	1889	-38	188	-226	0	-0.2%	-1	428	-429	:%	0.0%
Textiles	1260	952	986	-308	123	-431	0	-3.1%	34	215	-181	0	0.3%
Apparel	1236	1243	1387	7	120	-113	0	0.1%	144	281	-137	0	1.0%
Lumber & Wood	898	741	648	-157	87	-244	0	-2.1%	-93	168	-261	0	-1.2%
Furniture	393	404	479	11	38	-27	0	0.3%	75	91	-16	0	1.6%
Paper	486	583	703	97	47	50	0	2.0%	120	132	-12	0	1.7%
Print. Publish	815	955	1175	140	79	61	0	1.8%	220	216	4	0	1.9%
Chemicals	641	817	1057	176	62	114	0	2.7%	240	185	55	0	2.4%
Petro. Refin.	220	217	190	-3	21	-24	0	-0.2%	-27	49	-76	0	-1.2%
Rubber, Plas.	309	378	581	69	30	39	0	2.3%	203	86	117	0	4.0%
Leather	399	373	319	-26	39	-65	0	-0.7%	-54	84	-138	0	-1.4%
Stone, Clay	568	615	657	47	55	-8	0	0.9%	42	139	-97	0	0.6%
Primary Metals	1244	1193	1317	-51	121	-172	0	-0.5%	124	270	-146	0	0.9%
Fabricated Met	1062	1325	1727	263	103	160	0	2.5%	402	300	102	0	2.4%
Machinery	1262	1503	2032	241	123	118	0	2.0%	529	340	189	0	2.8%
Electric Mach.	987	1388	1927	401	96	305	0	3.9%	539	314	225	0	3.0%
Trans. Equip.	1261	1666	1744	405	123	282	0	3.1%	78	377	-299	0	0.4%
Instr., Misc.	683	763	923	80	66	14	0	1.2%	160	173	-13	0	1.7%
Trans. Service	2844	2547	2607	-297	277	-574	0	-1.2%	60	576	-516	0	0.2%
Comm., Pub. Ut	1285	1453	1819	168	125	43	0	1.4%	366	329	37	0	2.1%
Trade	10783	12059	15234	1276	1049	227	0	1.3%	3175	2729	446	0	2.1%
Fin.,Ins.,R.E.	2019	2695	3683	676	197	479	0	3.3%	988	610	378	0	2.9%
Services	7978	9815	13906	1837	776	1061	0	2.3%	4091	2221	1870	0	3.2%
Fed. Clv. Gov.	2003	2308	2816	305	195	110	0	1.6%	508	522	-14	0	1.8%
State & Local	3722	5291	8500	1569	362	1207	0	4.0%	3209	1197	2012	0	4.4%
Military	1026	1733	2032	707	100	607	0	6.0%	299	392	-93	0	1.5%
TOTAL	58472	64163	78682	5691	5688	0	0	1.0%	14519	14518	0	0	1.9%

Net Relative Change = 0   Net Relative Change = 0

Source: Georgia Department of Labor and Bureau of Economic Analysis, U.S. Department of Commerce.

However, not every industry grew at the 22.6 percent national rate for all industries combined; employment in some industries grew more rapidly; employment in others grew less rapidly or, in some cases, declined.

B.2.1 National growth component

The national growth component represents the growth that would have occurred in a particular industry if its employment had grown at the same rate as the average for all industries combined. For the 1959 to 1970 period, it can be computed by multiplying the individual industry employment totals for 1959 by the national *all-industry* growth rate, 22.6 percent. For example, Table B.2a shows the national growth component for apparel manufacturing to be 281,000. This figure represents the increase that would have occurred in the number of persons employed in apparel manufacturing in the United States between 1959 and 1970 if employment in this particular industry had increased at the national rate for all industries combined. It was computed by multiplying apparel manufacturing employment in 1959, 1,243,000, by the national all-industry growth rate, 22.6 percent.

B.2.2 Industrial mix component

Because structural changes such as demand patterns and technological innovation vary, employment in certain industries grows more rapidly than it does in others. These relative employment changes are indicated by the industrial mix component.[5] A negative value in this column indicates that employment in the industry grew at a slower rate than did employment for all industries combined. A positive value indicates that national employment in the industry grew at a faster rate than did employment for all industries combined. Using the apparel manufacturing industry once again as an example, the industrial mix component for the 1959 to 1970 period is computed as follows. First, an industrial mix percentage is derived by subtracting the national employment growth rate for all industry, 22.6 percent, from the 11.6 percent growth rate experienced by the apparel industry (computed by dividing the national change in apparel employment from 1959 to 1970, 144,000, by 1959 industry employment, 1,243,000). This industrial mix percentage, −11.0 percent, is then multiplied by the apparel manufacturing total in 1959 to determine the industrial mix component, −137,000. This represents the number of additional jobs that would have been available in the apparel industry in 1970 if this industry had grown at the national average for all industries during the 1959 to 1970 period. Conversely, the positive figure for electrical machinery manufacturing, 225,000, indicates the additional number of jobs created in this industry resulting from a growth rate higher than the national average rate for all industries.

Table B.2b Employment and components of employment change, Georgia, 1950-1959 and 1959-1970.

| | EMPLOYMENT IN | | | COMPONENTS OF EMPLOYMENT CHANGE | | | | | | | | | |
| | | | | 1950 to 1959 | | | | | 1959 to 1970 | | | | |
	1950	1959	1970	Tot Ch	Natl Growth	Ind Mix	Reg Share	% Ch	Tot Ch	Natl Growth	Ind Mix	Reg Share	Reg % Ch
Agriculture	237488	138932	82425	-98556	23114	-90559	-31111	-5.8%	-56507	31438	-72752	-15193	-4.6%
Mining	4152	6106	7581	1954	404	-1303	2853	4.4%	1475	1382	-2125	2218	2.0%
Contract Cons.	58607	73550	94678	14943	5704	-1652	10891	2.6%	21128	16643	-3953	8438	2.3%
LOW WAGE MFG.	244158	254240	315369	10082	23764	-58497	44815	0.5%	61129	57531	-49475	53073	2.0%
HIGH WAGE MFG.	50090	90330	153792	40240	4876	5852	29512	6.8%	63462	20441	-3263	46284	5.0%
Food Products	33845	44122	54042	10277	3294	-3961	10944	3.0%	9920	9984	-10007	9943	1.9%
Textiles	108469	100879	116232	-7590	10557	-37072	18925	-0.8%	15353	22827	-19924	11750	1.3%
Apparel	30445	46144	71354	15699	2963	-2791	15527	4.7%	25210	10442	-5096	19864	4.0%
Lumber & Wood	50538	34268	26406	-16270	4919	-13755	-7434	-4.2%	-7862	7754	-12055	-3561	-2.3%
Furniture	7298	8373	9826	1075	710	-506	871	1.5%	1453	1895	-340	-102	1.5%
Paper	11166	17327	25025	6161	1087	1142	3932	5.0%	7696	3921	-354	4129	3.4%
Print. Publish	8052	10907	16176	2855	784	599	1472	3.4%	5269	2468	45	2756	3.6%
Chemicals	8104	9455	13712	1351	789	1436	-874	1.7%	4257	2140	638	1479	3.4%
Petro. Refin.	556	882	863	326	54	-62	334	5.3%	-19	200	-309	90	-0.2%
Rubber, Plas.	227	1096	9803	869	22	29	818	19.1%	8707	248	341	8118	22.0%
Leather	2444	3772	4730	1328	238	-397	1487	4.9%	958	854	-1400	1504	2.1%
Stone, Clay	7568	10152	14052	2584	737	-110	1957	3.3%	3900	2297	-1604	3207	3.0%
Primary Metals	3192	4436	8412	1244	311	-442	1375	3.7%	3976	1004	-543	3515	6.0%
Fabricated Met	3932	6363	18391	2431	383	591	1457	5.5%	12028	1440	491	10097	10.1%
Machinery	6703	8752	14359	2049	652	628	769	3.0%	5607	1980	1100	2527	4.6%
Electric Mach.	978	4243	11656	3265	95	302	2868	17.7%	7413	960	688	5765	9.6%
Trans. Equip.	7407	27965	45200	20558	721	1658	18179	15.9%	17235	6328	-5019	15926	4.5%
Instr., Misc.	3324	5434	8924	2110	324	66	1720	5.6%	3490	1230	-90	2350	2.7%
Trans. Service	44224	45887	61495	1663	4304	-8923	6282	0.4%	15608	10383	-9302	14527	4.6%
Comm., Pub. Ut	21673	25169	41090	3496	2109	724	663	1.7%	15921	5695	645	9581	4.8%
Trade	192310	238674	324920	46364	18717	4040	23607	2.4%	86246	54008	8832	23406	2.8%
Fin., Ins., R.E.	26597	45586	75285	18989	2589	6517	9783	6.1%	29999	10247	6355	13397	4.7%
Services	183429	208612	265095	25183	17853	24383	-17053	1.4%	56483	47205	39746	-30468	2.2%
Fed. Civ. Gov.	45050	58251	79283	13201	4385	2475	6341	2.9%	21032	13181	-360	8211	2.8%
State & Local	68151	105584	186822	37433	6633	22096	8504	5.0%	81438	23847	40069	17522	5.3%
Military	37670	65885	84547	28215	3666	22291	2258	6.4%	18662	14909	-3541	7294	2.3%
TOTAL	1213599	1356306	1772382	142707	118818	-72756	97345	1.2%	416076	306910	-49124	158290	2.5%

Net Relative Change = 24589   Net Relative Change = 109166

Source: Georgia Department of Labor and Bureau of Economic Analysis,
U.S. Department of Commerce.

B.2.3 Regional share component

Just as the rate of employment growth in some industries is greater than or less than the national average rate for all industries combined, the rate of regional employment growth in a particular industry may be greater than or less than that experienced by the industry throughout the nation. For example, the data of Table B.2b show that if apparel manufacturing employment in Georgia had grown at the same rate during the 1959 to 1970 period as it did throughout the nation, then the state would have recorded an industry employment increase of only 5,346 during this period (the sum of a 10,442 national growth component and a −5,096 industrial mix component). Since the data show that Georgia apparel manufacturing actually increased by 25,210, the state must have gained a larger regional share of a nationally slow growth industry. This fact is indicated by the positive regional share component, 19,864. On the other hand, a negative regional share means that industry employment in the region did not grow as rapidly as, or declined more rapidly than, employment in the nation as a whole. The three components of employment change − national growth, industrial mix, and regional share − comprise the total Georgia employment change, 25,210, in the apparel manufacturing industry.

B.2.4 Net relative change

The sum of the industrial mix and regional share components for all industries represents the net relative change in employment for a region compared to the entire nation. A positive net relative change indicates the margin by which a region's employment growth exceeded the national growth rate for all industry. A negative figure indicates the number of additional jobs that would have been available if total employment in the region had grown at the national all-industry growth rate. Georgia enjoyed a positive net relative change of 109,166 during the 1959 to 1970 period, that is, the state's employment growth exceeded the national rate of growth by 109, 166.

B.3 PROJECTION METHODOLOGY

The shift and share technique can also be used to project future employment growth.[6] The additional requirements are an internal or external projection of national employment growth and some assumption regarding the stability of the regional share component over time.

The Georgia 1980 industry employment projections in Table B.3a provide an illustration of the projection method. Rates of national employment change by industry were computed from national figures supplied by the Bureau of Labor Statistics of the United States Department of Labor. These rates of change were then applied to the 1970 employment estimates to arrive at the national projections of 1980 employment by industry. From these estimates it was then possible to compute the national growth and industrial mix components of Georgia employment growth to 1980.

Table B.3a A shift-share projection of employment, Georgia, 1980.

	1970	Natl Growth	Ind Mix	Reg Share	Total Change	1980	Annual % Ch
Agriculture	82425	16003	-29335	-9354	-22686	59739	-3.2%
Mining	7581	1472	-1894	1366	944	8525	1.2%
Contract Cons.	94678	18382	-1429	5195	22148	116826	2.1%
Food Products	54042	10493	-15013	6121	1601	55643	0.3%
Textiles	116232	22567	-7124	7234	22677	138909	1.8%
Apparel	71354	13854	-7372	12229	18711	90065	2.4%
Lumber & Wood	26406	5127	-4190	-2192	-1255	25151	-0.5%
Furniture	9826	1908	1026	-63	2871	12697	2.6%
Paper	25023	4858	-3114	2542	4286	29309	1.6%
Print. Publish	16176	3141	-2012	1697	2826	19002	1.6%
Chemicals	13712	2662	-1287	911	2286	15998	1.6%
Petro. Refin.	863	168	-222	55	1	864	0.0%
Rubber, Plas.	9803	1903	847	4998	7748	17551	6.0%
Leather	4730	918	-1467	926	377	5107	0.8%
Stone, Clay	14052	2728	-1466	1974	3236	17288	2.1%
Primary Metals	8412	1633	-1256	2164	2541	10953	2.7%
Fabricated Met	18391	3571	-1675	6216	8112	26503	3.7%
Machinery	14359	2788	505	1556	4849	19208	3.0%
Electric Mach.	11656	2263	-473	3549	5339	16995	3.8%
Trans. Equip.	45200	8776	-1856	9805	16725	61925	3.2%
Instr., Misc.	8924	1733	-302	1447	2878	11802	2.8%
Trans. Service	61495	11940	-9463	8944	11421	72916	1.7%
Comm., Pub. Ut	41090	7978	-478	5899	13399	54489	2.9%
Trade	324920	63085	-1296	14410	76199	401119	2.1%
Fin., Ins.,R.E.	75285	14617	5640	8248	28505	103790	3.3%
Services	265095	51470	22496	-18758	55208	320303	1.9%
Fed. Civ. Gov.	79283	15393	1725	5055	22173	101456	2.5%
State & Local	186822	36272	47402	10788	94462	281284	4.2%
TOTAL	1687835	327703	-13083	92961	407582	2095417	2.1%

Relative Change= 79878

Source: Georgia Department of Labor and Bureau of Economic Analysis, U.S. Department of Commerce.

The final growth component, regional share, is the critical element in a regional projection, and is the one most subject to error. For example, it has been previously noted that Georgia's relatively rapid rate of employment growth in the apparel manufacturing industry between 1950 and 1970 occurred because the state was able to attract a greater proportionate share of a nationally slow growth industry. An important factor in this favorable competitive growth was the availability in Georgia of a large supply of labor willing to work for relatively low wages. Since most of this surplus labor pool has now been absorbed, it appears doubtful that the state can continue to attract apparel employment at the same relative rate in the future. Conversely, the development of a more highly skilled labor force or changes in other factors could possibly increase Georgia's competitive position in other industries.

In making the employment projections presented in Table B.3a it was assumed that the regional share during the 1970 to 1980 period will not be quite so important in the future, that is, that Georgia will be less competitive in attracting new employment, and that this growth component will fall to 75 percent of the 1959 to 1970 level when adjusted for the differing national base and time period.[7]

Two observations are appropriate regarding employment projections. First, the probability of error is inversely related to the size of the region. To make national projections one must analyze a few growth factors including changes in demand and technology. It is much more difficult to accurately project employment at the state, and particularly at the sub-state, level because to do this we must also estimate the spatial distribution of the employment change among many competitive areas.

Second, when making or using projections, one should remember that they are not predictions – they are extensions of existing or assumed trends. In other words, the projections of 1980 Georgia industry employment presented in this study are not predictions of what definitely will occur in the future. Rather, they are an attempt to show what will happen to the state's employment structure during the period if certain regional trends continue, assuming certain levels of national employment growth. Changes in either assumptions or economic policies would result, of course, in different levels of projected employment growth. The purpose is to make reasonable estimates of future employment change in order to provide a solid basis for rational economic policy decisions.

B.4 AN APPLICATION OF SHIFT AND SHARE ANALYSIS: GEORGIA EMPLOYMENT GROWTH, 1950–1980

The shift and share analysis highlights several characteristics of recent Georgia growth. First, like most of the states of the Southeast, Georgia's employment expansion has exceeded the national growth rate. Further reference to the data of Table B.2b shows that if the number of jobs in the state had increased at the national average annual compound rate between 1959 and 1970 (1.9 percent) instead of the actual 2.5 percent annual rate, Georgia employment would have been 109,166 smaller in 1970 (indicated by the 109,166 net relative change). For the previous nine-year period, the state's net relative change was only 24.589.

This relatively rapid employment growth since 1950 has been a product of Georgia's strong competitive position in attracting a greater proportionate share of new employment (indicated by the 158,290 regional share component for 1959-1970 and 97,345 for 1950-1959). The state's industry mix was quite unfavorable with regard to employment growth (indicated by the −72,756 industrial mix component for 1950-1959 and −49,124 for 1959-1970). If employment in each Georgia industry had grown at the same rate as its national counterpart, the total employment growth rate would have fallen well below the national rate in both periods. This can be attributed to relatively large concentrations in industries such as agriculture, forestry, and fisheries, food products, textile mill products, and lumber and wood products in which national employment was declining or growing very slowly.

The employment projections contained in Table B.3a indicate a continuing favorable employment growth trend for the Georgia economy to 1980. Georgia's projected employment growth rate is 2.4 percent annually, compared to the 2.0 percent national rate, resulting in a net relative change of 81,654. This will partially be a result of the diminished relative importance of the agricultural sector, one in which employment will continue to decline.

This very brief analysis of Georgia employment growth has raised many more questions than it has answered. For example, why was Georgia able to capture a greater proportionate share of national employment growth between 1950 and 1970? Will this favorable trend carry forward to 1980 and bevond? Will its effect be stronger or weaker in this future period? Was the rapid apparel manufacturing industry growth in Georgia only a temporary phenomenon resulting from the excess labor supply released from agriculture?

Use of shift and share analysis alone is not sufficient to answer questions such as these, for their complete analysis requires much deeper probing into the factors determining industrial location and regional growth. Shift and share is no more capable of furnishing simple answers to complex problems than any other technique, but it is a valuable aid in evaluating regional data to identify basic relationships and the direction of further analysis.

NOTES

1. David Creamer, 'Shifts of Manufacturing Industries,' Chapter 4 of *Industrial Location and National Resources* (Washington, D.C.: U.S. Government Printing Office, 1943), pp. 85-104; Edgar S. Dunn, Jr., 'A Statistical and Analytical Technique for Regional Analysis,' *Papers and Proceedings of the Regional Science Association*, Vol. VI, 1960. pp. 97-112, Edgar S. Dunn, Jr., *Recent Southern Economic Development*, University of Florida Monograph No. 14, Spring, 1962; and Lowell D. Ashby, 'The Geographical Redistribution of Employment: An Examination of the Elements of Change,' *Survey of Current Business*, Vol. 44, No. 10 (October 1964), pp. 13-20.
2. Lowell D. Ashby, *Growth Patterns in Employment By County, 1940-1950 and 1950-1960*, U.S. Department of Commerce, Office of Business Economics (Washington, D.C.: U.S. Government Printing Office, 1965).
3. For example, see: Federal Reserve Bank of Boston, 'Manufacturing Employment Changes in New England – 1947-1967,' *Business Review*, October 1967, pp. 8-11; Charles F. Floyd, *The Changing Structure of Employment and Income in the Title V Regions*, Economic Development Administration, 1971; M.A. Garrett, Jr., 'Growth of Manufacturing in the South, 1947-1958: A Study in Regional Industry Development,''

Southern Economic Journal, 33 (1968), pp. 352-364; and H.S. Perloff, E.S. Du nn, Jr., E.E. Lampard, and R.F. Muth, *Regions, Resources, and Economic Growth* (Baltimore: Johns Hopkins Press, 1960). Several recent British examples are: A.J. Brown, 'Regional Problems and Regional Policy,' *National Institute Economics Review*, November 1968, pp. 42-51; F.J.B. Stilwell, 'Regional Growth and Structural Adaptation,' *Urban Studies*, June 1969, pp. 162-178; and A.P. Thirlwall, 'A Measure of the Proper Distribution of Industry,' *Oxford Economic Papers*, March 1967, pp. 46-58.

4. Mathematically, the analysis can be represented as follows:

Let: E_i^1 = Regional employment in industry i in base period 1

   E_i^2 = Regional employment in industry i in period 2

   r_{oo} = United States all-industry employment growth rate between period 1 and period 2

   r_{10} = United States individual industry growth rate between period 1 and period 2

   r_{ij} = Regional individual industry growth rate between period 1 and period 2

   NG = National growth component of regional growth

   IM = Industrial mix component of regional growth

   RS = Regional share component of regional growth

   TC = Total change in regional employment between period 1 and period 2

Then:

$$NG = \sum_{i=1}^{n} \left[r_{oo} \, (E_i^1) \right]$$

$$IM = \sum_{i=1}^{n} \left[E_i^1 \, (r_{io} - r_{oo}) \right]$$

$$RS = \sum_{i=1}^{n} \left[(r_{ij} - r_{io}) \, E_i^1 \right] = TC - (NG - IM)$$

$$TC = \sum_{i=1}^{n} (E_i^2 - E_i^1) = NG + IM + RS$$

5. It is often said that economists would rather use each other's toothbrushes than their terminology. Shift and share analysis provides an excellent example of this maxim. In the literature, the industrial mix component is variously known as the structural component, proportionality shift, and composition effect. The regional share component is also known as differential growth and the competitive effect.

6. An exposition of the technique appears in L.D. Ashby, 'Regional Projections in a National Setting,' Regional Economics Division, U.S. Department of Commerce, No. 66143 (unpublished).

7. Mathematically, the projection technique can be represented as follows:

Let: E_i^2 = Regional employment in industry i in base period 2

E_i^3 = Projected employment in industry i in period 3

p_{oo} = United States projected all-industry employment growth rate between period 2 and period 3

p_{io} = United States projected individual industry growth rate between period 2 and period 3

NG' = Projected national growth component

IM' = Projected industry mix component

RS' = Projected regional share component

TC' = Projected total change in employment

RS_i = Regional share component for industry i in previous period

Then:

$$NG' = \sum_{i=1}^{n} (p_{oo} E_i^2)$$

$$IM' = \sum_{i=1}^{n} [(p_{io} - p_{oo}) E_i^2]$$

$$RS' = \sum_{i=1}^{n} (kRS_i) \text{ where}$$

RS_i is the Regional Share component in the previous period and k is a scalar equal to:

$$\frac{\text{U.S. employment base in period 2}}{\text{U.S. employment base in period 1}} \times \frac{t_3 - t_2}{t_2 - t_1}$$

In the present example:

$$k = \frac{78,682,000}{64,163,000} \times \frac{10}{11} = 1.115$$

The resulting RS_i' must be considered a first approximation because a continuation of the past regional share trend can lead to very low or even negative industry employment projections.

Since negative employment values are implausible, some adjustment must be made, either through the use of an algorithm as suggested by Ashby, or judgmentally as was done in the accompanying example.

When the projected regional share component has been determined, then:

$$TC_i' = NG_i' + IM_i' + RS_{i}', \text{ and}$$

$$E^3 = E_i^2 + NG_i' + IM_i' + RS_i'.$$

C. Tables

Table 1. Interindustry flow of goods and services in Georgia, 1970 (millions of dollars).

SELLING INDUSTRY	PURCHASING INDUSTRY NUMBER (SEE LEFT FOR TITLE)						
	1	2	3	4	5	6	7
1 AGRICULTURE (SIC 01, 07-9)	178.718	.000	5.476	498.168	8.845	3.219	29.519
2 MINING (SIC 10-4)	1.636	2.530	25.469	.446	.036	.000	.014
3 CONTRACT CONSTRUCTION (SIC 15-7)	12.313	1.623	.890	4.907	11.297	.509	1.846
4 FOOD AND KINDRED PRODUCTS (SIC 20-1)	105.615	.000	.076	170.167	.035	.001	.012
5 TEXTILE MILL PRODUCTS (SIC 22)	2.361	.005	1.217	2.064	527.851	207.302	.137
6 APPAREL AND RELATED PRODUCTS (SIC 23)	.544	.000	.517	1.748	4.727	30.558	.208
7 LUMBER AND WOOD PRODUCTS (SIC 24)	1.521	.052	80.078	.645	.006	.459	74.454
8 FURNITURE AND FIXTURES (SIC 25)	.000	.000	6.113	.007	.363	.177	.560
9 PAPER AND ALLIED PRODUCTS (SIC 26)	2.891	.052	6.871	41.943	27.694	2.981	1.302
10 PRINTING AND PUBLISHING (SIC 27)	.093	.003	.033	3.887	.063	.020	.026
11 CHEMICALS AND ALLIED PRODUCTS (SIC 28)	12.780	.913	12.514	10.992	46.108	.276	1.214
12 PETROLEUM REFINING (SIC 29)	.034	.288	16.370	.011	.009	.001	.015
13 RUBBER AND MISC. PLASTICS (SIC 30)	.605	2.345	10.189	7.362	16.267	3.780	.201
14 LEATHER AND LEATHER PRODUCTS (SIC 31)	.054	.000	.007	.014	.041	.537	.027
15 STONE, CLAY AND GLASS PROD. (SIC 32)	.392	3.694	145.651	31.142	.246	.006	.165
16 PRIMARY METAL INDUSTRIES (SIC 33)	.002	.506	9.778	.001	.003	.119	.310
17 FABRICATED METAL PRODUCTS (SIC 34, 19)	3.081	.149	99.464	22.940	.296	.138	1.444
18 MACHINERY, EXCEPT ELECTRICAL (SIC 35)	1.443	1.813	8.064	.781	3.074	.042	.315
19 ELECTRICAL MACHINERY & EQUIP (SIC 36)	.222	.139	15.176	.095	.022	.008	.029
20 TRANSPORTATION EQUIPMENT (SIC 37)	.105	.137	.163	.038	.008	.004	.054
21 MISCELLANEOUS MANUFACTURING (SIC 38-9)	.010	.001	1.538	.152	1.165	5.128	.139
22 TRANSPORTATION SERVICES (SIC 40-7)	10.212	1.313	41.478	31.305	26.241	2.291	5.803
23 COMMUNICATIONS & UTILITIES (SIC 48-9)	7.228	7.120	14.702	17.117	33.933	4.389	4.761
24 WHOLESALE AND RETAIL TRADE (SIC 50-9)	45.350	6.961	224.167	79.071	171.791	28.606	10.780
25 FINANCE, INS., REAL ESTATE (SIC 60-7)	35.690	7.616	25.600	19.605	27.183	9.042	5.511
26 SERVICES (SIC 70-9, 80-6, 89)	22.536	5.407	124.016	50.202	40.535	7.655	7.121
27 GOVERNMENT ENTERPRISES	.240	.455	2.121	2.361	4.141	1.657	.376
28 UNALLOCATED INDUSTRIES	2.666	1.473	13.002	6.764	12.452	3.432	1.516
29 TOTAL LOCAL PURCHASES	448.340	44.598	890.760	1003.936	964.432	312.336	147.858
30 HOUSEHOLDS	539.000	55.983	665.000	407.883	825.720	383.047	135.645
31 CAPITAL RESIDUAL	168.532	35.630	103.681	99.030	153.478	26.558	28.515
32 CITY AND COUNTY GOVERNMENT	45.465	1.826	25.806	10.154	13.340	1.436	7.000
33 STATE GOVERNMENT	.000	.666	9.280	7.619	11.413	2.694	11.002
34 FEDERAL GOVERNMENT	.000	8.931	101.824	73.216	104.281	32.314	17.808
35 IMPORTS	276.272	48.930	723.223	679.376	1617.976	239.171	140.128
36 TOTAL PURCHASES	1477.610	196.565	2519.575	2281.214	3690.639	997.556	487.956

Table 1. Interindustry flow of goods and services in Georgia, 1970 (millions of dollars).

	SELLING INDUSTRY	PURCHASING INDUSTRY NUMBER (SEE LEFT FOR TITLE)						
		8	9	10	11	12	13	14
1	AGRICULTURE (SIC 01, 07-9)	.000	.000	.000	.897	.000	.000	.000
2	MINING (SIC 10-4)	.000	6.964	.000	2.658	2.760	.225	.000
3	CONTRACT CONSTRUCTION (SIC 15-7)	.307	8.133	.520	2.913	.388	.808	.094
4	FOOD AND KINDRED PRODUCTS (SIC 20-1)	.000	1.455	.201	13.216	.015	.006	1.163
5	TEXTILE MILL PRODUCTS (SIC 22)	7.382	1.730	.154	.097	.000	12.298	1.517
6	APPAREL AND RELATED PRODUCTS (SIC 23)	.222	1.043	.000	.797	.014	.828	.785
7	LUMBER AND WOOD PRODUCTS (SIC 24)	15.159	45.548	.379	1.590	.036	.868	.373
8	FURNITURE AND FIXTURES (SIC 25)	2.645	.015	.570	.002	.000	.126	.008
9	PAPER AND ALLIED PRODUCTS (SIC 26)	1.952	174.525	38.846	15.551	2.410	3.203	.557
10	PRINTING AND PUBLISHING (SIC 27)	.011	3.547	7.551	.300	.000	.018	.024
11	CHEMICALS AND ALLIED PRODUCTS (SIC 28)	1.108	30.628	5.201	64.242	1.764	8.182	.356
12	PETROLEUM REFINING (SIC 29)	.001	.131	.001	1.136	.089	.022	.000
13	RUBBER AND MISC. PLASTICS (SIC 30)	7.435	4.591	.694	7.343	.749	2.293	2.233
14	LEATHER AND LEATHER PRODUCTS (SIC 31)	.031	.054	.007	.015	.001	.143	.519
15	STONE, CLAY AND GLASS PROD. (SIC 32)	.315	.276	.000	4.478	.004	.887	.002
16	PRIMARY METAL INDUSTRIES (SIC 33)	1.053	1.609	.007	.698	.442	.376	.001
17	FABRICATED METAL PRODUCTS (SIC 34, 19)	4.303	4.061	.125	11.318	.012	.909	.066
18	MACHINERY, EXCEPT ELECTRICAL (SIC 35)	.372	.937	.277	.601	.003	.308	.007
19	ELECTRICAL MACHINERY & EQUIP (SIC 36)	.034	.041	.023	.038	.002	.099	.002
20	TRANSPORTATION EQUIPMENT (SIC 37)	.494	.051	.807	.064	.002	.079	.002
21	MISCELLANEOUS MANUFACTURING (SIC 38-9)	.260	.422	.201	2.592	.981	1.554	.972
22	TRANSPORTATION SERVICES (SIC 40-7)	2.049	22.313	1.490	8.613	2.107	1.958	.332
23	COMMUNICATIONS & UTILITIES (SIC 48-9)	2.068	34.941	3.865	12.247	3.141	3.303	.474
24	WHOLESALE AND RETAIL TRADE (SIC 50-9)	10.365	45.104	7.257	26.589	.927	8.399	2.197
25	FINANCE, INS., REAL ESTATE (SIC 60-7)	4.616	12.484	9.819	8.326	1.093	2.784	.798
26	SERVICES (SIC 70-9, 80-6, 89)	4.181	22.875	8.383	25.311	.049	5.479	1.372
27	GOVERNMENT ENTERPRISES	.306	1.728	2.596	.955	.275	.306	.198
28	UNALLOCATED INDUSTRIES	1.402	24.298	4.064	6.010		1.942	.376
29	TOTAL LOCAL PURCHASES	68.074	449.504	93.218	218.597	17.278	57.405	14.428
30	HOUSEHOLDS	63.319	265.275	145.531	139.555	8.894	73.937	26.649
31	CAPITAL RESIDUAL	12.421	82.504	24.928	62.565	2.119	17.795	5.702
32	CITY AND COUNTY GOVERNMENT	1.290	13.399	1.976	7.533	.289	2.409	.328
33	STATE GOVERNMENT	.652	7.234	1.703	4.719	.082	1.670	.544
34	FEDERAL GOVERNMENT	8.700	60.671	13.820	46.570	.772	13.401	4.701
35	IMPORTS	78.455	336.838	59.769	236.874	20.055	79.028	25.492
36	TOTAL PURCHASES	232.911	1215.425	341.004	716.413	49.490	245.645	77.844

Table 1. Interindustry flow of goods and services in Georgia, 1970 (millions of dollars).

SELLING INDUSTRY	PURCHASING INDUSTRY NUMBER (SEE LEFT FOR TITLE)						
	15	16	17	18	19	20	21
1 AGRICULTURE (SIC 01, 07-9)	.000	.000	.000	.000	.000	.000	.280
2 MINING (SIC 10-4)	44.525	.358	.014	.007	.003	.024	.031
3 CONTRACT CONSTRUCTION (SIC 15-7)	2.823	1.060	.878	.649	.460	4.628	.458
4 FOOD AND KINDRED PRODUCTS (SIC 20-1)	.020	.000	.044	.407	.000	.000	.280
5 TEXTILE MILL PRODUCTS (SIC 22)	.054	.153	.241	.216	.248	2.279	1.268
6 APPAREL AND RELATED PRODUCTS (SIC 23)	2.950	.059	.225	.139	.086	3.023	.547
7 LUMBER AND WOOD PRODUCTS (SIC 24)	1.696	.647	1.720	5.858	.497	22.558	2.643
8 FURNITURE AND FIXTURES (SIC 25)	.512	.019	1.301	.180	.277	7.373	.741
9 PAPER AND ALLIED PRODUCTS (SIC 26)	3.377	.257	3.931	1.295	1.486	3.475	4.937
10 PRINTING AND PUBLISHING (SIC 27)	.020	.010	.897	.047	.034	.169	.828
11 CHEMICALS AND ALLIED PRODUCTS (SIC 28)	3.095	.690	3.840	3.733	1.522	4.420	2.336
12 PETROLEUM REFINING (SIC 29)	.193	.001	.034	.002	.003	.272	.012
13 RUBBER AND MISC. PLASTICS (SIC 30)	1.373	.117	1.500	2.954	4.743	9.247	4.521
14 LEATHER AND LEATHER PRODUCTS (SIC 31)	.019	.009	.016	.097	.009	.014	.316
15 STONE, CLAY AND GLASS PROD. (SIC 32)	11.218	.119	3.061	.632	.906	1.755	.369
16 PRIMARY METAL INDUSTRIES (SIC 33)	.813	5.965	35.882	7.393	6.701	38.849	1.622
17 FABRICATED METAL PRODUCTS (SIC 34, 19)	1.139	3.100	13.544	11.563	6.677	25.614	3.868
18 MACHINERY, EXCEPT ELECTRICAL (SIC 35)	.736	3.087	7.018	13.224	4.304	28.818	.957
19 ELECTRICAL MACHINERY & EQUIP (SIC 36)	.939	1.037	1.376	4.603	3.580	16.556	1.199
20 TRANSPORTATION EQUIPMENT (SIC 37)	.338	3.581	5.412	10.541	15.481	27.647	2.489
21 MISCELLANEOUS MANUFACTURING (SIC 38-9)	.107	.211	1.924	1.698	2.367	2.772	3.262
22 TRANSPORTATION SERVICES (SIC 40-7)	11.172	3.925	3.731	1.975	1.802	11.752	1.059
23 COMMUNICATIONS & UTILITIES (SIC 48-9)	15.780	6.408	5.302	3.259	3.107	22.219	2.193
24 WHOLESALE AND RETAIL TRADE (SIC 50-9)	15.888	9.133	15.044	12.302	11.659	58.756	9.334
25 FINANCE, INS., REAL ESTATE (SIC 60-7)	5.750	2.997	7.399	5.676	4.880	14.289	3.008
26 SERVICES (SIC 70-9, 80-6, 89)	10.400	4.297	8.537	6.467	6.045	58.204	6.692
27 GOVERNMENT ENTERPRISES	.880	.268	.472	.503	.392	3.236	.463
28 UNALLOCATED INDUSTRIES	3.232	7.832	3.364	3.025	2.797	20.011	2.175
29 TOTAL LOCAL PURCHASES	134.050	55.339	126.680	96.446	80.065	387.960	57.887
30 HOUSEHOLDS	119.554	72.868	151.700	126.829	108.872	577.707	62.549
31 CAPITAL RESIDUAL	19.916	12.816	28.723	29.194	24.820	199.473	19.203
32 CITY AND COUNTY GOVERNMENT	2.757	2.906	4.101	2.150	2.442	6.869	1.956
33 STATE GOVERNMENT	.989	1.271	2.710	1.997	1.391	20.656	1.574
34 FEDERAL GOVERNMENT	10.688	8.193	22.667	18.924	17.933	143.953	12.830
35 IMPORTS	101.064	134.103	187.538	147.917	125.364	1155.511	63.258
36 TOTAL PURCHASES	389.017	287.496	524.138	425.458	360.887	2492.129	219.256

Table 1. Interindustry flow of goods and services in Georgia, 1970 (millions of dollars).

SELLING INDUSTRY	PURCHASING INDUSTRY NUMBER (SEE LEFT FOR TITLE)						
	22	23	24	25	26	27	28
1 AGRICULTURE (SIC 01, 07-9)	1.082	.000	5.667	67.275	1.086	.059	2.009
2 MINING (SIC 10-4)	.001	.016	.403	1.429	.126	.002	.000
3 CONTRACT CONSTRUCTION (SIC 15-7)	29.958	40.594	13.764	108.649	62.430	51.318	.000
4 FOOD AND KINDRED PRODUCTS (SIC 20-1)	5.766	.017	22.272	3.594	7.133	.000	19.156
5 TEXTILE MILL PRODUCTS (SIC 22)	.161	.317	7.333	5.770	.889	.113	1.225
6 APPAREL AND RELATED PRODUCTS (SIC 23)	.104	.074	5.325	1.502	3.803	.155	.107
7 LUMBER AND WOOD PRODUCTS (SIC 24)	.033	.095	4.284	1.319	.000	.000	.052
8 FURNITURE AND FIXTURES (SIC 25)	.000	.002	1.390	.275	.000	.001	.000
9 PAPER AND ALLIED PRODUCTS (SIC 26)	.248	.983	14.755	7.231	1.983	.698	1.592
10 PRINTING AND PUBLISHING (SIC 27)	.454	.036	3.153	5.779	154.290	.358	26.278
11 CHEMICALS AND ALLIED PRODUCTS (SIC 28)	.486	.731	12.025	7.882	19.291	1.742	.396
12 PETROLEUM REFINING (SIC 29)	.120	.108	.639	.436	.039	.003	.001
13 RUBBER AND MISC. PLASTICS (SIC 30)	1.266	.001	4.172	1.351	2.986	.111	.232
14 LEATHER AND LEATHER PRODUCTS (SIC 31)	.000	.038	.308	.094	.118	.004	.169
15 STONE, CLAY AND GLASS PROD. (SIC 32)	.034	.199	4.603	1.204	3.179	.002	.015
16 PRIMARY METAL INDUSTRIES (SIC 33)	1.000	.000	.601	.266	.015	.001	2.441
17 FABRICATED METAL PRODUCTS (SIC 34, 19)	.390	.052	4.562	1.060	2.348	.018	1.135
18 MACHINERY, EXCEPT ELECTRICAL (SIC 35)	.344	.083	4.091	2.592	5.858	.029	1.199
19 ELECTRICAL MACHINERY & EQUIP (SIC 36)	1.463	.035	2.885	1.858	4.816	.031	.273
20 TRANSPORTATION EQUIPMENT (SIC 37)	16.688	.243	13.316	1.914	2.034	.042	1.017
21 MISCELLANEOUS MANUFACTURING (SIC 38-9)	.009	7.960	4.102	.454	10.662	.007	1.820
22 TRANSPORTATION SERVICES (SIC 40-7)	45.536	104.171	17.928	9.366	8.639	12.649	30.889
23 COMMUNICATIONS & UTILITIES (SIC 48-9)	16.786	8.869	84.245	59.896	210.358	10.830	.000
24 WHOLESALE AND RETAIL TRADE (SIC 50-9)	43.558	17.623	71.907	60.174	129.308	2.699	12.314
25 FINANCE, INS., REAL ESTATE (SIC 60-7)	41.170	43.156	192.104	683.316	232.622	7.829	.000
26 SERVICES (SIC 70-9, 80-6, 89)	46.314	81.309	177.843	190.198	257.190	12.189	27.250
27 GOVERNMENT ENTERPRISES	17.501	6.690	50.825	62.254	44.494	.301	.000
28 UNALLOCATED INDUSTRIES	9.322		35.398	37.503	74.798	2.462	.000
29 TOTAL LOCAL PURCHASES	279.792	313.417	759.958	1324.642	1240.493	103.651	129.570
30 HOUSEHOLDS	651.000	344.000	2385.000	1934.700	1482.000	191.437	.000
31 CAPITAL RESIDUAL	89.140	264.680	378.323	505.053	540.515	83.819	.000
32 CITY AND COUNTY GOVERNMENT	8.108	43.584	62.930	106.586	103.639	.000	.000
33 STATE GOVERNMENT	14.166	8.620	624.310	73.912	47.898	.000	.000
34 FEDERAL GOVERNMENT	43.137	117.805	299.220	80.248	271.268	.000	.000
35 IMPORTS	241.926	188.406	310.518	222.310	496.723	46.072	176.945
36 TOTAL PURCHASES	1327.270	1280.511	4820.279	4247.452	4182.537	424.979	306.514

Table 1. Interindustry flow of goods and services in Georgia, 1970 (millions of dollars).

	TOTAL LOCAL SALES	PERSONAL CONSUMPTION EXPENDITURES	GROSS PRIVATE INVESTMENT	LOCAL GOVERNMENT	STATE GOVERNMENT	FEDERAL GOVERNMENT (DEFENSE)	FEDERAL GOVERNMENT (OTHER)
1 AGRICULTURE (SIC 01, 07-9)	802.301	98.082	.000	.922	.770	.325	81.653
2 MINING (SIC 10-4)	89.673	.416	.000	.006	.006	4.119	.116
3 CONTRACT CONSTRUCTION (SIC 15-7)	364.218	.000	1079.334	305.786	312.563	47.628	57.326
4 FOOD AND KINDRED PRODUCTS (SIC 20-1)	350.682	790.937	.000	7.086	5.831	2.634	2.612
5 TEXTILE MILL PRODUCTS (SIC 22)	784.384	39.110	.945	.124	.120	.538	.054
6 APPAREL AND RELATED PRODUCTS (SIC 23)	60.089	109.538	.000	.515	.540	1.534	.510
7 LUMBER AND WOOD PRODUCTS (SIC 24)	262.569	3.525	.093	.061	.051	.135	.041
8 FURNITURE AND FIXTURES (SIC 25)	22.655	46.310	25.269	2.525	1.546	.378	.546
9 PAPER AND ALLIED PRODUCTS (SIC 26)	367.025	3.339	.000	1.159	.969	.441	.491
10 PRINTING AND PUBLISHING (SIC 27)	207.932	42.747	.000	3.842	2.240	2.918	.007
11 CHEMICALS AND ALLIED PRODUCTS (SIC 28)	258.467	54.090	.000	4.629	3.618	13.128	1.722
12 PETROLEUM REFINING (SIC 29)	19.480	.364	.000	.012	.008	8.624	.816
13 RUBBER AND MISC. PLASTICS (SIC 30)	100.033	13.301	.159	.888	.856	2.297	.154
14 LEATHER AND LEATHER PRODUCTS (SIC 31)	2.623	17.858	.000	.000	.000	.058	.014
15 STONE, CLAY AND GLASS PROD. (SIC 32)	215.139	2.130	.000	.118	.093	.492	.089
16 PRIMARY METAL INDUSTRIES (SIC 33)	116.214	.048	.060	.005	.002	2.460	.097
17 FABRICATED METAL PRODUCTS (SIC 34, 19)	223.755	4.881	10.707	.209	.110	6.693	.544
18 MACHINERY, EXCEPT ELECTRICAL (SIC 35)	90.374	2.679	63.675	2.360	1.369	9.585	1.992
19 ELECTRICAL MACHINERY & EQUIP (SIC 36)	56.651	5.636	10.839	.365	.305	10.303	1.606
20 TRANSPORTATION EQUIPMENT (SIC 37)	102.602	127.976	37.731	.937	.626	851.459	4.652
21 MISCELLANEOUS MANUFACTURING (SIC 38-9)	43.894	10.683	5.975	.397	.288	1.008	.508
22 TRANSPORTATION SERVICES (SIC 40-7)	324.763	116.697	8.110	8.458	5.740	17.730	2.494
23 COMMUNICATIONS & UTILITIES (SIC 48-9)	692.808	384.450	14.833	27.335	17.886	8.597	.870
24 WHOLESALE AND RETAIL TRADE (SIC 50-9)	1125.703	2563.370	128.670	11.643	8.792	9.375	2.285
25 FINANCE, INS., REAL ESTATE (SIC 60-7)	1388.663	1842.483	13.994	30.869	20.688	1.378	162.097
26 SERVICES (SIC 70-9, 80-6, 89)	1180.047	1875.131	.000	39.614	37.954	50.653	23.467
27 GOVERNMENT ENTERPRISES	280.385	43.536	.000	3.404	3.032	1.363	3.988
28 UNALLOCATED INDUSTRIES	288.283	.000	.000	7.601	6.263	1.190	3.178
29 TOTAL LOCAL PURCHASES	9822.713	8199.316	1400.396	460.870	432.267	1057.023	353.929
30 HOUSEHOLDS	11943.653	99.692	.000	841.975	563.397	880.000	1537.283
31 CAPITAL RESIDUAL	3019.133	871.570	.000	.000	.000	.000	.000
32 CITY AND COUNTY GOVERNMENT	480.300	377.900	.000	.000	445.900	.000	47.300
33 STATE GOVERNMENT	858.832	341.902	.000	22.117	.000	.000	408.770
34 FEDERAL GOVERNMENT	1533.898	2197.838	.000	.000	19.071	.000	.000
35 IMPORTS	8159.241	3777.787	802.113	138.838	115.806	.000	.000
36 TOTAL PURCHASES	35817.770	15866.004	2202.509	1463.800	1576.441	1937.023	2347.282

FINAL DEMAND

Table 1. Interindustry flow of goods and services in Georgia, 1970 (millions of dollars).

	NET EXPORTS	TOTAL FINAL DEMAND	TOTAL SALES
	FINAL DEMAND		
1 AGRICULTURE (SIC 01, 07-9)	493.562	675.314	1477.614
2 MINING (SIC 10-4)	102.230	106.893	196.566
3 CONTRACT CONSTRUCTION (SIC 15-7)	352.719	2155.356	2519.575
4 FOOD AND KINDRED PRODUCTS (SIC 20-1)	1121.431	1930.531	2281.214
5 TEXTILE MILL PRODUCTS (SIC 22)	2865.362	2906.254	3690.637
6 APPAREL AND RELATED PRODUCTS (SIC 23)	824.829	937.465	997.554
7 LUMBER AND WOOD PRODUCTS (SIC 24)	221.482	225.387	487.957
8 FURNITURE AND FIXTURES (SIC 25)	133.685	210.258	232.913
9 PAPER AND ALLIED PRODUCTS (SIC 26)	842.000	848.398	1215.423
10 PRINTING AND PUBLISHING (SIC 27)	81.319	133.072	341.004
11 CHEMICALS AND ALLIED PRODUCTS (SIC 28)	380.756	457.944	716.411
12 PETROLEUM REFINING (SIC 29)	19.787	29.610	49.490
13 RUBBER AND MISC. PLASTICS (SIC 30)	127.955	145.611	245.644
14 LEATHER AND LEATHER PRODUCTS (SIC 31)	57.290	75.220	77.843
15 STONE, CLAY AND GLASS PROD. (SIC 32)	170.956	173.879	389.018
16 PRIMARY METAL INDUSTRIES (SIC 33)	168.611	171.283	287.498
17 FABRICATED METAL PRODUCTS (SIC 34, 19)	277.239	300.382	524.137
18 MACHINERY, EXCEPT ELECTRICAL (SIC 35)	253.421	335.081	425.455
19 ELECTRICAL MACHINERY & EQUIP (SIC 36)	275.181	304.234	360.885
20 TRANSPORTATION EQUIPMENT (SIC 37)	1366.163	2389.525	2492.128
21 MISCELLANEOUS MANUFACTURING (SIC 38-9)	156.502	175.361	219.255
22 TRANSPORTATION SERVICES (SIC 40-7)	843.279	1002.509	1327.271
23 COMMUNICATIONS & UTILITIES (SIC 48-9)	133.734	587.704	1280.512
24 WHOLESALE AND RETAIL TRADE (SIC 50-9)	970.441	3694.577	4820.280
25 FINANCE, INS., REAL ESTATE (SIC 60-7)	787.279	2858.789	4247.453
26 SERVICES (SIC 70-9, 80-6, 89)	974.793	3001.592	4182.539
27 GOVERNMENT ENTERPRISES	89.253	144.596	424.981
28 UNALLOCATED INDUSTRIES	.000	18.232	306.514
29 TOTAL LOCAL PURCHASES	14091.257	25995.058	35817.771
30 HOUSEHOLDS	.000	3922.347	15866.000
31 CAPITAL RESIDUAL	.000	871.570	3890.703
32 CITY AND COUNTY GOVERNMENT	.000	871.100	1351.400
33 STATE GOVERNMENT	.000	772.789	1631.621
34 FEDERAL GOVERNMENT	.000	2216.909	3750.807
35 IMPORTS	.000	4834.543	12993.784
36 TOTAL PURCHASES	14091.257	39484.316	75302.086

Table 2. Direct requirements per dollar of gross output, Georgia, 1970 (in percent).

SELLING INDUSTRY	PURCHASING INDUSTRY NUMBER (SEE LEFT FOR TITLE)						
	1	2	3	4	5	6	7
1 AGRICULTURE (SIC 01, 07-9)	12.10	.00	.22	21.84	.24	.32	6.05
2 MINING (SIC 10-4)	.11	1.29	1.01	.02	.00	.00	.00
3 CONTRACT CONSTRUCTION (SIC 15-7)	.83	.83	.04	.22	.31	.05	.38
4 FOOD AND KINDRED PRODUCTS (SIC 20-1)	7.15	.00	.00	7.46	.30	.00	.00
5 TEXTILE MILL PRODUCTS (SIC 22)	.16	.00	.05	.09	14.30	20.78	.03
6 APPAREL AND RELATED PRODUCTS (SIC 23)	.04	.00	.02	.08	.13	3.06	.04
7 LUMBER AND WOOD PRODUCTS (SIC 24)	.10	.03	3.18	.03	.00	.05	15.26
8 FURNITURE AND FIXTURES (SIC 25)	.00	.00	.24	.00	.01	.02	.11
9 PAPER AND ALLIED PRODUCTS (SIC 26)	.20	.03	.27	1.84	.00	.30	.27
10 PRINTING AND PUBLISHING (SIC 27)	.01	.00	.00	.17	.75	.00	.01
11 CHEMICALS AND ALLIED PRODUCTS (SIC 28)	.86	.46	.50	.48	1.25	.03	.25
12 PETROLEUM REFINING (SIC 29)	.00	.15	.65	.00	.00	.03	.00
13 RUBBER AND MISC. PLASTICS (SIC 30)	.04	1.19	.40	.32	.44	.38	.04
14 LEATHER AND LEATHER PRODUCTS (SIC 31)	.00	.00	.00	.00	.00	.05	.01
15 STONE, CLAY AND GLASS PROD. (SIC 32)	.03	1.88	5.78	1.37	.01	.00	.03
16 PRIMARY METAL INDUSTRIES (SIC 33)	.00	.26	.39	.00	.00	.01	.06
17 FABRICATED METAL PRODUCTS (SIC 34, 19)	.21	.08	3.95	1.01	.01	.01	.30
18 MACHINERY, EXCEPT ELECTRICAL (SIC 35)	.10	.92	.32	.03	.08	.00	.06
19 ELECTRICAL MACHINERY & EQUIP (SIC 36)	.02	.07	.60	.00	.00	.00	.01
20 TRANSPORTATION EQUIPMENT (SIC 37)	.01	.07	.01	.00	.00	.00	.01
21 MISCELLANEOUS MANUFACTURING (SIC 38-9)	.00	.00	.06	.01	.00	.00	.03
22 TRANSPORTATION SERVICES (SIC 40-7)	.69	.67	1.65	1.37	.71	.51	1.19
23 COMMUNICATIONS & UTILITIES (SIC 48-9)	.49	3.62	.58	.75	.92	.44	.98
24 WHOLESALE AND RETAIL TRADE (SIC 50-9)	3.07	3.54	8.90	3.47	4.65	2.87	2.21
25 FINANCE, INS., REAL ESTATE (SIC 60-7)	2.42	3.87	1.02	.86	.74	.91	1.13
26 SERVICES (SIC 70-9, 80-6, 89)	1.53	2.75	4.92	2.20	1.10	.77	1.46
27 GOVERNMENT ENTERPRISES	.02	.23	.08	.10	.11	.17	.08
28 UNALLOCATED INDUSTRIES	.18	.75	.52	.30	.34	.34	.31
29 TOTAL LOCAL PURCHASES	30.34	22.69	35.35	44.01	26.13	31.31	30.30
30 HOUSEHOLDS	36.48	28.48	26.39	17.88	22.37	38.40	27.80
31 CAPITAL RESIDUAL	11.41	18.13	4.12	4.34	4.16	2.66	5.84
32 CITY AND COUNTY GOVERNMENT	3.08	.93	1.02	.45	.36	.14	1.43
33 STATE GOVERNMENT	.00	.34	.37	.33	.31	.27	2.25
34 FEDERAL GOVERNMENT	.00	4.54	4.04	3.21	2.83	3.24	3.65
35 IMPORTS	18.70	24.89	28.70	29.78	43.84	23.98	28.72
36 TOTAL PURCHASES	100.00	100.00	100.00	100.00	100.00	100.00	100.00

Table 2. Direct requirements per dollar of gross output, Georgia, 1970 (in percent).

SELLING INDUSTRY	\[PURCHASING INDUSTRY NUMBER (SEE LEFT FOR TITLE)\] 8	9	10	11	12	13	14
1 AGRICULTURE (SIC 01, 07-9)	.00	.00	.00	.13	.00	.00	.00
2 MINING (SIC 10-4)	.00	.57	.00	.37	5.58	.09	.00
3 CONTRACT CONSTRUCTION (SIC 15-7)	.13	.67	.15	.41	.78	.33	.12
4 FOOD AND KINDRED PRODUCTS (SIC 20-1)	.00	.12	.08	1.84	.03	.00	1.49
5 TEXTILE MILL PRODUCTS (SIC 22)	3.17	.14	.05	.01	.00	5.01	1.95
6 APPAREL AND RELATED PRODUCTS (SIC 23)	.10	.09	.00	.11	.03	.34	1.01
7 LUMBER AND WOOD PRODUCTS (SIC 24)	6.51	3.75	.11	.22	.07	.35	.48
8 FURNITURE AND FIXTURES (SIC 25)	1.14	.00	.17	.00	.00	.05	.01
9 PAPER AND ALLIED PRODUCTS (SIC 26)	.84	14.36	11.39	2.17	4.87	1.30	.72
10 PRINTING AND PUBLISHING (SIC 27)	.00	.29	2.21	.04	.00	.01	.03
11 CHEMICALS AND ALLIED PRODUCTS (SIC 28)	.48	2.52	1.53	8.97	3.56	3.53	.46
12 PETROLEUM REFINING (SIC 29)	.00	.01	.00	.16	.18	.01	.00
13 RUBBER AND MISC. PLASTICS (SIC 30)	3.19	.38	.20	1.03	.03	.93	2.87
14 LEATHER AND LEATHER PRODUCTS (SIC 31)	.01	.00	.00	.00	.00	.06	.67
15 STONE, CLAY AND GLASS PROD. (SIC 32)	.14	.02	.00	.00	.00	.36	.00
16 PRIMARY METAL INDUSTRIES (SIC 33)	.45	.13	.00	.63	1.51	.15	.08
17 FABRICATED METAL PRODUCTS (SIC 34, 19)	1.85	.33	.04	.10	.01	.37	.01
18 MACHINERY, EXCEPT ELECTRICAL (SIC 35)	.16	.08	.08	1.58	.89	.13	.00
19 ELECTRICAL MACHINERY & EQUIP (SIC 36)	.01	.00	.01	.08	.02	.04	.00
20 TRANSPORTATION EQUIPMENT (SIC 37)	.21	.00	.25	.01	.01	.03	.00
21 MISCELLANEOUS MANUFACTURING (SIC 38-9)	.11	.03	.08	.01	.00	.63	1.25
22 TRANSPORTATION SERVICES (SIC 40-7)	.88	1.84	.44	.36	1.98	.80	.43
23 COMMUNICATIONS & UTILITIES (SIC 48-9)	.89	2.87	1.13	1.20	4.26	1.34	.61
24 WHOLESALE AND RETAIL TRADE (SIC 50-9)	4.45	3.71	2.13	1.71	6.35	3.42	2.82
25 FINANCE, INS., REAL ESTATE (SIC 60-7)	1.98	1.03	2.88	3.71	1.87	1.13	1.02
26 SERVICES (SIC 70-9, 80-6, 89)	1.80	1.88	2.46	1.16	2.21	2.23	1.76
27 GOVERNMENT ENTERPRISES	.13	.14	.76	3.53	.10	.12	.25
28 UNALLOCATED INDUSTRIES	.60	2.00	1.19	.13	.56	.79	.48
29 TOTAL LOCAL PURCHASES	29.23	36.98	27.34	.84	34.91	23.37	18.53
30 HOUSEHOLDS	27.19	21.83	42.68	30.51	17.97	30.10	34.23
31 CAPITAL RESIDUAL	5.33	6.79	7.31	19.48	4.28	7.24	7.33
32 CITY AND COUNTY GOVERNMEN'	.55	1.10	.58	8.73	.58	.98	.42
33 STATE GOVERNMENT	.28	.60	.52	1.05	.17	.68	.70
34 FEDERAL GOVERNMENT	3.74	4.99	4.05	.66	1.56	5.46	6.04
35 IMPORTS	33.68	27.71	17.53	6.50	40.52	32.17	32.75
36 TOTAL PURCHASES	100.00	100.00	100.00	33.06	100.00	100.00	100.00

Table 2. Direct requirements per dollar of gross output, Georgia, 1970 (in percent).

SELLING INDUSTRY	PURCHASING INDUSTRY NUMBER (SEE LEFT FOR TITLE)						
	15	16	17	18	19	20	21
1 AGRICULTURE (SIC 01, 07-9)	.00	.00	.00	.00	.00	.00	.13
2 MINING (SIC 10-4)	11.45	.12	.00	.00	.00	.00	.01
3 CONTRACT CONSTRUCTION (SIC 15-7)	.73	.37	.17	.15	.13	.19	.21
4 FOOD AND KINDRED PRODUCTS (SIC 20-1)	.01	.00	.00	.10	.00	.00	.13
5 TEXTILE MILL PRODUCTS (SIC 22)	.01	.05	.05	.05	.07	.09	.58
6 APPAREL AND RELATED PRODUCTS (SIC 23)	.76	.02	.04	.03	.02	.12	.25
7 LUMBER AND WOOD PRODUCTS (SIC 24)	.44	.22	.33	1.38	.14	.91	1.21
8 FURNITURE AND FIXTURES (SIC 25)	.13	.01	.25	.04	.08	.30	.34
9 PAPER AND ALLIED PRODUCTS (SIC 26)	.87	.09	.75	.30	.41	.14	2.25
10 PRINTING AND PUBLISHING (SIC 27)	.01	.09	.17	.01	.01	.01	.38
11 CHEMICALS AND ALLIED PRODUCTS (SIC 28)	.80	.24	.73	.88	.42	.18	1.07
12 PETROLEUM REFINING (SIC 29)	.05	.00	.01	.00	.00	.01	.01
13 RUBBER AND MISC. PLASTICS (SIC 30)	.35	.04	.29	.69	1.31	.37	2.06
14 LEATHER AND LEATHER PRODUCTS (SIC 31)	.00	.00	.00	.02	.00	.00	.14
15 STONE, CLAY AND GLASS PROD. (SIC 32)	2.88	.04	.58	.15	.25	.07	.17
16 PRIMARY METAL INDUSTRIES (SIC 33)	.21	2.07	6.85	1.74	1.86	1.56	.74
17 FABRICATED METAL PRODUCTS (SIC 34, 19)	.29	1.08	2.58	2.72	1.85	1.03	1.76
18 MACHINERY, EXCEPT ELECTRICAL (SIC 35)	.19	1.07	1.34	3.11	1.19	1.16	.44
19 ELECTRICAL MACHINERY & EQUIP (SIC 36)	.24	.36	.26	1.08	.99	.66	.55
20 TRANSPORTATION EQUIPMENT (SIC 37)	.09	1.25	1.03	2.48	4.29	1.11	1.13
21 MISCELLANEOUS MANUFACTURING (SIC 38-9)	.03	.07	.37	.40	.66	.11	1.49
22 TRANSPORTATION SERVICES (SIC 40-7)	2.87	1.37	.71	.46	.50	.47	.48
23 COMMUNICATIONS & UTILITIES (SIC 48-9)	4.06	2.23	1.01	.77	.86	.89	1.00
24 WHOLESALE AND RETAIL TRADE (SIC 50-9)	2.80	3.18	2.87	2.89	3.23	2.36	4.26
25 FINANCE, INS., REAL ESTATE (SIC 60-7)	1.48	1.04	1.41	1.33	1.35	.57	1.37
26 SERVICES (SIC 70-9, 80-6, 89)	2.67	1.49	1.63	1.52	1.67	2.34	3.05
27 GOVERNMENT ENTERPRISES	.23	.09	.09	.12	.11	.13	.21
28 UNALLOCATED INDUSTRIES	.83	2.72	.64	.71	.78	.80	.99
29 TOTAL LOCAL PURCHASES	34.46	19.25	24.17	23.14	22.19	15.57	26.40
30 HOUSEHOLDS	30.73	25.35	28.94	29.81	30.17	23.18	28.53
31 CAPITAL RESIDUAL	5.12	4.46	5.48	6.86	6.88	8.00	8.76
32 CITY AND COUNTY GOVERNMENT	.71	1.01	.78	.51	.68	.28	.89
33 STATE GOVERNMENT	.25	.44	.52	.47	.39	.83	.72
34 FEDERAL GOVERNMENT	2.75	2.85	4.33	4.45	4.97	5.78	5.85
35 IMPORTS	25.98	46.65	35.78	34.77	34.74	46.37	28.85
36 TOTAL PURCHASES	100.00	100.00	100.00	100.00	100.00	100.00	100.00

Table 2. Direct requirements per dollar of gross output, Georgia, 1970 (in percent).

SELLING INDUSTRY	22	23	24	25	26	27	28
			PURCHASING INDUSTRY NUMBER (SEE LEFT FOR TITLE)				
1 AGRICULTURE (SIC 01, 07-9)	.08	.00	.12	1.58	.03	.01	.66
2 MINING (SIC 10-4)	.00	.00	.01	.03	.00	.00	.00
3 CONTRACT CONSTRUCTION (SIC 15-7)	2.26	3.17	.29	2.56	1.49	12.00	6.00
4 FOOD AND KINDRED PRODUCTS (SIC 20-1)	.43	.00	.46	.08	.17	.00	6.25
5 TEXTILE MILL PRODUCTS (SIC 22)	.01	.02	.15	.14	.02	.03	.40
6 APPAREL AND RELATED PRODUCTS (SIC 23)	.01	.01	.11	.04	.09	.04	.03
7 LUMBER AND WOOD PRODUCTS (SIC 24)	.00	.01	.09	.03	.00	.00	.02
8 FURNITURE AND FIXTURES (SIC 25)	.00	.00	.03	.01	.00	.00	.00
9 PAPER AND ALLIED PRODUCTS (SIC 26)	.02	.08	.31	.17	.05	.16	.52
10 PRINTING AND PUBLISHING (SIC 27)	.03	.00	.07	.14	.00	.08	.00
11 CHEMICALS AND ALLIED PRODUCTS (SIC 28)	.04	.06	.25	.19	3.69	.41	8.57
12 PETROLEUM REFINING (SIC 29)	.01	.00	.01	.01	.46	.08	.13
13 RUBBER AND MISC. PLASTICS (SIC 30)	.10	.01	.09	.03	.07	.03	.08
14 LEATHER AND LEATHER PRODUCTS (SIC 31)	.00	.00	.01	.00	.00	.00	.06
15 STONE, CLAY AND GLASS PROD. (SIC 32)	.00	.00	.10	.03	.08	.00	.00
16 PRIMARY METAL INDUSTRIES (SIC 33)	.08	.02	.01	.01	.00	.00	.00
17 FABRICATED METAL PRODUCTS (SIC 34, 19)	.03	.00	.09	.02	.06	.00	.37
18 MACHINERY, EXCEPT ELECTRICAL (SIC 35)	.03	.00	.08	.06	.14	.01	.39
19 ELECTRICAL MACHINERY & EQUIP (SIC 36)	.11	.01	.06	.04	.12	.01	.09
20 TRANSPORTATION EQUIPMENT (SIC 37)	1.26	.00	.28	.05	.05	.01	.33
21 MISCELLANEOUS MANUFACTURING (SIC 38-9)	.00	.02	.09	.01	.25	.00	.59
22 TRANSPORTATION SERVICES (SIC 40-7)	3.43	.62	.37	.22	.21	2.98	10.08
23 COMMUNICATIONS & UTILITIES (SIC 48-9)	1.26	8.14	1.75	1.41	5.03	2.55	.00
24 WHOLESALE AND RETAIL TRADE (SIC 50-9)	3.28	.69	1.49	1.42	3.09	.64	4.02
25 FINANCE, INS., REAL ESTATE (SIC 60-7)	3.10	1.38	3.99	16.09	5.56	1.84	.00
26 SERVICES (SIC 70-9, 80-6, 89)	3.49	3.37	3.69	4.48	6.15	2.87	8.89
27 GOVERNMENT ENTERPRISES	1.32	6.35	1.05	1.47	1.06	.07	.00
28 UNALLOCATED INDUSTRIES	.70	.52	.73	.88	1.79	.58	.00
29 TOTAL LOCAL PURCHASES	21.08	24.48	15.77	31.19	29.66	24.39	42.27
30 HOUSEHOLDS	49.05	26.86	49.48	45.55	35.43	45.05	.00
31 CAPITAL RESIDUAL	6.72	20.67	7.85	11.89	12.92	19.72	.00
32 CITY AND COUNTY GOVERNMENT	.61	3.40	1.31	2.51	2.48	.00	.00
33 STATE GOVERNMENT	1.07	.67	12.95	1.74	1.15	.00	.00
34 FEDERAL GOVERNMENT	3.25	9.20	6.21	1.89	6.49	.00	.00
35 IMPORTS	18.23	14.71	6.44	5.23	11.88	10.84	57.73
36 TOTAL PURCHASES	100.00	100.00	100.00	100.00	100.00	100.00	100.00

Table 2. Direct requirements per dollar of gross output, Georgia, 1970 (in percent).

	TOTAL LOCAL SALES	PERSONAL CONSUMPTION EXPENDITURES	GROSS PRIVATE INVESTMENT	LOCAL GOVERNMENT	STATE GOVERNMENT	FEDERAL GOVERNMENT (DEFENSE)	FEDERAL GOVERNMENT (OTHER)
1 AGRICULTURE (SIC 01, 07-9)	2.24	.62	.00	.06	.05	.02	3.48
2 MINING (SIC 10-4)	.25	.00	.00	.00	.00	.21	.00
3 CONTRACT CONSTRUCTION (SIC 15-7)	1.02	.00	49.00	20.89	19.83	2.46	2.44
4 FOOD AND KINDRED PRODUCTS (SIC 20-1)	.98	4.99	.00	.48	.37	.14	.11
5 TEXTILE MILL PRODUCTS (SIC 22)	2.19	.25	.04	.01	.01	.03	.00
6 APPAREL AND RELATED PRODUCTS (SIC 23)	.17	.69	.00	.04	.03	.08	.02
7 LUMBER AND WOOD PRODUCTS (SIC 24)	.73	.02	.00	.00	.00	.01	.00
8 FURNITURE AND FIXTURES (SIC 25)	.06	.29	1.15	.17	.10	.02	.02
9 PAPER AND ALLIED PRODUCTS (SIC 26)	1.02	.02	.00	.08	.06	.02	.02
10 PRINTING AND PUBLISHING (SIC 27)	.58	.27	.00	.26	.14	.15	.00
11 CHEMICALS AND ALLIED PRODUCTS (SIC 28)	.72	.34	.00	.32	.23	.68	.07
12 PETROLEUM REFINING (SIC 29)	.06	.08	.00	.06	.00	.45	.03
13 RUBBER AND MISC. PLASTICS (SIC 30)	.28	.11	.01	.01	.05	.12	.01
14 LEATHER AND LEATHER PRODUCTS (SIC 31)	.01	.01	.00	.01	.01	.00	.00
15 STONE, CLAY AND GLASS PROD. (SIC 32)	.60	.00	.00	.00	.00	.03	.00
16 PRIMARY METAL INDUSTRIES (SIC 33)	.32	.03	.00	.00	.00	.13	.00
17 FABRICATED METAL PRODUCTS (SIC 34, 19)	.62	.02	.49	.01	.01	.35	.02
18 MACHINERY, EXCEPT ELECTRICAL (SIC 35)	.25	.04	2.89	.16	.09	.49	.08
19 ELECTRICAL MACHINERY & EQUIP (SIC 36)	.16	.81	.49	.02	.02	.53	.07
20 TRANSPORTATION EQUIPMENT (SIC 37)	.29	.07	1.71	.06	.04	43.96	.20
21 MISCELLANEOUS MANUFACTURING (SIC 38-9)	.12	.27	.27	.03	.02	.05	.02
22 TRANSPORTATION SERVICES (SIC 40-7)	.91	.74	.37	.58	.36	.92	.11
23 COMMUNICATIONS & UTILITIES (SIC 48-9)	1.93	2.42	.67	1.87	1.13	.44	.04
24 WHOLESALE AND RETAIL TRADE (SIC 50-9)	3.14	16.16	5.84	.80	.56	.48	.10
25 FINANCE, INS., REAL ESTATE (SIC 60-7)	3.88	11.61	.64	2.11	1.31	.07	6.91
26 SERVICES (SIC 70-9, 80-6, 89)	3.30	11.82	.00	2.71	2.41	2.51	1.00
27 GOVERNMENT ENTERPRISES	.78	.27	.00	.23	.19	.07	.17
28 UNALLOCATED INDUSTRIES	.80	.00	.00	.52	.40	.06	.14
29 TOTAL LOCAL PURCHASES	27.42	51.68	63.58	31.48	27.42	54.57	15.08
30 HOUSEHOLDS	33.35	.63	.00	57.52	35.74	45.43	65.49
31 CAPITAL RESIDUAL	8.43	5.49	.00	.00	.00	.00	.00
32 CITY AND COUNTY GOVERNMENT	1.34	2.38	.00	.00	28.29	.00	2.02
33 STATE GOVERNMENT	2.40	2.15	.00	1.51	.00	.00	.00
34 FEDERAL GOVERNMENT	4.28	13.85	.00	.00	1.21	.00	17.41
35 IMPORTS	22.78	23.81	36.42	9.48	7.35	.00	.00
36 TOTAL PURCHASES	100.00	100.00	100.00	100.00	100.00	100.00	100.00

FINAL DEMAND

Table 2. Direct requirements per dollar of gross output, Georgia, 1970 (in percent).

| | FINAL DEMAND | | |
	NET EXPORTS	TOTAL FINAL DEMAND	TOTAL SALES
1 AGRICULTURE (SIC 01, 07-9)	3.50	1.71	1.96
2 MINING (SIC 10-4)	.73	.27	.26
3 CONTRACT CONSTRUCTION (SIC 15-7)	2.50	5.46	3.35
4 FOOD AND KINDRED PRODUCTS (SIC 20-1)	7.96	4.89	3.03
5 TEXTILE MILL PRODUCTS (SIC 22)	20.33	7.36	4.90
6 APPAREL AND RELATED PRODUCTS (SIC 23)	5.85	2.37	1.32
7 LUMBER AND WOOD PRODUCTS (SIC 24)	1.57	.57	.65
8 FURNITURE AND FIXTURES (SIC 25)	.95	.53	.31
9 PAPER AND ALLIED PRODUCTS (SIC 26)	5.98	2.15	1.61
10 PRINTING AND PUBLISHING (SIC 27)	.58	.34	.45
11 CHEMICALS AND ALLIED PRODUCTS (SIC 28)	2.70	1.16	.95
12 PETROLEUM REFINING (SIC 29)	.14	.07	.07
13 RUBBER AND MISC. PLASTICS (SIC 30)	.91	.37	.33
14 LEATHER AND LEATHER PRODUCTS (SIC 31)	.41	.19	.10
15 STONE, CLAY AND GLASS PROD. (SIC 32)	1.21	.44	.52
16 PRIMARY METAL INDUSTRIES (SIC 33)	1.20	.43	.38
17 FABRICATED METAL PRODUCTS (SIC 34, 19)	1.97	.76	.70
18 MACHINERY, EXCEPT ELECTRICAL (SIC 35)	1.80	.85	.56
19 ELECTRICAL MACHINERY & EQUIP (SIC 36)	1.95	.77	.48
20 TRANSPORTATION EQUIPMENT (SIC 37)	9.70	6.05	3.31
21 MISCELLANEOUS MANUFACTURING (SIC 38-9)	1.11	.44	.29
22 TRANSPORTATION SERVICES (SIC 40-7)	5.98	2.54	1.76
23 COMMUNICATIONS & UTILITIES (SIC 48-9)	.95	1.49	1.70
24 WHOLESALE AND RETAIL TRADE (SIC 50-9)	6.89	9.36	6.40
25 FINANCE, INS., REAL ESTATE (SIC 60-7)	5.59	7.24	5.64
26 SERVICES (SIC 70-9, 80-6, 89)	6.92	7.60	5.55
27 GOVERNMENT ENTERPRISES	.63	.37	.56
28 UNALLOCATED INDUSTRIES	.00	.05	.41
29 TOTAL LOCAL PURCHASES	100.00	65.84	47.57
30 HOUSEHOLDS	.00	9.93	21.07
31 CAPITAL RESIDUAL	.00	2.21	5.17
32 CITY AND COUNTY GOVERNMENT	.00	2.21	1.79
33 STATE GOVERNMENT	.00	1.96	2.17
34 FEDERAL GOVERNMENT	.00	5.61	4.98
35 IMPORTS	.00	12.24	17.26
36 TOTAL PURCHASES	100.00	100.00	100.00

Table 3. Total requirements (direct and indirect) per dollar of delivery to final demand, Georgia, 1970.

(Each entry approximates the total output required from the sector at the beginning of each row for every dollar of delivery to final demand by the sector numbered at the head of each column.)

SELLING INDUSTRY	PURCHASING INDUSTRY NUMBER (SEE LEFT FOR TITLE)						
	1	2	3	4	5	6	7
1 AGRICULTURE (SIC 01, 07-9)	1.1611	.0016	.0064	.2749	.0041	.0053	.0836
2 MINING (SIC 10-4)	.0019	1.0157	.0178	.0027	.0003	.0002	.0004
3 CONTRACT CONSTRUCTION (SIC 15-7)	.0125	.0134	1.0050	.0080	.0058	.0032	.0076
4 FOOD AND KINDRED PRODUCTS (SIC 20-1)	.0906	.0014	.0021	1.1030	.0015	.0012	.0073
5 TEXTILE MILL PRODUCTS (SIC 22)	.0027	.0011	.0016	.0025	1.1678	.2508	.0010
6 APPAREL AND RELATED PRODUCTS (SIC 23)	.0007	.0003	.0010	.0013	.0017	1.0321	.0007
7 LUMBER AND WOOD PRODUCTS (SIC 24)	.0023	.0014	.0390	.0024	.0009	.0012	1.1809
8 FURNITURE AND FIXTURES (SIC 25)	.0001	.0001	.0028	.0001	.0002	.0003	.0014
9 PAPER AND ALLIED PRODUCTS (SIC 26)	.0056	.0019	.0062	.0259	.0114	.0066	.0047
10 PRINTING AND PUBLISHING (SIC 27)	.0018	.0025	.0035	.0041	.0014	.0012	.0016
11 CHEMICALS AND ALLIED PRODUCTS (SIC 28)	.0123	.0067	.0042	.0102	.0170	.0046	.0047
12 PETROLEUM REFINING (SIC 29)	.0001	.0016	.0066	.0001	.0001	.0000	.0001
13 RUBBER AND MISC. PLASTICS (SIC 30)	.0012	.0127	.0052	.0042	.0056	.0054	.0008
14 LEATHER AND LEATHER PRODUCTS (SIC 31)	.0001	.0001	.0000	.0000	.0000	.0006	.0001
15 STONE, CLAY AND GLASS PROD. (SIC 32)	.0026	.0207	.0608	.0164	.0007	.0004	.0011
16 PRIMARY METAL INDUSTRIES (SIC 33)	.0043	.0033	.0075	.0011	.0009	.0003	.0012
17 FABRICATED METAL PRODUCTS (SIC 34, 19)	.0015	.0021	.0449	.0128	.0012	.0007	.0044
18 MACHINERY, EXCEPT ELECTRICAL (SIC 35)	.0005	.0101	.0047	.0011	.0012	.0004	.0011
19 ELECTRICAL MACHINERY & EQUIP (SIC 36)	.0005	.0011	.0067	.0004	.0002	.0001	.0003
20 TRANSPORTATION EQUIPMENT (SIC 37)	.0003	.0014	.0018	.0007	.0004	.0003	.0006
21 MISCELLANEOUS MANUFACTURING (SIC 38-9)	.0003	.0004	.0013	.0004	.0006	.0057	.0005
22 TRANSPORTATION SERVICES (SIC 40-7)	.0112	.0103	.0224	.0204	.0104	.0057	.0166
23 COMMUNICATIONS & UTILITIES (SIC 48-9)	.0110	.0460	.0182	.0166	.0153	.0102	.0162
24 WHOLESALE AND RETAIL TRADE (SIC 50-7)	.0439	.0431	.1014	.0536	.0590	.0447	.0329
25 FINANCE, INS., REAL ESTATE (SIC 60-7)	.0397	.0542	.0268	.0269	.0159	.0176	.0230
26 SERVICES (SIC 70-9, 80-6, 89)	.0275	.0397	.0655	.0383	.0199	.0162	.0251
27 GOVERNMENT ENTERPRISES	.0025	.0072	.0048	.0040	.0036	.0037	.0032
28 UNALLOCATED INDUSTRIES	.0041	.0102	.0093	.0064	.0056	.0056	.0053
29 TOTAL LOCAL PURCHASES	1.4427	1.3102	1.4787	1.6387	1.3515	1.4244	1.4264

Table 3. Total requirements (direct and indirect) per dollar of delivery to final demand, Georgia, 1970.

(Each entry approximates the total output required from the sector at the beginning of each row for every dollar of delivery to final demand by the sector numbered at the head of each column.)

SELLING INDUSTRY	|	PURCHASING INDUSTRY NUMBER (SEE LEFT FOR TITLE)						
	|	8	9	10	11	12	13	14
1 AGRICULTURE (SIC 01, 07-9)	|	.0067	.0056	.0023	.0085	.0019	.0017	.0054
2 MINING (SIC 10-4)	|	.0005	.0073	.0011	.0055	.0594	.0018	.0003
3 CONTRACT CONSTRUCTION (SIC 15-7)	|	.0049	.0124	.0067	.0085	.0141	.0065	.0037
4 FOOD AND KINDRED PRODUCTS (SIC 20-1)	|	.0017	.0049	.0031	.0239	.0027	.0021	.0176
5 TEXTILE MILL PRODUCTS (SIC 22)	|	.0400	.0029	.0013	.0016	.0007	.0603	.0275
6 APPAREL AND RELATED PRODUCTS (SIC 23)	|	.0014	.0013	.0003	.0016	.0007	.0038	.0108
7 LUMBER AND WOOD PRODUCTS (SIC 24)	|	.0789	.0525	.0080	.0049	.0045	.0057	.0067
8 FURNITURE AND FIXTURES (SIC 25)	|	1.0117	.0002	.0018	.0001	.0001	.0006	.0002
9 PAPER AND ALLIED PRODUCTS (SIC 26)	|	.0122	1.1705	.1377	.0300	.0594	.0179	.0107
10 PRINTING AND PUBLISHING (SIC 27)	|	.0021	.0072	.0261	.0037	.0027	.0024	.0021
11 CHEMICALS AND ALLIED PRODUCTS (SIC 28)	|	.0084	.0337	.0218	1.1010	.0423	.0390	.0075
12 PETROLEUM REFINING (SIC 29)	|	.0001	.0003	.0001	.0018	1.0021	.0002	.0001
13 RUBBER AND MISC. PLASTICS (SIC 30)	|	.0332	.0052	.0031	.0120	.0020	1.0106	.0299
14 LEATHER AND LEATHER PRODUCTS (SIC 31)	|	.0002	.0001	.0000	.0001	.0000	.0006	1.0068
15 STONE, CLAY AND GLASS PROD. (SIC 32)	|	.0022	.0016	.0007	.0083	.0181	.0046	.0008
16 PRIMARY METAL INDUSTRIES (SIC 33)	|	.0064	.0024	.0006	.0028	.0014	.0023	.0004
17 FABRICATED METAL PRODUCTS (SIC 34, 19)	|	.0203	.0056	.0018	.0190	.0110	.0052	.0019
18 MACHINERY, EXCEPT ELECTRICAL (SIC 35)	|	.0024	.0015	.0013	.0016	.0014	.0018	.0004
19 ELECTRICAL MACHINERY & EQUIP (SIC 36)	|	.0004	.0003	.0003	.0004	.0004	.0007	.0002
20 TRANSPORTATION EQUIPMENT (SIC 37)	|	.0030	.0009	.0031	.0009	.0009	.0009	.0005
21 MISCELLANEOUS MANUFACTURING (SIC 38-9)	|	.0017	.0009	.0012	.0045	.0006	.0069	.0132
22 TRANSPORTATION SERVICES (SIC 40-7)	|	.0131	.0274	.0105	.0175	.0258	.0118	.0069
23 COMMUNICATIONS & UTILITIES (SIC 48-9)	|	.0162	.0426	.0216	.0275	.0573	.0206	.0110
24 WHOLESALE AND RETAIL TRADE (SIC 50-9)	|	.0555	.0530	.0328	.0500	.0767	.0443	.0359
25 FINANCE, INS., REAL ESTATE (SIC 60-7)	|	.0324	.0235	.0428	.0245	.0357	.0209	.0181
26 SERVICES (SIC 70-9, 80-6, 89)	|	.0294	.0357	.0378	.0508	.0388	.0328	.0256
27 GOVERNMENT ENTERPRISES	|	.0041	.0062	.0110	.0051	.0071	.0041	.0045
28 UNALLOCATED INDUSTRIES	|	.0089	.0260	.0169	.0123	.0101	.0105	.0068
29 TOTAL LOCAL PURCHASES	|	1.3982	1.5516	1.3960	1.4286	1.4781	1.3205	1.2553

Table 3. Total requirements (direct and indirect) per dollar of delivery to final demand, Georgia, 1970.

(Each entry approximates the total output required from the sector at the beginning of each row for every dollar of delivery to final demand by the sector numbered at the head of each column.)

	SELLING INDUSTRY	PURCHASING INDUSTRY NUMBER (SEE LEFT FOR TITLE)						
		15	16	17	18	19	20	21
1	AGRICULTURE (SIC 01, 07-9)	.0018	.0015	.0013	.0024	.0011	.0015	.0042
2	MINING (SIC 10-4)	.1201	.0015	.0011	.0005	.0005	.0003	.0008
3	CONTRACT CONSTRUCTION (SIC 15-7)	.0139	.0067	.0046	.0041	.0038	.0040	.0056
4	FOOD AND KINDRED PRODUCTS (SIC 20-1)	.0017	.0026	.0014	.0025	.0013	.0011	.0034
5	TEXTILE MILL PRODUCTS (SIC 22)	.0028	.0011	.0013	.0015	.0021	.0020	.0094
6	APPAREL AND RELATED PRODUCTS (SIC 23)	.0083	.0004	.0007	.0006	.0006	.0014	.0029
7	LUMBER AND WOOD PRODUCTS (SIC 24)	.0068	.0036	.0056	.0179	.0032	.0117	.0168
8	FURNITURE AND FIXTURES (SIC 25)	.0015	.0002	.0027	.0007	.0010	.0031	.0036
9	PAPER AND ALLIED PRODUCTS (SIC 26)	.0120	.0024	.0106	.0053	.0065	.0027	.0293
10	PRINTING AND PUBLISHING (SIC 27)	.0029	.0037	.0038	.0021	.0022	.0022	.0069
11	CHEMICALS AND ALLIED PRODUCTS (SIC 28)	.0110	.0036	.0097	.0114	.0064	.0030	.0147
12	PETROLEUM REFINING (SIC 29)	.0008	.0001	.0001	.0001	.0001	.0002	.0001
13	RUBBER AND MISC. PLASTICS (SIC 30)	.0057	.0009	.0037	.0080	.0142	.0043	.0220
14	LEATHER AND LEATHER PRODUCTS (SIC 31)	.0001	.0001	.0001	.0003	.0001	.0012	.0015
15	STONE, CLAY AND GLASS PROD. (SIC 32)	1.0331	.0011	.0067	.0023	.0032	.0175	.0026
16	PRIMARY METAL INDUSTRIES (SIC 33)	.0032	1.0229	.0727	.0213	.0218	.0118	.0098
17	FABRICATED METAL PRODUCTS (SIC 34, 19)	.0044	.0125	1.0286	.0303	.0209	.0127	.0199
18	MACHINERY, EXCEPT ELECTRICAL (SIC 35)	.0036	.0120	.0154	1.0334	.0137	.0071	.0055
19	ELECTRICAL MACHINERY & EQUIP (SIC 36)	.0029	.0041	.0034	.0118	1.0108	.0125	.0060
20	TRANSPORTATION EQUIPMENT (SIC 37)	.0020	.0140	.0126	.0273	.0451	1.0115	.0128
21	MISCELLANEOUS MANUFACTURING (SIC 38-9)	.0007	.0012	.0042	.0047	.0072	.0015	1.0158
22	TRANSPORTATION SERVICES (SIC 40-7)	.0347	.0187	.0111	.0079	.0082	.0073	.0090
23	COMMUNICATIONS & UTILITIES (SIC 48-9)	.0559	.0284	.0173	.0134	.0144	.0137	.0179
24	WHOLESALE AND RETAIL TRADE (SIC 50-9)	.0412	.0387	.0375	.0371	.0400	.0292	.0527
25	FINANCE, INS., REAL ESTATE (SIC 60-7)	.0321	.0186	.0238	.0225	.0261	.0123	.0252
26	SERVICES (SIC 70-9, 80-6, 89)	.0430	.0251	.0260	.0245	.0225	.0305	.0426
27	GOVERNMENT ENTERPRISES	.0081	.0041	.0034	.0053	.0034	.0032	.0050
28	UNALLOCATED INDUSTRIES	.0122	.0296	.0105	.0099	.0106	.0101	.0134
29	TOTAL LOCAL PURCHASES	1.4665	1.2593	1.3200	1.3071	1.2910	1.2080	1.3595

Table 3. Total requirements (direct and indirect) per dollar of delivery to final demand, Georgia, 1970.

(Each entry approximates the total output required from the sector at the beginning of each row for every dollar of delivery to final demand by the sector numbered at the head of each column.)

SELLING INDUSTRY	PURCHASING INDUSTRY NUMBER (SEE LEFT FOR TITLE)						
	22	23	24	25	26	27	28
1 AGRICULTURE (SIC 01, 07-9)	.0036	.0010	.0041	.0230	.0032	.0018	.0259
2 MINING (SIC 10-4)	.0006	.0009	.0004	.0012	.0007	.0023	.0005
3 CONTRACT CONSTRUCTION (SIC 15-7)	.0282	.0450	.0077	.0354	.0227	.1249	.0066
4 FOOD AND KINDRED PRODUCTS (SIC 20-1)	.0062	.0009	.0063	.0041	.0042	.0012	.0712
5 TEXTILE MILL PRODUCTS (SIC 22)	.0006	.0006	.0024	.0023	.0010	.0008	.0055
6 APPAREL AND RELATED PRODUCTS (SIC 23)	.0003	.0002	.0013	.0006	.0012	.0006	.0007
7 LUMBER AND WOOD PRODUCTS (SIC 24)	.0014	.0020	.0017	.0021	.0015	.0050	.0020
8 FURNITURE AND FIXTURES (SIC 25)	.0001	.0001	.0003	.0002	.0002	.0004	.0003
9 PAPER AND ALLIED PRODUCTS (SIC 26)	.0014	.0020	.0047	.0038	.0074	.0004	.0209
10 PRINTING AND PUBLISHING (SIC 27)	.0031	.0026	.0034	.0053	.0428	.0034	.0926
11 CHEMICALS AND ALLIED PRODUCTS (SIC 28)	.0014	.0018	.0037	.0037	.0072	.0060	.0054
12 PETROLEUM REFINING (SIC 29)	.0003	.0003	.0002	.0004	.0002	.0008	.0001
13 RUBBER AND MISC. PLASTICS (SIC 30)	.0014	.0005	.0012	.0008	.0013	.0011	.0019
14 LEATHER AND LEATHER PRODUCTS (SIC 31)	.0000	.0000	.0001	.0000	.0001	.0000	.0006
15 STONE, CLAY AND GLASS PROD. (SIC 32)	.0019	.0028	.0017	.0027	.0024	.0077	.0017
16 PRIMARY METAL INDUSTRIES (SIC 33)	.0014	.0006	.0005	.0006	.0006	.0011	.0090
17 FABRICATED METAL PRODUCTS (SIC 34, 19)	.0019	.0020	.0017	.0021	.0021	.0055	.0057
18 MACHINERY, EXCEPT ELECTRICAL (SIC 35)	.0008	.0004	.0012	.0012	.0020	.0008	.0048
19 ELECTRICAL MACHINERY & EQUIP (SIC 36)	.0016	.0005	.0008	.0009	.0016	.0010	.0014
20 TRANSPORTATION EQUIPMENT (SIC 37)	.0135	.0004	.0031	.0009	.0011	.0008	.0057
21 MISCELLANEOUS MANUFACTURING (SIC 38-9)	.0003	.0005	.0011	.0005	.0031	.0004	.0066
22 TRANSPORTATION SERVICES (SIC 40-7)	1.0384	.0113	.0063	.0062	.0069	.0350	.1083
23 COMMUNICATIONS, & UTILITIES (SIC 48-9)	.0195	1.0946	.0239	.0240	.0630	.0334	.0124
24 WHOLESALE AND RETAIL TRADE (SIC 50-9)	.0411	.0154	1.0202	.0253	.0411	.0227	.0569
25 FINANCE, INS., REAL ESTATE (SIC 60-7)	.0451	.0247	.0532	1.1999	.0775	.0302	.0200
26 SERVICES (SIC 70-9, 80-6, 89)	.0469	.0472	.0463	.0642	1.0792	.0439	.1095
27 GOVERNMENT ENTERPRISES	.0166	.0708	.0137	.0203	.0176	1.0046	.0052
28 UNALLOCATED INDUSTRIES	.0095	.0078	.0094	.0127	.0218	.0085	1.0058
29 TOTAL LOCAL PURCHASES	1.2872	1.3368	1.2206	1.4444	1.4135	1.3474	1.5869

Table 4. Total requirements (direct, indirect, and induced) per dollar of delivery to final demand, Georgia, 1970.

(Each entry approximates the total output required from the sector at the beginning of each row for every dollar of delivery to final demand by the sector numbered at the head of each column.)

SELLING INDUSTRY	1	2	3	4	5	6	7
1 AGRICULTURE (SIC 01, 07-9)	1.1788	.0152	.0214	.2884	.0154	.0228	.0981
2 MINING (SIC 10-4)	.0022	1.0160	.0182	.0030	.0006	.0005	.0007
3 CONTRACT CONSTRUCTION (SIC 15-7)	.0198	.0190	1.0113	.0136	.0105	.0104	.0136
4 FOOD AND KINDRED PRODUCTS (SIC 20-1)	.1317	.0330	.0369	1.1344	.0279	.0418	.0409
5 TEXTILE MILL PRODUCTS (SIC 22)	.0068	.0043	.0051	.0056	1.1705	.2549	.0043
6 APPAREL AND RELATED PRODUCTS (SIC 23)	.0061	.0045	.0056	.0055	.0052	1.0375	.0051
7 LUMBER AND WOOD PRODUCTS (SIC 24)	.0035	.0022	.0399	.0033	.0016	.0023	1.1818
8 FURNITURE AND FIXTURES (SIC 25)	.0023	.0018	.0046	.0018	.0016	.0024	.0032
9 PAPER AND ALLIED PRODUCTS (SIC 26)	.0087	.0043	.0088	.0283	.0134	.0097	.0073
10 PRINTING AND PUBLISHING (SIC 27)	.0084	.0077	.0092	.0092	.0057	.0078	.0070
11 CHEMICALS AND ALLIED PRODUCTS (SIC 28)	.0170	.0103	.0121	.0138	.0200	.0092	.0085
12 PETROLEUM REFINING (SIC 29)	.0003	.0017	.0067	.0002	.0001	.0001	.0002
13 RUBBER AND MISC. PLASTICS (SIC 30)	.0024	.0137	.0063	.0052	.0064	.0067	.0019
14 LEATHER AND LEATHER PRODUCTS (SIC 31)	.0009	.0007	.0007	.0007	.0006	.0014	.0008
15 STONE, CLAY AND GLASS PROD. (SIC 32)	.0040	.0218	.0620	.0175	.0016	.0018	.0023
16 PRIMARY METAL INDUSTRIES (SIC 33)	.0009	.0036	.0078	.0014	.0005	.0007	.0015
17 FABRICATED METAL PRODUCTS (SIC 34, 19)	.0058	.0032	.0432	.0139	.0018	.0021	.0056
18 MACHINERY, EXCEPT ELECTRICAL (SIC 35)	.0022	.0106	.0053	.0017	.0016	.0011	.0017
19 ELECTRICAL MACHINERY & EQUIP (SIC 36)	.0010	.0016	.0072	.0008	.0006	.0011	.0008
20 TRANSPORTATION EQUIPMENT (SIC 37)	.0070	.0064	.0072	.0057	.0046	.0068	.0059
21 MISCELLANEOUS MANUFACTURING (SIC 38-9)	.0013	.0012	.0021	.0012	.0013	.0067	.0014
22 TRANSPORTATION SERVICES (SIC 40-7)	.0197	.0168	.0296	.0269	.0159	.0141	.0236
23 COMMUNICATIONS & UTILITIES (SIC 48-9)	.0410	.0691	.0437	.0396	.0347	.0399	.0408
24 WHOLESALE AND RETAIL TRADE (SIC 50-9)	.1703	.1404	.2084	.1503	.1403	.1696	.1362
25 FINANCE, INS., REAL ESTATE (SIC 60-7)	.1539	.1920	.1234	.1142	.0893	.1305	.1163
26 SERVICES (SIC 70-9, 80-6, 89)	.1323	.1202	.1541	.1183	.0872	.1197	.1106
27 GOVERNMENT ENTERPRISES	.0108	.0136	.0118	.0104	.0089	.0118	.0099
28 UNALLOCATED INDUSTRIES	.0087	.0137	.0132	.0099	.0085	.0102	.0090
29 HOUSEHOLDS	.7121	.5476	.6026	.5442	.4579	.7037	.5818
30 TOTAL LOCAL PURCHASES	2.6598	2.2462	2.5086	2.5689	2.1341	2.6272	2.4208

PURCHASING INDUSTRY NUMBER (SEE LEFT FOR TITLE)

Table 4. Total requirements (direct, indirect, and induced) per dollar of delivery to final demand, Georgia, 1970.

(Each entry approximates the total output required from the sector at the beginning of each row for every dollar of delivery to final demand by the sector numbered at the head of each column.)

PURCHASING INDUSTRY NUMBER (SEE LEFT FOR TITLE)

SELLING INDUSTRY	8	9	10	11	12	13	14
1 AGRICULTURE (SIC 01, 07-9)	.0206	.0185	.0212	.0197	.0135	.0155	.0201
2 MINING (SIC 10-4)	.0008	.0076	.0015	.0058	.0596	.0021	.0006
3 CONTRACT CONSTRUCTION (SIC 15-7)	.0106	.0177	.0145	.0131	.0189	.0122	.0097
4 FOOD AND KINDRED PRODUCTS (SIC 20-1)	.0340	.0347	.0471	.0499	.0297	.0341	.0517
5 TEXTILE MILL PRODUCTS (SIC 22)	.0432	.0059	.0057	.0042	.0034	.0635	.0310
6 APPAREL AND RELATED PRODUCTS (SIC 23)	.0057	.0052	.0061	.0050	.0043	.0081	.0153
7 LUMBER AND WOOD PRODUCTS (SIC 24)	.0798	.0533	.0092	.0056	.0052	.0065	.0077
8 FURNITURE AND FIXTURES (SIC 25)	1.0134	.0018	.0042	.0015	.0016	.0023	.0020
9 PAPER AND ALLIED PRODUCTS (SIC 26)	.0147	1.1728	.1410	.0320	.0614	.0204	.0132
10 PRINTING AND PUBLISHING (SIC 27)	.0074	.0121	1.0332	.0079	.0071	.0076	.0076
11 CHEMICALS AND ALLIED PRODUCTS (SIC 28)	.0121	.0370	.0267	1.1040	.0453	.0427	.0114
12 PETROLEUM REFINING (SIC 29)	.0002	.0004	.0002	.0019	1.0021	.0003	.0001
13 RUBBER AND MISC. PLASTICS (SIC 30)	.0342	.0062	.0045	.0129	.0029	1.0116	.0310
14 LEATHER AND LEATHER PRODUCTS (SIC 31)	.0008	.0007	.0009	.0006	.0006	.0013	1.0075
15 STONE, CLAY AND GLASS PROD. (SIC 32)	.0033	.0026	.0023	.0092	.0191	.0057	.0019
16 PRIMARY METAL INDUSTRIES (SIC 33)	.0067	.0027	.0010	.0030	.0017	.0026	.0007
17 FABRICATED METAL PRODUCTS (SIC 34, 19)	.0215	.0067	.0034	.0199	.0120	.0064	.0031
18 MACHINERY, EXCEPT ELECTRICAL (SIC 35)	.0029	.0020	.0020	.0021	.0018	.0023	.0010
19 ELECTRICAL MACHINERY & EQUIP (SIC 36)	.0009	.0008	.0010	.0008	.0009	.0011	.0008
20 TRANSPORTATION EQUIPMENT (SIC 37)	.0081	.0056	.0100	.0050	.0052	.0060	.0059
21 MISCELLANEOUS MANUFACTURING (SIC 38-9)	.0025	.0017	.0023	.0051	.0012	.0077	.0141
22 TRANSPORTATION SERVICES (SIC 40-7)	.0198	.0336	.0196	.0229	.0314	.0184	.0140
23 COMMUNICATIONS & UTILITIES (SIC 48-9)	.0398	.0644	.0538	.0465	.0771	.0441	.0360
24 WHOLESALE AND RETAIL TRADE (SIC 50-9)	.1547	.1448	.1680	.1298	.1597	.1430	.1409
25 FINANCE, INS., REAL ESTATE (SIC 60-7)	.1219	.1064	.1649	.0965	.1106	.1100	.1129
26 SERVICES (SIC 70-9, 80-6, 89)	.1115	.1117	.1498	.1169	.1076	.1145	.1126
27 GOVERNMENT ENTERPRISES	.0106	.0122	.0198	.0103	.0125	.0105	.0113
28 UNALLOCATED INDUSTRIES	.0126	.0293	.0219	.0152	.0131	.0141	.0107
29 HOUSEHOLDS	.5584	.5172	.7613	.4495	.4672	.5557	.5913
30 TOTAL LOCAL PURCHASES	2.3526	2.4156	2.6971	2.1969	2.2766	2.2703	2.2661

Table 4. Total requirements (direct, indirect, and induced) per dollar of delivery to final demand, Georgia, 1970.

(Each entry approximates the total output required from the sector at the beginning of each row for every dollar of delivery to final demand by the sector numbered at the head of each column.)

SELLING INDUSTRY	PURCHASING INDUSTRY NUMBER (SEE LEFT FOR TITLE)						
	15	16	17	18	19	20	21
1 AGRICULTURE (SIC 01, 07-9)	.0177	.0131	.0048	.0161	.0147	.0118	.0180
2 MINING (SIC 10-4)	.1205	.0018	.0014	.0007	.0008	.0005	.0011
3 CONTRACT CONSTRUCTION (SIC 15-7)	.0205	.0115	.0102	.0097	.0095	.0083	.0113
4 FOOD AND KINDRED PRODUCTS (SIC 20-1)	.0388	.0294	.0327	.0342	.0330	.0252	.0357
5 TEXTILE MILL PRODUCTS (SIC 22)	.0065	.0038	.0045	.0047	.0053	.0044	.0126
6 APPAREL AND RELATED PRODUCTS (SIC 23)	.0132	.0039	.0048	.0048	.0047	.0046	.0072
7 LUMBER AND WOOD PRODUCTS (SIC 24)	.0078	.0043	.0065	.0188	.0041	.0124	.0177
8 FURNITURE AND FIXTURES (SIC 25)	.0035	.0016	.0044	.0024	.0027	.0044	.0054
9 PAPER AND ALLIED PRODUCTS (SIC 26)	.0148	.0045	.0129	.0077	.0089	.0045	.0317
10 PRINTING AND PUBLISHING (SIC 27)	.0089	.0080	.0089	.0072	.0073	.0061	.0121
11 CHEMICALS AND ALLIED PRODUCTS (SIC 28)	.0152	.0066	.0132	.0150	.0100	.0057	.0184
12 PETROLEUM REFINING (SIC 29)	.0009	.0001	.0047	.0001	.0001	.0002	.0002
13 RUBBER AND MISC. PLASTICS (SIC 30)	.0068	.0017	.0047	.0090	.0152	.0051	.0230
14 LEATHER AND LEATHER PRODUCTS (SIC 31)	.0008	.0006	.0007	.0009	.0007	.0005	.0022
15 STONE, CLAY AND GLASS PROD. (SIC 32)	1.0344	.0020	.0078	.0034	.0043	.0020	.0037
16 PRIMARY METAL INDUSTRIES (SIC 33)	.0036	1.0231	.0729	.0216	.0221	.0177	.0100
17 FABRICATED METAL PRODUCTS (SIC 34, 19)	.0058	.0134	1.0298	.0314	.0221	.0127	.0210
18 MACHINERY, EXCEPT ELECTRICAL (SIC 35)	.0042	.0124	.0160	1.0339	.0143	.0131	.0060
19 ELECTRICAL MACHINERY & EQUIP (SIC 36)	.0035	.0046	.0039	.0123	1.0113	.0075	.0065
20 TRANSPORTATION EQUIPMENT (SIC 37)	.0078	.0182	.0175	.0323	.0501	1.0162	.0179
21 MISCELLANEOUS MANUFACTURING (SIC 38-9)	.0016	.0019	.0050	.0055	.0080	.0021	1.0166
22 TRANSPORTATION SERVICES (SIC 40-7)	.0424	.0243	.0176	.0145	.0147	.0123	.0157
23 COMMUNICATIONS & UTILITIES (SIC 48-9)	.0830	.0481	.0402	.0366	.0376	.0313	.0415
24 WHOLESALE AND RETAIL TRADE (SIC 50-9)	.1551	.1213	.1339	.1348	.1374	.1031	.1519
25 FINANCE, INS., REAL ESTATE (SIC 60-7)	.1350	.0932	.1109	.1107	.1105	.0790	.1148
26 SERVICES (SIC 70-9, 80-6, 89)	.1373	.0936	.1058	.1054	.1068	.0917	.1247
27 GOVERNMENT ENTERPRISES	.0155	.0095	.0097	.0097	.0097	.0080	.0115
28 UNALLOCATED INDUSTRIES	.0163	.0326	.0140	.0135	.0142	.0128	.0170
29 HOUSEHOLDS	.6413	.4654	.5429	.5501	.5486	.4162	.5585
30 TOTAL LOCAL PURCHASES	2.5626	2.0548	2.2479	2.2474	2.2287	1.9194	2.3141

Table 4. Total requirements (direct, indirect, and induced) per dollar of delivery to final demand, Georgia, 1970.

(Each entry approximates the total output required from the sector at the beginning of each row for every dollar of delivery to final demand by the sector numbered at the head of each column.)

SELLING INDUSTRY	PURCHASING INDUSTRY NUMBER (SEE LEFT FOR TITLE)						
	22	23	24	25	26	27	28
1 AGRICULTURE (SIC 01, 07-9)	.0243	.0143	.0239	.0447	.0204	.0213	.0334
2 MINING (SIC 10-4)	.0010	.0011	.0009	.0016	.0010	.0027	.0006
3 CONTRACT CONSTRUCTION (SIC 15-7)	.0368	.0505	.0159	.0444	.0299	.1330	.0097
4 FOOD AND KINDRED PRODUCTS (SIC 20-1)	.0542	.0318	.0524	.0545	.0445	.0466	.0886
5 TEXTILE MILL PRODUCTS (SIC 22)	.0054	.0037	.0070	.0074	.0051	.0053	.0072
6 APPAREL AND RELATED PRODUCTS (SIC 23)	.0066	.0043	.0074	.0073	.0065	.0066	.0030
7 LUMBER AND WOOD PRODUCTS (SIC 24)	.0027	.0028	.0030	.0035	.0026	.0063	.0024
8 FURNITURE AND FIXTURES (SIC 25)	.0027	.0018	.0028	.0029	.0023	.0028	.0012
9 PAPER AND ALLIED PRODUCTS (SIC 26)	.0050	.0043	.0082	.0077	.0104	.0069	.0222
10 PRINTING AND PUBLISHING (SIC 27)	.0109	.0076	.0108	.0134	.0493	.0107	.0955
11 CHEMICALS AND ALLIED PRODUCTS (SIC 28)	.0069	.0053	.0089	.0095	.0117	.0112	.0074
12 PETROLEUM REFINING (SIC 29)	.0004	.0004	.0003	.0005	.0003	.0010	.0001
13 RUBBER AND MISC. PLASTICS (SIC 30)	.0029	.0014	.0026	.0024	.0026	.0025	.0024
14 LEATHER AND LEATHER PRODUCTS (SIC 31)	.0010	.0006	.0010	.0011	.0009	.0009	.0009
15 STONE, CLAY AND GLASS PROD. (SIC 32)	.0036	.0039	.0033	.0044	.0038	.0092	.0023
16 PRIMARY METAL INDUSTRIES (SIC 33)	.0018	.0009	.0009	.0010	.0009	.0015	.0092
17 FABRICATED METAL PRODUCTS (SIC 34, 19)	.0036	.0031	.0019	.0039	.0035	.0071	.0063
18 MACHINERY, EXCEPT ELECTRICAL (SIC 35)	.0016	.0009	.0015	.0020	.0026	.0015	.0051
19 ELECTRICAL MACHINERY & EQUIP (SIC 36)	.0023	.0009	.0015	.0017	.0022	.0017	.0017
20 TRANSPORTATION EQUIPMENT (SIC 37)	.0211	.0052	.0104	.0089	.0075	.0080	.0084
21 MISCELLANEOUS MANUFACTURING (SIC 38-9)	.0015	.0012	.0023	.0017	.0041	.0015	.0070
22 TRANSPORTATION SERVICES (SIC 40-7)	1.0063	.0177	.0158	.0167	.0153	.0444	.1119
23 COMMUNICATIONS & UTILITIES (SIC 48-9)	.0547	1.1172	.0576	.0609	.0925	.0656	.0251
24 WHOLESALE AND RETAIL TRADE (SIC 50-9)	.1888	.1104	1.1620	.1803	.1648	.1622	.1104
25 FINANCE, INS., REAL ESTATE (SIC 60-7)	.1785	.1105	.1812	1.3399	.1893	.1561	.0682
26 SERVICES (SIC 70-9, 80-6, 89)	.1693	.1259	.1637	.1925	1.1817	.1594	.1538
27 GOVERNMENT ENTERPRISES	.0263	.0770	.0230	.0304	.0256	1.0137	.0086
28 UNALLOCATED INDUSTRIES	.0149	.0113	.0146	.0184	.0263	.0136	1.0077
29 HOUSEHOLDS	.8319	.5352	.7983	.8727	.6968	.7853	.3011
30 TOTAL LOCAL PURCHASES	2.7091	2.2516	2.5850	2.9360	2.6045	2.6897	2.1015

Table 4. Total requirements (direct, indirect, and induced) per dollar of delivery to final demand, Georgia, 1970.

(Each entry approximates the total output required from the sector at the beginning of each row for every dollar of delivery to final demand by the sector numbered at the head of each column.)

PURCHASING INDUSTRY NUMBER (SEE LEFT FOR TITLE)

SELLING INDUSTRY	29
1 AGRICULTURE (SIC 01, 07-9)	.0345
2 MINING (SIC 10-4)	.0008
3 CONTRACT CONSTRUCTION (SIC 15-7)	.0143
4 FOOD AND KINDRED PRODUCTS (SIC 20-1)	.0803
5 TEXTILE MILL PRODUCTS (SIC 22)	.0080
6 APPAREL AND RELATED PRODUCTS (SIC 23)	.0107
7 LUMBER AND WOOD PRODUCTS (SIC 24)	.0022
8 FURNITURE AND FIXTURES (SIC 25)	.0043
9 PAPER AND ALLIED PRODUCTS (SIC 26)	.0061
10 PRINTING AND PUBLISHING (SIC 27)	.0130
11 CHEMICALS AND ALLIED PRODUCTS (SIC 28)	.0091
12 PETROLEUM REFINING (SIC 29)	.0002
13 RUBBER AND MISC. PLASTICS (SIC 30)	.0025
14 LEATHER AND LEATHER PRODUCTS (SIC 31)	.0016
15 STONE, CLAY AND GLASS PROD. (SIC 32)	.0028
16 PRIMARY METAL INDUSTRIES (SIC 33)	.0007
17 FABRICATED METAL PRODUCTS (SIC 34, 19)	.0029
18 MACHINERY, EXCEPT ELECTRICAL (SIC 35)	.0013
19 ELECTRICAL MACHINERY & EQUIP (SIC 36)	.0012
20 TRANSPORTATION EQUIPMENT (SIC 37)	.0127
21 MISCELLANEOUS MANUFACTURING (SIC 38-9)	.0020
22 TRANSPORTATION SERVICES (SIC 40-7)	.0166
23 COMMUNICATIONS & UTILITIES (SIC 48-9)	.0588
24 WHOLESALE AND RETAIL TRADE (SIC 50-9)	.2470
25 FINANCE, INS., REAL ESTATE (SIC 60-7)	.2230
26 SERVICES (SIC 70-9, 80-6, 89)	.2046
27 GOVERNMENT ENTERPRISES	.0161
28 UNALLOCATED INDUSTRIES	.0090
29 HOUSEHOLDS	1.3911
30 TOTAL LOCAL PURCHASES	2.3776

Selected references

Many excellent bibliographies on regional input-output studies now exist. We have found the ones by Bourque and Cox (1970) and by Hewings (1970) particularly useful and refer the reader to them for more complete references. We list here only a fraction of the sources which have contributed to our education and, specifically, only the publications referred to in the text.

Bahl, Roy W. and Kenneth L. Sh ellhammer. 'Evaluating the State Business Tax Structure: 'An Application of Input-Output Analysis,' *National Tax Journal*, XXII (June 1969), 203-16.

Barnard, Jerald R. *Design and Use of Social Accounting Systems in State Development Planning.* Iowa City: Bureau of Business and Economic Research, The University of Iowa, 1967.

Beyers, William B., Philip J. Bourque, Warren R. Seyfried, and Eldon E. Weeks. *Input-Output Tables for the Washington Economy, 1967.* Seattle: Graduate School of Business Administration, University of Washington, 1970.

Billings, R. Bruce. 'The Mathematical Identity of the Multipliers Derived from the Economic Base Model and the Input-Output Model,' *Journal of Regional Science*, IX (1969), 471-3.

Bourque, Philip J. 'An Input-Output Analysis of Economic Change in Washington State,' *University of Washington Business Review*, XXX (Summer 1971), 5-22.

Bourque, Philip J. 'Income Multipliers for the Washington Economy,' *University of Washington Business Review*, XXVIII (Winter 1969), 5-15.

Bourque, Philip J., *et al. The Washington Economy: An Input-Output Study.* Seattle: Graduate School of Business Administration, University of Washington, 1967.

Bourque, Philip J. and Millicent Cox. *An Inventory of Regional Input-Output Studies in the United States.* Seattle: Graduate School of Business Administration, University of Washington, 1970.

Bradley, Iver E. 'Utah Interindustry Study: An Input-Output Analysis,' *Utah Economic and Business Review*, XXVII (July-August 1967), 1-13.

Carden, John G.D. and F.G. Whittington, Jr. *Studies in the Economic Structure of the State of Mississippi.* Jackson: Mississippi Industrial and Technological Research Commission, 1964.

Cheatham, Berrien M. (ed.). *1971 Georgia Manufacturing Directory.* Atlanta: Georgia Department of Industry and Trade, 1971.

Chenery, Hollis B. and Paul G. Clark. *Interindustry Economics.* New York: John Wiley and Sons, 1966.

Clark, David H. and John D. Coupe. *The Bangor Area Economy: Its Present and Future.* Bangor: College of Business Administration, University of Maine, March 1967.

Cleland, Sherrill. 'Local Input-Output Analysis: A New Business Tool,' *Michigan Business Topics*, VII (Autumn 1959), 41-8.

Conference on Research in Income and Wealth. *Input-Output Analysis: An Appraisal.* Princeton: Princeton University Press, 1955.

Davidson, Lawrence S. and William A. Schaffer. 'An Economic-Base Multiplier for Atlanta, 1961-1970,' *Atlanta Economic Review*, XXIII-4 (July-August 1973), 52-4.

Elrod, Robert H., Kemal El-Sheshai, and William A. Schaffer. *Interindustry Study of Forestry Sectors for Georgia Economy.* Macon: Georgia Forest Research Council, Report 31, November 1972.

Emerson, M. Jarvin. *Interindustry Projections of the Kansas Economy*. Manhattan: Department of Economics, Kansas State University (no date).

Emerson, M. Jarvin. *The Interindustry Structure of the Kansas Economy*. Manhattan: Kansas Office of Economic Analysis, 1969.

Fuerst, E. 'The Matrix as a Tool of Macro-Accounting,' *Review of Economics and Statistics*, XXVII (1955), 35-47.

Gamble, Hays B. and David L. Raphael. *A Microregional Analysis of Clinton County, Pennsylvania*. University Park: The Pennsylvania Regional Analysis Group, The Pennsylvania State University, February 1965.

Garnick, Daniel H. 'Differential Regional Multiplier Models,' *Journal of Regional Science*, X (1970), 35-47.

Graham, Robert E., Jr., Henry L. Degraff, and Edward A. Trott, Jr. 'State Projections of Income, Employment, and Population,' *Survey of Current Business* (April 1972), 22-48.

Grubb, Herbert W. *The Structure of the Texas Economy*, Volumes I and II. Austin: Office of the Governor, Office of Information Services, March 1973.

Hansen, W. Lee and Charles M. Tiebout. 'An Intersectoral Flows Analysis of the California Economy,' *The Review of Economics and Statistics*, XLV (November 1963), 409-18.

Harmston, Floyd K. and Richard E. Lund. *Application of an Input-Output Framework to a Community Economic System*. Columbia: University of Missouri Press, 1967.

Hewings, Geoffrey J.D. 'Regional Input-Output Analysis in the United States: A Bibliography,' Center for Research in the Social Sciences, University of Kent at Canterbury, Discussion Paper 3, September 1970.

Hirsch, Werner Z. 'Interindustry Relations of a Metropolitan Area,' *Review of Economics and Statistics*, XLI (1959), 360-9.

Hite, James C. and Eugene A. Laurent. *Environmental Planning: An Economic Analysis*. New York: Praeger Publishers, 1972.

Hochwald, Werner (ed.). *Design of Regional Accounts*. Baltimore: The Johns Hopkins Press, 1961.

Interplan, Inc. *The Socio-Economic Consequences of the Appalachian Highway in the North Georgia Area*. Atlanta: Georgia Department of Transportation, 1974.

Isard, Walter, *et al. Ecologic-Economic Analysis for Regional Development*. New York: The Free Press, 1972.

Isard, Walter. *Methods of Regional Analysis*. Cambridge: The MIT Press, 1960.

Isard, Walter. 'Regional Commodity Balances and Interregional Commodity Flows,' *The American Economic Review*, XLIII (May 1953), 167-180.

Isard, Walter and Thomas W. Langford. *Regional Input-Output Study: Recollections, Reflections, and Diverse Notes on the Philadelphia Experience*. Cambridge: The MIT Press, 1971.

Isard, Walter, Thomas W. Langford, Jr., and Eliahu Romanoff. *Philadelphia Region Input-Output Study, Working Papers*, Volumes 1-4. Philadelphia: Regional Science Research Institute, 1966-1968.

Laurent, Eugene A. and James C. Hite. *Economic-Ecologic Analysis in the Charleston Metropolitan Region: An Input-Output Study*. Report 19, Water Resources Research Institute, Clemson University, April 1971.

Leontief, Wassily. 'The Structure of Development,' *Scientific American*, CCIX (September 1963), 148-66.

Leven, Charles L. 'Regional and Interregional Accounts in Perspective,' *Regional Science Association Papers*, XIII (1964), 127-44.

Leven, Charles L. 'Regional Income and Product Accounts: Construction and Application,' in Hochwald (1961), 148-95.

Liebling, Herman I. 'Interindustry Economics and National Income Theory,' in Conference on Research in Income and Wealth (1955), 291-315.

Lindberg, Carolyn G. *A Technical Supplement to the Input-Output Study for New Mexico*.

Albuquerque: Bureau of Business Research, The University of New Mexico, September 1966.

Lindberg, Carolyn G. 'New Mexico's Imports and Exports,' *New Mexico Business* (September 1966).

Miernyk, William H. *The Elements of Input-Output Analysis*. New York: Random House, 1965.

Miernyk, William H., Ernest R. Bonner, John H. Chapman, Jr., and Kenneth Shellhammer. *Impact of the Space Program on a Local Economy*. Morgantown: West Virginia University Library, 1967.

Miernyk, William H., Kenneth L. Shellhammer, Douglas M. Brown, Ronald L. Coccari, Charles J. Gallagher, and Wesley H. Wineman. *Simulating Regional Economic Development*. Lexington: D.C. Heath and Co., 1970.

Moore, Frederick T. and James W. Petersen, 'Regional Analysis: An Interindustry Model of Utah,' *Review of Economics and Statistics*, XXXVII (1955), 368-81.

National Economics Division. 'Input-Output Structure of the U.S. Economy: 1963,' *Survey of Current Business* (November 1969), 16-47.

National Economics Division. 'Personal Consumption Expenditures in the 1963 Input-Output Study,' *Survey of Current Business* (January 1971), 34-38.

Niemi, Albert W., Jr. *Gross State Product and Productivity in the Southeast*. Chapel Hill: The University of North Carolina Press, 1975.

Rapkin, Chester. *Industrial Renewal: Determining the Potential and Accelerating the Economy of the Utica Urban Area*. New York: New York State Division of Housing and Community Renewal, 1963.

Richardson, Harry W. *Elements of Regional Economics*. New York: Praeger Publishers, 1969.

Richardson, Harry W. *Input-Output and Regional Economics*. New York: John Wiley and Sons, 1972.

Richardson, Harry W. *Regional Growth Theory*. New York: John Wiley and Sons, 1973.

Schaffer, William A. 'A Synthesis of Regional Input-Output Techniques,' presented at the Second Advanced Studies Institute in Regional Science, Institut für Regionalwissenschaft der Universität Karlsruhe, August 1972.

Schaffer, William A. 'Estimating Regional Input-Output Coefficients,' *Review of Regional Studies*, II-3 (Spring 1972), 57-71.

Schaffer, William A., 'Measuring the Potential Impact of Alternative Highway Locations,' presented at the Third Advanced Studies Institute in Regional Science, Institut für Regionalwissenschaft der Universität Karlsruhe, August 1974 (available from the author as Working Paper E-74-07, College of Industrial Management, Georgia Institute of Technology).

Schaffer, William A. and Kong Chu. 'Nonsurvey Techniques for Constructing Regional Interindustry Models,' *Regional Science Association Papers*, XXIII (1969), 83-101.

Schaffer, William A. and Kong Chu. 'Simulating Regional Interindustry Models for Western States,' *Papers of the First Pacific Regional Science Conference, 1969*, (Tokyo: University of Tokyo Press, 1971), 123-40.

Schaffer, William A., Eugene A. Laurent, and Ernest M. Sutter, Jr. 'The Georgia Economic Model – A Nontechnical Lesson in Input-Output Analysis,' *Atlanta Economic Review*, XXIII-2 (March-April 1973), 34-40.

Schaffer, William A., Eugene A. Laurent, and Ernest M. Sutter, Jr. 'Gross State Product Accounts and State Input-Output Models,' Regional Development Program, College of Industrial Management, Georgia Institute of Technology, Discussion Paper 17, 1972.

Schaffer, William A., Eugene A. Laurent, and Ernest M. Sutter, Jr. *Introducing the Georgia Economic Model*. Atlanta: Georgia Department of Industry and Trade, 1972.

Schaffer, William A., Eugene A. Laurent, and Ernest M. Sutter, Jr. 'The Economic Structure of Georgia,' *Georgia Business*, XXXI-11 (May 1971), 1-9.

Schaffer, William A., with the assistance of Teh C. Liang, Ernest M. Sutter, Jr., Glenn Ifuku, Lynn Zane, and Young P. Joun. *Interindustry Study of the Hawaiian Economy*. Honolulu: Department of Planning and Economic Development, State of Hawaii, 1972.

Shang, Yung-Cheng, William H. Albrecht, William Wan, *et al. Hawaii's Income and Expenditures, 1961-1964, with Certain Revisions of Previous Estimates, 1958-1960.* Honolulu: Economic Research Center, University of Hawaii, 1967.

Schang, Yung C., William H. Albrecht, and Glenn Ifuku. *Hawaii's Income and Expenditure Accounts, 1958-68.* Honolulu: Economic Research Center, University of Hawaii, 1970.

Smith, P. and W.I. Morrison. *Simulating the Urban Economy.* London: Pion Limited, 1974.

Tiebout, Charles M. 'An Empirical Regional Input-Output Projection Model: The State of Washington, 1980,' *Review of Economics and Statistics, LI* (1969), 334-40.

Tiebout, Charles M. 'Input-Output and the Firm: A Technique for Using National and Regional Tables,' *Review of Economics and Statistics,* XLIX (May 1967), 260-2.

Tiebout, Charles M. *The Community Economic Base Study.* Committee for Economic Development, Supplementary Paper 16, 1962.

U.S. Department of Labor, Bureau of Labor Statistics. *Patterns of U.S. Economic Growth.* BLS Bulletin 1672.

U.S. Department of Labor, Bureau of Labor Statistics. *The U.S. Economy in 1980: A Summary of BLS Projections.* BLS Bulletin 1673.

Studies in applied regional science

Vol. 1
On the use of input-output models for regional planning
W. A. Schaffer

This volume is devoted to the use of input-output techniques in regional planning. The study provides a clear
introduction to the essential ideas of input-output analysis.
Particular emphasis is placed on the intricate problems of
data collection at a regional level.
Attention is focused on the applicability of input-output
analysis in the field of regional planning. Alternative
methods such as shift-and-share techniques are discussed.
For means of clear illustration an extensive regional study
of the Georgia economy has been capably employed.

ISBN 90 207 0626 8

Vol. 2
Forecasting transportation impacts upon land use
P. F. Wendt

This reader concentrates on transportation problems in
urban areas. After a survey of model techniques for
analyzing transportation and land use problems, several
new methods in the field of transportation and land-use
planning (including Delphi-methods and interaction
models) are developed. In the study particular attention
is paid to forecasting techniques for regional-urban developments. The book is exemplified by an extensive set of
applied methods in transportation land-use planning for
the Georgia region.

ISBN. 90 207 0627 6

Martinus Nijhoff Social Sciences Division Leiden 1976

Vol. 3
Estimation of stochastic input-output models
S. D. Gerking

The primary objective of this monograph is to develop a
method for measuring the uncertainty in estimates of the
technical coefficients in an input-output model. Specifically, it is demonstrated that if two-stage least squares is
used to estimate these parameters, then uncertainty may
be judged according to the magnitude of the standard
errors of these estimates.
This study also describes three further applications of the
two-stage least squares estimation technique in an input-
output context. The techniques and applications are
illustrated using cross-sectional input-output data from
West Virginia.

ISBN 90 207 0628 4